THE NINE WAVES
OF CREATION

"*The Nine Waves of Creation* presents a speculative cosmology supported by the recent discovery that galaxies in the universe are not located randomly but ordered in a way that radically challenges previous cosmological assumptions. If Calleman's ideas—which are refreshingly wild but rationally argued—are even partially correct, today's assumptions about the nature of evolution and the evolution of nature will need to be reconsidered."

DEAN RADIN, PH.D.,
CHIEF SCIENTIST AT THE INSTITUTE OF NOETIC SCIENCES,
PROFESSOR AT THE CALIFORNIA INSTITUTE OF INTEGRAL STUDIES,
AND AUTHOR OF *SUPERNORMAL* AND *ENTANGLED MINDS*

PRAISE FOR PREVIOUS WORKS
BY CARL JOHAN CALLEMAN

"[*The Global Mind and the Rise of Civilization* contains] the first novel idea about the rise of civilization in many decades."

JAMES REDFIELD, AUTHOR OF
THE CELESTINE PROPHECY AND *THE TWELFTH INSIGHT*

"*The Global Mind and the Rise of Civilization* addresses one of the crucial issues of our time, on which our future may depend: the relationship between human consciousness and the brain. Let Calleman be your guide on this exciting journey."

LARRY DOSSEY, M.D., AUTHOR OF
*ONE MIND: HOW OUR INDIVIDUAL MIND IS
PART OF A GREATER CONSCIOUSNESS AND WHY IT MATTERS*

"In *The Global Mind and the Rise of Civilization,* Carl Johan Calleman formulates a unique outlook on human civilization, one that is deeply rooted in metaphysical changes in human consciousness. The effect is to reconcile diverse aspects of symbolism, myth, and theology, drawn from a wide range of ancient cultures."

LAIRD SCRANTON, AUTHOR OF *THE SCIENCE OF THE DOGON*
AND *POINT OF ORIGIN: GOBEKLI TEPE AND
THE SPIRITUAL MATRIX FOR THE WORLD'S COSMOLOGIES*

"In *The Global Mind and the Rise of Civilization,* Calleman examines how the two hemispheres of the brain have parallels with the East and West civilizations and suggests that the global mind is connected to the Earth's inner core. . . . fascinating book."

NEXUS MAGAZINE

"Between the simplicity of religion and the absurdity of an empty randomness, Carl Johan Calleman proposes a brilliant but plausible third way: The Tree of Life. In *The Purposeful Universe* we have finally a modern theory of the origin and evolution of life that unifies the most recent discoveries of science with ancient wisdom. Without ever imposing God on us, this great book brings agnostics like myself to face the evidence."

JEAN-CLAUDE PEREZ, PH.D., AUTHOR OF
CODEX BIOGENESIS: LES 13 CODES DE l'AND
[THE 13 CODES OF DNA]

THE NINE WAVES
OF CREATION

Quantum Physics, Holographic Evolution,
and the Destiny of Humanity

Carl Johan Calleman, Ph.D.

Bear & Company
Rochester, Vermont • Toronto, Canada

Bear & Company
One Park Street
Rochester, Vermont 05767
www.BearandCompanyBooks.com

Text stock is SFI certified

Bear & Company is a division of Inner Traditions International

Library of Congress Cataloging-in-Publication Data

Names: Calleman, Carl Johan, author.
Title: The nine waves of creation : quantum physics, holographic evolution,
    and the destiny of humanity / Carl Johan Calleman, Ph.D.
Description: Rochester, VT : Bear & Company, 2016. | Includes bibliographical
    references and index.
Identifiers: LCCN 2016013883 (print) | LCCN 2016037274 (e-book) |
    ISBN 9781591432777 (pbk.) | ISBN 9781591432784 (e-book)
Subjects: LCSH: Cosmology. | Consciousness—Miscellanea. | Evolution
    (Biology)—Philosophy. | Quantum theory. | Maya cosmology.
Classification: LCC BD511 .C28 2016 (print) | LCC BD511 (e-book) |
    DDC 113—dc23
LC record available at https://lccn.loc.gov/2016013883

Printed and bound in the United States by Lake Book Manufacturing, Inc.
The text stock is SFI certified. The Sustainable Forestry Initiative® program promotes sustainable forest management.

10 9 8 7 6 5 4 3 2 1

Text design by Debbie Glogover and layout by Priscilla Baker
This book was typeset in Garamond Premier Pro with Eremitage, Helvetica Neue, and Gill Sans used as display typefaces

To send correspondence to the author of this book, mail a first-class letter to the author c/o Inner Traditions • Bear & Company, One Park Street, Rochester, VT 05767, and we will forward the communication, or contact the author directly at **cjcalleman@swipnet.se.**

Contents

Foreword

Everything "out there" is frequencies or waves interpreted by our minds when we observe things. I believe in this definition of the material world based on quantum physics, yet I struggle to comprehend it. I have strove to attain this view, which is the basis of most technological advances during the past hundred years. *The Nine Waves of Creation* reveals the cosmic aspect of this counterintuitive description of the reality that we "see." Carl Calleman decodes what is, and has been, happening in our quantum-holographic world by proving that the fabled Tree of Life is the central organizer of space-time. Because I resonate with the tree as a shaman, Calleman's observation opened my eyes. Maybe I can see because we've come to the end of our 16.4-billion-year climb through the nine waves of creation that now function simultaneously? These waves reveal stunning new patterns in reality that initially shocked me during 2012. After reading Calleman's latest book, these patterns make more sense.

Reality changed fundamentally when the climb through the waves completed on October 28, 2011; many of my colleagues and I could palpably feel it. During March 9 through October 28, 2011, a small but significant group of researchers led by Calleman observed world events during the DAYS and NIGHTS of the Ninth Wave, which was the final acceleration of evolutionary time. I was one of the researchers. Many groups of people clamored for a more idealistic world during

2011, such as the Arab Spring in the Middle East when an instinctual signal went out through people in the streets to demand a better life. These collective forces aimed to shred the political and social structures that had run the world for the past five thousand years, forces that are in a backlash as millions of refugees stream out of their homelands. These refugees will not tolerate oppression any more; they'd rather die. Nobody knows what will happen next with European nations weakening and buckling under this enormous influx, a global malaise inspired by repressed desires that will not be denied. Calleman's hugely important book accesses the root causes of these fantastic events and seeks ways we can move human society into the higher waves.

Calleman asked me for a few insights on the new world with all nine waves functioning simultaneously, the first time this has happened on Earth according to his interpretation of the Mayan calendar. In *Alchemy of Nine Dimensions,* I wrote about the opening of nine dimensions of human consciousness that would occur at the end of the Mayan calendar. Calleman's description of all nine waves functioning simultaneously is synchronistic with my work on nine dimensions. For example, he wants us to become quantum activists in a holographic universe, which is exactly how we are when we become multidimensional. I think deep contemplation of the nine waves is a necessity now that the final acceleration in 2011 is oscillating twenty times faster. We each need to process the positive and negative aspects of the previous eight waves. *The Nine Waves of Creation* demonstrates that the wave or waves we resonate with indicate the direction of our personal work.

Here is my story about this intriguing idea: Starting in early 2012, I created two Seventh Wave projects, while having no idea that was what I was doing. The simultaneity of all nine waves was so intense, confusing, and overwhelming that I felt I had to manifest solid things just to survive. At the end of 2011, everything that seemed to be moving forward to an end point just dissolved! It felt like time ended. I countered this bizarre halt with action: I fulfilled my long-suppressed desire to build a simple yet beautiful house for my family. Shredded daily by chaos and losing my grip on reality, I had to create something of lasting value. Also, since I always do two things at once, I satisfied another long-unfulfilled desire—to write a novel. In 2012 my partner, Gerry Clow, and I stopped teaching, and we started building a house. And I wrote a novel that came out in 2015—*Revelations of the Ruby Crystal*.

Reading *The Nine Waves of Creation* has clarified my obsessive drives: I was resonating with the Seventh Wave that began in 1755! When the Ninth Wave's "unity consciousness" flooded the world with its exquisite beauty during 2011, the Seventh Wave was my safety zone while Sixth Wave patriarchal structures collapsed amid the chaos brought on by Eighth Wave technologies. For example, the refugees streaming out of the Middle East have been able to move through old barriers because of their cell phones, iPhones, Blackberries, and iPads. For me, as a Seventh Wave aficionado, the world was becoming a zone of trancelike nuttiness. Everywhere I went, people were staring at lit screens and digitalizing with both hands while they stumbled blindly across busy streets, deaf from plugs in their ears that blasted them with loud music. The frequencies emanating from these devices were toxic, so it made me sick to get on elevators where everybody was furiously texting. Worse than that, while the Sixth and Eighth Wave creations transformed reality, horrible Fourth Wave tribal cruelty appeared; for example, mass shootings throughout the United States and ISIS atrocities in the Middle East.

Young people processed the tribal Fourth Wave and took action against the patriarchal Sixth Wave by sporting nose rings, tattoos, and tongue piercings. But I resonated with the Fifth, Seventh, and Ninth Waves, the unitized frequencies, so I created beautiful things inspired by the Seventh Wave. The Arts and Crafts movement in Europe and America was a grassroots movement that valued simple yet beautiful handcrafted homes in reaction to the negative aspects of industrialization that manifested at the peak of the Seventh Wave in 1883. Its proponents believed every person should enjoy a fine home; comfort and art was for all, not just the rich. So, Gerry and I built a small Craftsman bungalow on an island, while we cringed at shoddy towers going up in nearby Vancouver, where "open plan" boxes replaced cozy old bungalows. The novel evolved all the way through the Seventh Wave to help readers explore psychology, love, and the meaning of life, the themes I explore with my characters as they resonate with the Ninth Wave.

Calleman says people born in the Seventh Wave were "born into the wave that had the highest frequency at his or her birth." This is the vast majority of people at this time, and our ancestral memory fits right into this time frame. The reader will need to consider Calleman's thoughts about the Seventh Wave. As the result of my own creative experiences since 2011, I think the ability to manifest the higher levels of the Seventh Wave *is the key to holding things together while Sixth Wave patriarchal structures collapse and more egalitarian societies emerge through positive Seventh Wave frequencies*—globalization, equality, and materialism. The Eighth Wave (digitalization, addressing economic inequality) and the Ninth Wave (total equality and unity consciousness) require a firm material basis during the physical collapse of nation-states and patriarchal dominance.

Possibly the most fascinating idea in this book is Calleman's belief that we must deactivate the Hologram of Good and Evil, which has negatively contaminated the Sixth Wave in the Middle East. Beyond this dualistic and mostly unconscious Sixth Wave trap, Seventh Wave creations are quite well understood, easily utilized, and appreciated, especially its economies, laws, and treaties. Industrialists developed things independently unlike the imaginary judgmental Sixth Wave god that consumes our bodies in war and our minds in the media. Calleman says if the negative frequencies of the Sixth Wave continue to dominate, our climb into the higher waves will abort. I agree. At this time, the Seventh Wave is like a life jacket, like the life jackets worn by refugees crossing the seas. As for resonating with the Eighth and Ninth Waves, those born before 1999 struggle to do so, yet this will come naturally through the consciousness of those born into these high-frequency waves. Meanwhile, those born into the Seventh Wave must use its highest frequencies to manifest egalitarian social structures and economies for their grandchildren. They will manifest the high levels of the Eighth and Ninth Waves that will eventually create a much less material world, something we cannot yet envisage, yet it will come.

BARBARA HAND CLOW
OCTOBER 2016

BARBARA HAND CLOW is an internationally acclaimed teacher, author, and Mayan calendar researcher. Her numerous books include *The Mayan Code: Time Acceleration and the World Mind*, *Revelations of the Ruby Crystal*, *The Pleiadian Agenda*, *Alchemy of Nine Dimensions*, and *Awakening the Planetary Mind*. She has taught at sacred sites throughout the world and maintains an astrological website, www.HandClow2012.com.

Acknowledgments

My gratitude goes to my partner, Margo Baldwin, who provided ongoing feedback and advice as this book project developed and corrected some of my linguistic errors. Great thanks also go to Bengt Sundin, who displayed a brilliant ability to create images for this book.

The reader will notice that many of the references in this book are to *Wikipedia,* as was done in my book *Global Mind and the Rise of Civilization.* Since the paradigm shift I am proposing is so radical, it is my intention to base my books only on what is currently considered established fact by the scientific community. Defining each of those commonly accepted scientific understandings within the body of this work is not possible, so I have used the resource of *Wikipedia* to offer readers the chance to explore each of those premises on their own—so that we are all using the same base of understanding. *Wikipedia* offers readers a convenient way to familiarize themselves with the complex building blocks of my theories and serves as a jumping-off point for interested readers to further explore these and related subjects.

1
The Origin of The Universe

OUR CURRENT WORLD SITUATION

This book describes what I believe to be a deep and long-lasting new paradigm about where we come from and the underlying factors that drive evolution in all of its aspects, including those that are behind the course of human history. As with all true new paradigms, this is based on new facts and discoveries that may change how we look at the universe we live in, discoveries with consequences that until fairly recently would have been considered unthinkable. This new paradigm is, however, not merely theoretical but has very direct consequences for how we understand the world at the present moment and what we may be able to do about it.

The world people are experiencing now, at the time of writing (July 2016), is quite different from only a few years ago. In the United States, the number of mass shootings is multiplying, and politicians are saying things that would have seemed horrifying up until quite recently. The feeling of a mental crisis driven by fear is quite apparent, and the rules of the system are no longer as set as previously. Rationality and wisdom seem to be at risk of disappearing, and many fundamental values of freedom and democracy are threatened. On the other side of the ocean, in the Middle East, jihadist terrorists are displaying a brutality that has not been seen for centuries. Violence is not a new thing in human history, but what seems very marked at the current time is the disappearance of boundaries and the lack of respect for life that goes with them. It seems fair to say that we are in a deepgoing civilizational

1

crisis, which includes the world's religions. But what are the roots of all these changes? Most answers that political commentators propose point to immediate reasons, based on a short-term perspective of events. We will here instead ask if there are deepgoing long-term factors behind them, which originate in how the evolution of the universe is designed. To answer this I will here present a scientific theory for the evolution of the universe from the Big Bang to the current time that explains what is happening in the world today. That would also imply that humanity has a destiny that we all need to connect to if we are to be able to move forward successfully.

That there is such an underlying time plan for the evolution of the universe is indeed what I am suggesting. I do not think it is possible to understand what is going on today without a fundamental paradigm shift in how we are thinking about evolution. In this book, I thus provide a new context for understanding human history, a long-term perspective the reader has likely not heard before. At the very least, I hope to explain why the world is so different from only a few years ago. At the end of the book, in chapter 9, I also provide what I believe to be useful tools and guidelines that the reader may work with to align with the destiny of humanity. Hence, in the midst of the chaos we should not miss out on the current constructive possibilities for aligning with the higher purpose of humanity that have now opened up to us. Maybe the chaos is there to create space for a better world to emerge. Perhaps it is because of these new possibilities—generated by the Ninth Wave of creation—that more and more people are beginning to see that everything is connected with everything else. Maybe they are also the reasons that you are holding this book in your hand.

In this new perspective, no one is powerless. Yet, you may need to summon your inner courage and ask your higher self for guidance, as what is presented here may be different from many established ideas in both science and religion. I can, however, assure the reader that the perspective is rational, and I have attempted to present it in such a way that not too big leaps of faith need to be made. Hence, the book begins with this chapter about the birth of the universe, which provides a new framework for understanding our origins. We will then in a sequence of chapters study how and why life has emerged from this origin to what it is today and compare this to ancient creation stories. Regardless of whether the reader shares my conclusions, I think it is indisputable that this theory removes the boundaries between many thought systems and disciplines that previously seemed entirely separate. In chapters 7 and 8 we will return to look at our present situation, and hopefully the reader will, by then, have gained a completely new way of understanding the world. This may then serve for guidance to the Era of Fulfillment that will be discussed in the ninth and final chapter. Let us begin by gaining a new perspective of what our origins are through some very dramatic new findings in cosmology.

THE BIRTH OF THE UNIVERSE

How did the universe that we are living in come to be in the first place? To answer this question—fundamental for understanding the purpose of life—all human societies have had some form of creation stories, explanations of how the universe, the Earth, and human beings themselves have come into existence, and maybe also why it all exists in the first place. Ancient creation stories for the most part include some Creator God, or creator gods, and give the reasons he/they had for creating the world and the human beings. The major monotheist religions see a single God as the source of our existence, and in the Western world the creation story that dominated people, at least up until the seventeenth century, has been the biblical creation story (to be discussed further in chapter 5). For a long time this was interpreted to mean that the world was only six thousand years old and that all the species, including the humans, had been created "as is" at that point in time. As the mid-1700s brought a new way of thinking (to be discussed in chapter 6) it became increasingly clear, however, that the universe was much older than this and that the current Earth had been developed by geological processes over hundreds of millions of years. Evidence of fossilized species that no longer existed also made it clear that biologically speaking an evolution had taken place that was not consistent with the notion that all species were only a few thousand years old.

As a result, during the course of the nineteenth century the biblical creation story gradually lost ground in intellectual circles and step-by-step its various tenets had to be given up. As the beginning of the time line of evolution was gradually pushed backward, a void was thus created as to what was the true origin of the universe, a void that scientists, rather than priests, were now trying to fill. However, while it had already become clear that life on our own planet had been evolving for a very long time, evidence of evolution on a cosmic scale was late in coming, and as Einstein published his general theory of relativity in 1915 he still adhered to a model of a universe that was not evolving.

In the 1920s, however, the Belgian astronomer (and Catholic priest) Georges Lemaître[1] was the first to propose what later has become known as the Big Bang theory. Based on observations of the movements of galaxies he proposed the theory that the universe was expanding and had its origin in a "primeval atom" or "cosmic egg" and developed a mathematical theory for such an origin of the universe. In 1927, the American astronomer Edwin Hubble[2] confirmed the validity of Lemaître's ideas through a systematic study of the red-shift of galaxies, a study that then led Einstein to revise his earlier negativity toward an evolving universe. Einstein in fact at one point exclaimed that Lemaître's theory was "the most beautiful and satisfactory explanation of creation to which I have ever listened."[3] Hence, there was a point when the primordial atom theory would be seen as something that could unify science and religion, and some scientists were open-minded about this. Later, in 1951, Pope Pius XII declared that Lemaître's theory provided a scientific validation for the Catholic view of creation. Lemaître himself, however, objected to this proclamation, arguing that his theory was neutral and that there was neither a connection nor a contradiction between his religion and his theory.[4] We can only speculate about Lemaître's motives, but presumably Lemaître did not want to alienate parts of the scientific community from his theory (known since 1949 as the Big Bang theory[5]) and so persuaded the pope to stop discussing its consequences for creation.

Ironically then, despite the fact that the originator of the Big Bang theory was himself a devout Catholic and priest, Lemaître's stance opened the field for the purely materialist interpretations for the birth of the universe, which have dominated this area of research ever since. Eventually more or less the entire scientific community was also won over to the Big Bang theory, notably through the discovery in the 1960s of the so-called cosmic microwave background radiation (CMBR) by radioastronomers Penzias and Wilson.[6] This CMBR is an afterglow from the very high initial temperatures in the Big Bang when the universe reached billions of degrees. Although the universe has since cooled down considerably, the CMBR can still be measured and provides information about how the temperatures were distributed at the time the universe was born. Since the temperature measured in this CMBR was consistent with what was predicted, the discovery of the CMBR, similar to the discovery of the expansion of galaxies, pointed to an origin of the universe in a singularity in the distant past. The Big Bang came to be conceived of much as a giant explosion occurring for no reason, and even if scientists will consider such a description an oversimplification, it captures the gist of this view.

Following the discovery of the CMBR a fairly consistent standard model of cosmology has been developed within the scientific community describing how after the Big Bang space-time emerged in an inflationary manner, and how elementary particles and forces of nature, as well as galaxies, stars, and planets, subsequently came into existence. The technicalities of this model are too complex for most people to engage themselves in, and the Big Bang theory as it is presented by academia has become a "secular" alternative to the creation stories of the past. It has been stripped of everything that is not measurable and has neither a creator nor a purpose. Through this trajectory, official science has arrived at a view of the world that exists for no other reason than that some fifteen billion years ago there was a big explosion. Or, in the words of Nobel Prize–winner Steven Weinberg, who wrote a much acclaimed book about the Big Bang theory titled *The First Three Minutes,* "The more the universe seems comprehensible, the more it also seems pointless."[7] Naturally, even if the vast majority of humanity still believes in a higher power behind the existence of the universe and themselves, it seems difficult for an intellectually astute person to simply neglect such a theory as the Big Bang theory, which is supported by so many observations and is sanctioned by official science. We are thus faced with a momentous question: Are we just by-products of a giant explosion, or is there something amiss in how official science has interpreted the birth of the universe?

It then deserves to be pointed out that most cosmologists working with the Big Bang theory in the past fifty years have had a fundamentally atheist-materialist agenda and have sought to create a model where "God" can be taken out of the picture and the various steps in the continued evolution of the universe can be explained as a series of accidents. This does not mean that they are producing false data, but it does mean that they look at reality through a filter, which makes them look away from every hint of knowledge that may point to the existence of a higher spiritual power. Not surprisingly then, people at large have come to perceive the Big Bang as being in conflict with an intelligent design of the universe. Remarkably few books on spirituality or critical new thought has even discussed the birth of the universe, despite the fact that this would seem to be absolutely critical for understanding who we are and why we are here.

EMERGING PROBLEMS
WITH THE STANDARD MODEL
OF THE BIG BANG THEORY

I should here say that I do not on my own part question the central tenets of the Big Bang theory or that some fifteen billion years ago there was a point of beginning for the universe. Yet, as we shall see, there are very serious problems with the official interpretation of the Big Bang theory and data have been accumulating, especially more recently, making this even clearer. One obvious such problem is that the world that has resulted from the initial explosion does not look like the aftermath of an explosion. How did you, reading this book, emerge from a universe of billions of degrees? The world we are living in in fact looks very structured also at the largest levels of the universe with its galaxies, star systems, and planets. Official science explains the emergence of such structures by reference to "random fluctuations," and life itself is seen as something that has accidentally "popped up" on our own planet and then evolved through "random mutations." How likely does this seem? In fact, in the models of modern physics and biology, life is still essentially considered as an accidental spin-off effect of the laws of physics and chemistry rather than the very reason for the existence of the universe. However, common sense tells us that such an immensely intricate and complex phenomenon as a human being could not just be a result of an undirected explosion, and we must ask: How did the universe as a whole become structured?

As a second more general problem pertaining to the standard model of cosmology, astronomers have discovered that stars in galaxies do not behave as expected from Newtonian physics and that galaxies are moving away from each other at an accelerating speed. This has led them to postulate that 95 percent of the matter of the universe exists in two unknown forms termed "dark matter" and "dark energy"[8] even though there is no direct evidence that either one of these entities actually exists. Abstract ideas based on mathematical models rather than actual observations are thus now being used to patch up a model of the universe that is bursting at its seams. Although cosmologists will congratulate themselves on being able to explain certain phenomena by their standard model, it can hardly be considered a success that 95 percent of the matter of the universe cannot be accounted for in this model. There are thus reasons to wonder how long a model with so little explanatory power will survive. This obviously also sets question marks for many other things that this model is said to have explained, including the purported randomness of the birth of the universe. Some cosmologists representing the official view of science are also recognizing that this branch of science is in a crisis[9] and that we may be approaching a significant paradigm shift.

To scrutinize the validity of the current theory about the birth of the universe it seems that we should first study the data upon which it is based. The main source of information that we currently possess about the birth of the universe is the abovementioned CMBR. The CMBR reflects the distribution of temperatures at a time of only about three hundred thousand years after the Big Bang (which took place about fifteen billion years ago), and so measurements of the CMBR really give an infant picture of the universe (compared to the age of the universe this is like taking a photograph of a child only twelve hours after it was born). This is as close in time that we may currently come to the birth of the universe, because no light existed before this, and so the CMBR is important if we want to learn about the nature of the universe at its inception.

Up until the twenty-first century, the predominant idea was that at the largest scale the universe had no structure, an idea that was codified in the so-called cosmological principle.[10] This theory stated that at the largest scale the universe was homogeneous and isotropic, meaning similar in all directions. This was a principle, or assumption, upon which much of modern physics, and especially the general theory of relativity, was based. If the cosmological principle were true it would have to be expected that the universe also at the very early point in time measured by the CMBR would have no structure or favored directions. This assumption, however, had to be tested, and so the COBE satellite (see fig. 1.1a on p. 10)[11] was sent up in 1989 to measure the microwave radiation and map out its distribution in the universe.

The COBE satellite (fig 1.1a) did discover anisotropies (non-uniformities) in the distribution of the CMBR but no significant structuring factor that could be used to explain any aspects of the further evolution of the universe. This supported the previously predominant belief that the universe at its largest scale was homogenous and isotropic as the anisotropies found appeared random in nature. The cosmological principle thus seemed supported. It was, however, recognized that the resolution of the COBE measurements was relatively low, and the question remained as to whether a satellite able to measure the CMBR with a higher resolution would still validate this principle.

THE TREE OF LIFE HYPOTHESIS FOR THE ORIGIN OF THE UNIVERSE

From my own perspective, having studied ancient cosmologies and especially that of the Maya, it seemed, however, that the universe should have a Tree of Life, or, if you like, a World Tree, at its center. Something should account for how the entire universe is connected and has a coordinated direction. Yet, based partly on the abovementioned measurements of the COBE satellite, at the time of the writing of *Solving the Greatest Mystery of Our Time: The Mayan Calendar* (2001), I had to admit that there was no hard evidence that a Cosmic Tree of Life existed in the center of the universe, despite the fact that this was a central tenet of so many ancient traditions. Nonetheless, because Trees of Life (or axis mundi)[12] could be identified on the planetary and galactic levels as their rotational axes, it seemed reasonable that such a tree would exist

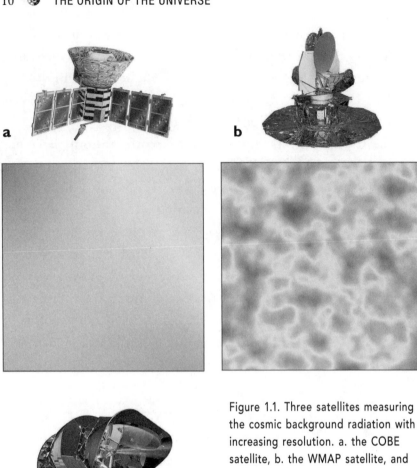

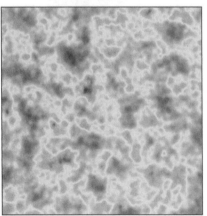

Figure 1.1. Three satellites measuring the cosmic background radiation with increasing resolution. a. the COBE satellite, b. the WMAP satellite, and c. the Planck satellite. Only the WMAP and Planck satellites had a sufficient resolution to identify the Cosmic Tree of Life (see fig. 1.2) in the infant universe. (*Courtesy of NASA/JPL-Caltech/ESA*)

also on a level encompassing the entire cosmos. In *The Mayan Calendar and the Transformation of Consciousness* (2004), I thus hypothesized the existence of such a Cosmic Tree of Life. But visions and ideas are one thing; hard evidence is another. Even then I had to recognize that the latter was still missing. The radiation from the Big Bang measured by the COBE satellite was essentially consistent with the notion that this was homogenously distributed in the early universe. This corroborated the consensus view in the scientific community that the early universe had no structure.

In 2003, new satellite measurements of the CMBR had, however, begun to be recorded by means of the Wilkinson Microwave Anisotropy Probe, which provided much more accurate data of the afterglow from the Big Bang (WMAP, fig. 1.1b).[13] Unexpectedly, when the WMAP data set was analyzed mathematically, an axis and polarized fields of temperature were discovered; the findings were published in 2004 by Max Tegmark and coworkers.[14] These fields were organized somewhat like the panels of a basketball, which defined the direction of an axis through the early universe (fig. 1.2).

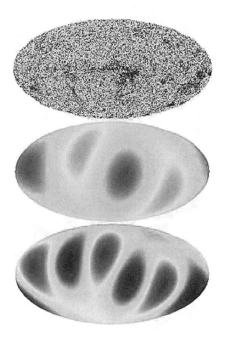

Figure 1.2. The cosmic microwave background with the "axis of evil" as measured by the WMAP satellite. Top: The cosmic microwave background in the original image from the WMAP study. Middle: After mathematical processing of the temperature variation a structure in the quadrupole axis becomes evident. Bottom: An octupole axis aligned with the quadrupole was discovered, which demonstrates the existence of an axis of evil. (*Source: NASA and the WMAP team; used with permission: de Oliveira-Costa, Tegmark, Zaldarriaga, and Hamilton, "The Significance of the Largest Scale CMBR Fluctuations in WMAP"*)

Katharine Land and Joao Magueijo of Oxford University later verified these findings in an article titled "The Axis of Evil,"[15] an unfor-
tunate label with associations to President George W. Bush's foreign
policy. The name has, however, remained, partly because it is catchy
and partly because the discovery of this axis seemed so disturbing to
the established cosmology. As it appears from the WMAP, the early
cosmos was thus not homogeneous but organized like a meatball on a
toothpick. The center of the meatball, what seems to be the center of
the universe, is located in the direction of the constellation of Virgo.[16]
Curiously, the associated great axis, which exists on an unfathomably
supergalactic scale (a galaxy is a speck of dust in this context), lies
in the plane of the ecliptic and has a direction that may be parallel to the equinoxes of our own Earth's planetary orbit.[17] Although
this may be an accident, it may also mean that our own particular
planet is aligned with the Cosmic Axis in a way that is conducive to
the emergence of life here and that we are in a special place in the
universe.

Already the very finding that the temperatures in the afterglow of
the Big Bang lined up with an axis was remarkable, because according to established cosmology this universe is supposed to have come
into existence by accident and should not at the largest scale display
any structure (which could indicate that it may have an intelligent
divine source). Naturally, as the existence of such an axis would put
in question many of the assumptions of official science, with potentially far-reaching consequences for cosmology, the finding of this was
questioned early on.[18] Nonetheless, soon afterward, other studies were
performed that validated the existence of the axis in dramatic ways:
First it was found that the polarization of light from quasars (some of
the brightest and most massive astronomical objects known, emitting
huge amounts of radio waves) was influenced by their proximity to
the axis.[19] An interesting twist of this particular study was that the
polarization seemed to *corkscrew* around the axis, and its authors suggested that a potential explanation to this effect is that the entire uni-

verse rotates around what in fact is its central axis. This would then be consistent with the idea that *the universe as a whole is a spinning vortex generated by the axis and that it emerged as such from the very beginning*. Professor Michael Longo at the University of Michigan, who studied the handedness of spiral galaxies (whether they revolved clockwise or counterclockwise) throughout the universe, made a second, equally dramatic finding. He found that a line separating the preference for the two types of handedness approximately lined up with the axis previously discovered in the WMAP study (fig. 1.2),[20] thus generating a mirroring effect.

These findings regarding the Cosmic Axis were very exciting, as they indicated this might also play a role for the structuring and large-scale evolution of the universe. The mirroring effect might also point to a fundamental polarity of the universe. The universe was not without a basic structure after all, and the Cosmic Axis seemed to have something to do with how this was created. In support of this, the study of the handedness of galaxies had been made independently of the WMAP study and could not have been distorted by some unknown influence from our own Earth or galaxy. Longo thus concluded that "a well-defined axis for the universe on a scale of ~170 Mpc would mean a small, but significant, violation of the Cosmological Principle and of Lorentz symmetry and thus of the underpinnings of special and general relativity."[21] If Longo is right, his data points to a universe that was polarized from the very beginning by the Cosmic Axis, resulting in the separation of galaxies that were either left- or right-handed from our own particular perspective. It hinted at the possibility that the Cosmic Axis created a basic duality throughout the universe.

What is more, if the handedness and spin axes of galaxies are directly related to the central axis of the universe, then this would mean that the formation of galaxies is not just a result of random fluctuations, which caused them to rotate. The spins of the galaxies would instead be related to that of the Cosmic Axis and probably have emerged in resonance with this. This would mean that all the galaxies of the universe are connected with this Cosmic Axis and so also with one another. If the different galaxies of the universe are not independent but retain a connection to its overall polarized structure created by the Cosmic Axis, this would also favor the idea that their evolution is connected and synchronized, something that may be crucial for the evolution of life. The most important aspect of this discovery is, however, that *the existence of the Cosmic Axis shows that there was structure in the universe from its very inception,* which puts in question the whole randomness philosophy and purported purposelessness of the universe that is upheld by official science.

That there are directions in the universe may at first seem hard to accept as we have all grown up with a view of the universe as having no "up" or "down," with galaxies seemingly floating around in space with no connection to anything else. An overall structuring factor such as the Cosmic Tree of Life also seems at odds with Carl Sagan's view that "our planet is a lonely speck in the great enveloping cosmic dark."[22] Nonetheless, in the view that is now emerging, and more evidence will be provided for this shortly, the entire universe with all of its galaxies has an overarching structure with directions emanating for the Cosmic Axis.

It was based on the above findings that I wrote *The Purposeful Universe* (2009), which presents an alternative theory not only to Darwinism but also to the scientific consensus view of the evolution of the universe at large. I then identified the so-called axis of evil as the Tree of Life of the ancients and especially of the Maya in whose time-based cosmology this had played a significant part. Very notably, since this Cosmic Axis had been discovered in the original microwave background radiation, I drew the conclusion that *it was not the Big Bang that had created the Tree of Life but the emergence of the Tree of Life that had created the giant inflationary expansion called the Big Bang.* Based on this model, it became possible to understand not only why and how the constants of nature had gained their particular values but also why the large-scale evolutionary processes of biological species followed wave patterns. It seemed that the discovery of the axis of evil was the icebreaker and that humanity was now beginning to rediscover the Cosmic Tree of Life, and maybe some steps would be taken toward unifying science and spirituality.

THE COVER-UP OF THE EXISTENCE OF THE TREE OF LIFE

As we will see later, the existence of a central axis in the universe at its inception has very profound and immediate consequences for how we can understand what is happening in today's world. It also immediately touches upon the question about the nature of God and how the universe was created. Yet, the discovery of the Cosmic Axis did not reach the public in the way that it deserved, and it is quite obvious why. This is a case where a finding is so disturbing to the ruling paradigm that it may seem best for its adherents to cover it up by pretending that it is unimportant. All paradigm shifts obviously are uncomfortable for established science, but in this case the consequences are unusually far reaching as it affects our view of the very origin of the universe. Such a finding would in turn affect all branches of science, and this was too much for the scientific establishment to bear.

Thus, the Cosmic Axis has been essentially ignored in popular documentaries about cosmology (except for the independently made *The Principle*,[23] which several of the participating scientists later rejected).[24] This downplaying of the importance of the axis was true even after new measurements of the CMBR collected by the Planck satellite (fig. 1.1c) were published in 2013.[25] This satellite had a considerably higher resolution than the data recorded by the WMAP and *verified the earlier findings of the existence of the axis of evil*. Moreover, the detection method used by the Planck satellite was entirely different from that of the WMAP, showing that the axis did not come out of an instrumental error. In the words of George Efstathiou, a member of the team who made the study, "We can be extremely confident that these anomalies are not caused by galactic emissions and not caused by instrumental effects, because our two instruments see very similar features."[26] Based on this, you would have expected that the scientists involved would have publicly announced that one of the most significant principles that science has been based on for four hundred years, the cosmological principle, now had to go out the window.

Yet, established science has held on to the old paradigm of randomness and meaninglessness. *Wikipedia,* which generally expresses the views of mainstream science, refers to the Cosmic Axis as the "axis of evil" under "other anomalies": "Recent observations with the Planck telescope, which is very much more sensitive than WMAP and has a larger angular resolution, confirm the observation of the axis of evil. Since two different instruments recorded the same anomaly, instrumental error (but not foreground contamination) appears to be ruled out. Coincidence is a possible explanation. Chief scientist from WMAP, Charles L. Bennett suggested coincidence and human psychology were involved, 'I do think there is a bit of a psychological effect; people want to find unusual things.'"[27]

The desire to suppress the scientific finding is quite evident in this *Wikipedia* article. To an outsider it may seem strange that mainstream science expresses such negativity toward a seemingly neutral finding, labeling it as the "axis of evil" and disregarding the actual data by referring to them as a "psychological effect." This attitude has been maintained despite the fact that the studies were performed and evaluated mathematically by groups of scientists from very prestigious institutions and that two consecutive mappings by satellites with increasing resolution showed the same Cosmic Axis.

Despite this, the verification by the Planck satellite of the existence of the Cosmic Axis created a certainty about its existence that has triggered new research, which has pointed even more strongly to its crucial role for how the universe is organized. A recent study (2016), for instance, indicates that the jet streams emanating from black holes are preferentially aligned with the Cosmic Axis,[28,29] adding to the already existing studies that show that this axis is an overriding space-time organizer of the universe. This would imply that black holes are connected to the Cosmic Axis, and we come back to the theme that ultimately the entire universe is connected to the Cosmic Tree of Life.

THE ORIGIN OF YIN AND YANG

Equally dramatically, another study[30] has shown that the so-called axis of evil divided the universe in two halves, sky regions, with widely different numbers of quasars and galaxies. In one half of the sky separated by a plane through the Earth, the author, A. K. Singal, found thirty-three quasars and in the other only fifteen. He concluded: "If we include all the observed asymmetries in the sky distributions of quasars and radio galaxies in the 3CRR sample, the probability of their occurrence by a chance combination reduces to $\sim 2 \times 10^{-5}$." These asymmetries were created along the central Cosmic Axis that then separates the universe into a light and a dark hemisphere (at least when it comes to quasars as radiation sources), with the Earth located in a very special place: the plane that separates these hemispheres. In another study comparing these cosmic hemispheres,[31] the authors conclude: "Our results suggest that the Universe is intrinsically anisotropic with the axis of anisotropy pointing roughly towards the CMBR dipole direction." This is obviously technical language, but what "intrinsically anisotropic" means is that the universe at large is divided into a light and a dark hemisphere, at least when it comes to certain forms of radio emissions, and that it is the Cosmic Axis that separates these two hemispheres. To me at least, the picture that is now emerging of the cosmos and its origin is truly mind-blowing, because it is so fundamentally different from what we have been taught and from our own experience of the night sky. When we look at this it may seem that the various stars are relatively evenly distributed in the sky. Yet, if we limit ourselves to certain large distant radio sources, which we cannot see with our eyes, it turns out that the radiation they emit divides the sky in two different hemispheres. This rings a bell of ancient cosmologies explaining the emergence of duality.

These findings imply that the axis (or as I prefer to say, the Cosmic Tree of Life) has introduced a duality on the largest scale of the universe, which in turn creates two separate fields of radiation. We may in fact talk about one half of the sky, the brighter, as yang, and the darker half as yin, separated by the Cosmic Tree of Life as a fundamental duality, which actually pervades the cosmos and reflects physical differences between the hemispheres of the universe (fig. 1.3). This duality, as we will see later, has most likely played a significant role in the evolution of life in the universe and is the very origin of the concept of duality. I should here admit that I have myself up until now always looked upon the duality of yin and yang as something "metaphysical," but what

Figure 1.3. The Aztec hunab-ku symbol showing the duality of the Universe. (*Reproduction based on the* Codex Magliabenchiano; *courtesy of Famsi.org*)

these data are suggesting is that this polarity is intrinsic to how our universe was created in a direct physical sense. A worldview is thus now emerging where the separation between "metaphysical" and "physical" is beginning to disappear.

I should also mention here that there is evidence coming forth[32] that, as I proposed in *The Purposeful Universe,* the Tree of Life can be likened to a three-dimensional coordinate system. The Tree of Life is thus not merely an axis, but the source of space in all three dimensions, presumably with the potential of expressing much more complicated geometries as well. A relevant report regarding this was published in *Nature* magazine[33] in 2014, which also implied the existence of a Tree of Life at the center of the universe. This report described a computer simulation based on the largest data set of astronomical objects ever studied. By means of this, the evolution of the universe from only twelve million years after the Big Bang to our present time was followed. The remarkable thing is that this study shows that the universe in its entirety at its outset appears as a Cosmic Tree (fig. 1.4 on p. 20), which later develops into a bundle of branchlike filaments. A short video[34] of the simulation of the evolution of the universe can be watched on the Internet, and I recommend the reader to see it.

It is noteworthy that this simulation was published in *Nature,* the most prestigious of the scientific journals, because this means that its data has undergone a very strict scrutiny. Yet, it seems the scientists involved have been unable to see the full picture of the Tree of Life, which to an unbiased observer seems quite obvious. The conclusion to draw from this series of discoveries, going from the WMAP identification of the axis of evil to its verification by the Planck satellite to studies showing what role the Cosmic Tree of Life has in structuring the universe, is that *far from being created as a random explosion called the Big Bang, all of the evolution of the universe is a result of the emergence of a Cosmic Axis, referred to by the ancients as the Tree of Life, and it is from this that the universe has gained the structure that it currently has.*

It is exciting that this phenomenon, the Tree of Life, whose existence I had hypothesized prior to its discovery, has been found on the largest scale of the universe and that evidence is increasingly coming forth to support that this indeed plays a central organizing role for the universe. These findings allow us to create a holistic view of the universe that explains the emergence and evolution of life in a meaningful way and provides a basis for unifying science and spiritu-

Figure 1.4. Image of the Cosmic Tree. (*Used with permission from Bolshoi Cosmological Simulations, http://hipacc.ucsc.edu/Bolshoi/FAQ.html*)

ality. Yet, I do not think that these recent discoveries, with enormous consequences for how we look at our own role in the big scheme of things, have received the kind of attention that they deserve. Hence, it has not come to the public's attention that a Cosmic Tree of life, a widespread component of the cosmologies of ancient peoples, has been verified by modern scientific techniques. In my view, the Big Bang was thus far from a random explosion. It was instead a stage-setting event, and in the next chapter we will see how the continued evolution of the universe is brought about through creation waves broadcast by the Tree of Life.

The creation of the universe, in other words, begins at the Big Bang with a vibration, which is to say a wave emanating from this axis. Or as it is stated in the Bible: "In the Beginning was the word" (John 1:1). The axis mundi, from which the waves of creation emanate, with the size of the diameter of the universe, may generate vibrational holograms creating conscious observers all over the universe who are in resonance with these waves. *It is the origin of creation waves in the Cosmic Tree of Life that makes the evolution of the universe understandable and purposeful.*

To summarize, over the past decade data have been forthcoming that have shattered not only the Cosmological Principle but also the view that the universe is essentially directionless and random in nature. We now know things about the birth of the universe that will be highly meaningful for understanding the way life on Earth has evolved. From the recent discoveries three conclusions may be drawn that especially deserve to be highlighted.

1. The entire universe has from its very inception been organized in relation to a Central Cosmic Axis, presumably its primeval organizer of space-time, and called by the ancient cultures of our planet the Tree of Life.
2. The Big Bang did not create the Tree of Life. Instead, the

emergence of the Tree of Life created the Big Bang, space-time, the inflationary expansion of the universe, and all the subsequently emerging galaxies, star systems, and the life they harbor.

3. The Cosmic Axis induces a yin/yang polarity across the universe. The Earth is located on the plane that separates the yin and yang of the cosmos.

THE FRACTAL-HOLOGRAPHIC MODEL OF THE UNIVERSE

Geometry existed before the Creation. It is co-eternal with the mind of God. . . . Geometry is God himself.

JOHANNES KEPLER, *HARMONICES MUNDI* (1618)

It needs to be pointed out that the Cosmic Tree of Life is not a "thing" made of matter. Rather, it is the geometric source of the space-time through which the matter of the universe is organized. The Tree of Life is a name for a particular form of pure geometry, which underlies the structure of the universe. When this geometry was activated at the birth of the universe, its structure, and the effect of this on the energy released in the Big Bang, provided the basis for the evolution of life. You may then say that the Divine manifests itself as pure geometry, created through the effects this has on energy. The geometry of the Tree of Life is the chief space-time organizer of the universe, and it was through its activation and initial vibration that the evolution of the universe was set in motion. From this Cosmic Tree of Life, as we will see in the next chapter, waves are constantly emitted that give rise to vibrational holograms that shape the physical and mental aspects of life all over the universe. When we talk about manifesting the purpose of this creation, the discussion is based on an understanding that this started with the activation of an immensely powerful, overriding geometry from which the continued evolution of the universe may be understood.

The life of the universe can only emerge and be sustained if it is created by a synchronization of processes at many different levels. Systems such as galaxies, solar systems, or planets that seem partially autonomous are in fact synchronized in their movements with the evolutionary process so that they are able to sustain life. This synchronization of the different systems of the universe takes place because the Cosmic Tree of Life is reproduced at several lower levels, as was discussed in detail in *The Purposeful Universe.* Each level has a "tree"—a coordinate system made from pure geometry (see fig. 1.5 on p. 24)—at its core and these "trees" are entangled with the Cosmic Tree of Life according to a model where parts are subordinate to wholes. The creation of the universe thus depends on the coordination and synchronization of the geometries of the Tree of Life on several different levels. Understanding the evolution of life in the universe thus requires what may be called a fractal-holographic model,[35] according to which its different levels are connected in such a way that the microcosm reflects the macrocosm.

What is important to note in figure 1.5 is that the Cosmic Tree of Life discussed in this chapter represents the most encompassing level of the universe and is what the geometries of all the lower levels ultimately are connected to. What this means is that all life in the universe, including what we call extraterrestrial life in other galaxies or star systems, ultimately finds its origin and evolves based on wave information emanating from this same Cosmic Tree of Life. The model is called fractal-holographic, as the universe is not just one big hologram but instead is composed of a nested hierarchy of holograms within holograms, which also at lower levels have Trees of Life at their centers. It is the existence of Trees of Life at several different levels that makes the universe fractal and holographic in the first place. Each of these levels has a certain autonomy as the boundaries of the different systems are defined by the pure geometries of trees at different levels.

The fractal-holographic model means that what goes on at our own human (or organismic) level is profoundly conditioned by the

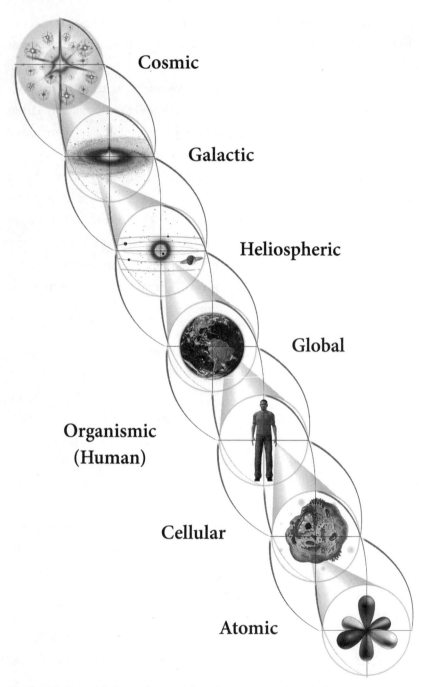

Figure 1.5. Fractal-holographic model of the universe where holograms are created at different levels by a fractal expansion of Trees of Life. (*Diagram from* The Purposeful Universe *by the author, design courtesy of Bengt Sundin*)

systems, such as the galaxy and the solar system that are senior to our own system (our bodies), and, as we shall see, the creation waves affect the different levels in synchrony. Similarly, what happens at the cellular or atomic microlevels is determined by the context created by our own human level. That different levels or subsystems of the universe are connected in this way has been amply verified in earlier books of mine. The model explains how changes taking place in different subholograms are synchronized with the whole to produce the coherent universe that we experience. Thus, the universe has not come into existence as a random amassment of atoms; it is not created in a reductionist way from below to above. The systems of life at all levels are integrated as parts in a whole, and *the organizing principles of the universe act from above to below based on creation waves emanating from the Cosmic Tree of Life, which ensures that its coherence is always maintained.*

GOD

What the ancient traditions said about the Tree of Life will be discussed later, but we should already note that in several of these traditions the Tree of Life was looked upon as the Creator itself. If indeed we look upon the Tree of Life as the Divine that manifests itself as pure geometry, we can also explain three common traditional perceptions regarding the Divine. One is that the Divine is not of a material nature, another is that the Divine is everywhere, and a third is that the Divine is invisible. That God is not material fits well with the pure geometry of the Tree of Life, because this is not of a material nature. The pure geometry would also exist everywhere through the hierarchy of trees of which the fractal-holographic model is made up (fig. 1.5). Hence, if the Divine is expressed through this pure geometry it would indeed be omnipresent. Each living species, including our own, would also be created by this pure geometry, and so if the Tree of Life is the Creator it would also be invisible. This view is also consistent with another common idea about the nature of God, namely that God is in everyone. A fourth prevalent religious idea, namely that man has been created in the image of God, is also consistent with this model. If in figure 1.5 we identify the Tree of Life at the cosmic level with the Divine, then we can understand that the holographic projection of the human level is a reflection of the Divine created in its image.

Maybe then the Creator is not separate from the Tree of Life, and it becomes understandable why the ancients placed so much emphasis on worshipping this tree. A Creator taking the form of a Cosmic Axis of pure geometry brings us to the heart of the conflict between today's established science and religion. In contrast to the towering pioneers of science, beginning with Kepler and even up to Einstein, today's scientists are largely antireligious and are trying to cover up everything that may point to the existence of an intelligent design of the universe. The focus of today's scientists is on measuring aspects of the material reality and denying the existence of everything else. Because the Creator is not by nature material, but pure geometry as in the model presented here, it should be obvious that the Creator's existence will never be proved by such measurements. To say that the Divine cannot in any way be measured is the same thing as saying that it is indeed invisible.

Yet, obviously this does not mean that the Creator does not exist. What we can see through the new discoveries in cosmology is that indeed there is a pure geometry, which measurably influences physical reality and guides the evolution of the universe. If we identify this pure geometry with the Tree of Life, and in turn with God, we can make sense of reality and how the spiritual aspects of reality indeed are directly connected to the physical even if they are not the same. The Divine depends on material reality to manifest its creation, but it is never identical with that physical reality, and the physical reality would not have come into existence in the first place without the Divine. This may not be proof of the existence of God, as this may not even be possible given the invisible nature of the Divine. Yet, it is a way of look-ing at how science and spirituality are related in a way where they can coexist and each has its place. Science and spirituality are not mutually exclusive but complementary. Meaningful science can only be produced with a spiritual understanding, but on the other hand without science spirituality may lose much of its foundation.

2
The Nine Waves of Creation

QUANTUM THEORY—EVERYTHING IS WAVES

Up until the end of the nineteenth century, physicists essentially believed the world to be made up of solid matter in the form of indivisible particles called atoms. People in general also believed they were living in a solid universe that behaved according to known mathematical laws. But then, similarly to how our own century has begun with dramatic findings regarding the macrocosmic birth of the universe, the twentieth century began with some dramatic discoveries about the microcosmos, which would forever change the science of physics.

In the first few years of the twentieth century, the apparent solidity of matter was shattered by experiments performed by Max Planck (black-body radiation, 1900)[1] and Albert Einstein (photoelectric effect, 1905),[2] effectively birthing the new era of quantum physics. These experiments would be the initial steps by means of which pioneers such as Max Planck, Albert Einstein, Niels Bohr, Werner Heisenberg, and Erwin Schrödinger would enter the world of the subatomic cosmos and, in the first decades of the twentieth century, develop the basic concepts of quantum physics.[3] Following the proposal of Niels Bohr's atom model in 1913 (fig. 2.1a), the existence of electrons, protons, and neutrons was verified, and the idea of the indivisibility of the atom could no longer be maintained. As the nature of matter was studied on smaller and smaller scales, particles were found to behave as *quanta*, or energy packages, which could be described or quantified in accordance with Einstein's famous formula $E = mc^2$: the old physics of solid matter disappeared.

One of the most remarkable concepts of quantum physics prompted by several experiments was the wave-particle duality.[4] What this meant was that elementary particles, such as photons and electrons, were also waves whose energies could be determined by their frequencies. Depending on the experimental settings, matter could be seen as constituted of either particles or waves. The atom, for instance, could be seen as composed of a nucleus surrounded by electron particles moving in circular orbits much like planets as in figure 2.1a. But the model that has become favored is indeed the one in figure 2.1b, where the electrons do not behave as particles in definable positions but appear to exist as electron "clouds," or wave patterns, that determine the respective chemical properties of the different kinds of atoms.

In the latter model, the basic building blocks of matter, such as in this case the electrons, may then be seen as waves whose precise location in space cannot be determined. They only exist as potentialities. Accordingly, the locations of electrons in atoms (fig. 2.1b) really do not have fixed positions as implied in figure 2.1a. Instead they should be described as electron clouds, which reflects the different probabilities that an electron exists in a certain location of this cloud. Surprising as

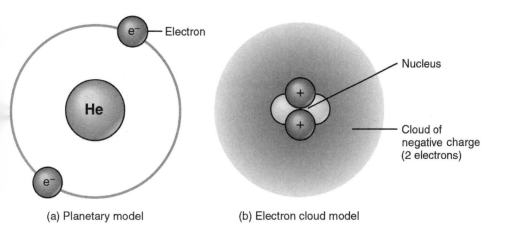

(a) Planetary model   (b) Electron cloud model

Figure 2.1. a. Bohr's original (particle) atom model. b. The orbital (wave) atom model (both for helium).

it may seem, electrons and other elementary particles are thus not solid particles with clearly defined positions in time and space. Only a conscious observer will bring about the "wave function collapse," allowing the electron to behave as, and be measurable as, a particle.

This wave function collapse has consequences for what happens when a human brain receives a quantum, for instance in the form of an electromagnetic light wave. We do not actually see this in the form that it exists out there: like a wave. Instead, as the quantum is being observed by us, the "wave function" collapses and is transformed into electrical signals that in the brain give rise to an experience, for instance of a yellow color. A remarkable consequence of this is that we never really see reality as it exists "out there"—in the form of waves—and this fact may make us wonder about how "real" the "reality" we experience really is.

Although quantum physics is now accepted science, it is easy to understand how scientists like Einstein raised questions about the worldview underlying this new branch of physics. He is famously known to have said, "Quantum mechanics is certainly imposing. But an inner voice tells me that it is not yet the real thing. The theory says a lot but does not really bring us any closer to the secret of the 'old one' [his expression for God]. I, at any rate, am convinced that He does not throw dice."[5] After all, we may all ask the question regarding where our coherent experience of the universe would come from if an indeterminate and probabilistic quantum field is all that exists.

I believe that what Einstein was saying was that he found it difficult to reconcile the probabilistic model of quantum theory with the notion of a coherent universe that has a purpose and a direction as well as an intelligent source. For such a reconciliation to happen I believe that quantum physics now has to be reconstituted within a new and wider framework of nine waves of creation emanating from the structure provided by the Cosmic Tree of Life, which was described in the previous chapter. What this would mean is that the probabilistic and indeterminate processes that go on at the atomic level in figure 1.5 (p. 24) are subordinated to creation waves that develop the large-scale structure of the universe as well as of ourselves.

This implies including quantum theory in a broader wave theory. While quantum theory within established physics is usually confined to the subatomic microcosmos and applied only to the electromagnetic wave spectrum, strictly speaking the word *quantum* refers to anything that can be quantized, and as we shall see soon the creation waves do meet this criterion. For this reason I will also refer to the study of the basic creation waves as quantum theory, because these have very precise and discrete frequencies. In this way we will be able to see that the statement that "everything is waves" is meaningful also when it comes to the macrocosmos. Hence, with an expansion into a new frequency range of a fractal-holographic universe it will become clear that God does not play dice. It is by integrating the waves that the Cosmic Axis emits into this scientific framework that we may expand our understanding of our existence. From this perspective, we will better understand where we come from, where in the evolution of the cosmos we are now (2016), and in what direction the universe intends to take us.

WAVE INTERFERENCE AND HOLOGRAPHY

A critical property of waves, and especially of their interference patterns, is that they may carry information. This property is made use of in all modern communication technologies, such as radio, TV, mobile phones, and so on. As the waves reach their receivers, for instance TVs, a reality that we can experience through our senses is reproduced on a screen from the interference patterns transmitted by carrier waves.

Holography is an example of how the interference patterns of waves can be reproduced to create a physical reality. Technically speaking, a three-dimensional hologram is produced in two steps. In the first, laser beams (producing coherent light of a specific wavelength) are split (fig. 2.2, p. 32) so that one beam goes unobstructed to a recording film while another is reflected by an object.[6] As the two beams come together on holographic film, on which they have been focused, an interference pattern is produced that incorporates all the information about the size and shape of the object.

This information is then stored on the two-dimensional film as an interference pattern of the two beams. To produce a holographic image of an apple, a beam of light is directed to the film, which results in a three-dimensional image that may be projected into thin air. Most of us have seen such three-dimensional images or holograms, in which we can see depth and behind corners, produced on a two-dimensional surface, but maybe this is also a model for how the universe is created on a larger scale.

Even though the interference pattern of waves as such has no meaning to us, the information held in it may. It is this information, as well as the possibility of transmitting such information through waveforms, that will primarily be of interest to us here. It gives an example of

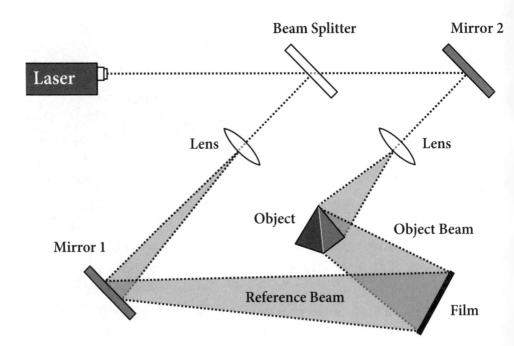

Figure 2.2. The production of a hologram on holographic film by means of two beams of light. (*Courtesy of Bengt Sundin*)

how interference patterns between waves, even if we cannot see them directly, may re-create a view of reality that we can experience. Hence, wave patterns in the quantum field may provide an essential invisible underlying reality to the one we experience, and this model forms a significant principle throughout this book. Holographic images produced in our brains are then seen as projections generated by wave patterns in the quantum field. They generate these projections for the simple reason that we are conscious and are able to make the wave function collapse.

The holographic principle for creating three-dimensional images "in thin air" was suggested by theoretical physicist David Bohm as the basis for a holographic model of the universe.[7] Similarly, brain researcher Karl Pribram has likened the human mind to a hologram.[8] This is relevant here as we will demonstrate a holographic model, which shows how the human mind is created by the Tree of Life. A good book discussing the consequences of their findings is *The Holographic Universe* by Michael Talbot,[9] and an informative video series exists on YouTube that goes by the same name.[10] Recently, physicist Leonard Susskind[11] has also proposed the idea that the universe in its entirety is a hologram created from the two-dimensional surface, or boundary area, of the universe. This is an intuitively attractive idea but leaves many questions unanswered, for instance: Who designed this two-dimensional surface? What, in my view, is missing in these accounts is an identification of the Source of the waves, which created the holograms that pervade the universe. I assert this Source is the Cosmic Tree of Life and that the holograms it transmits are broadcast by creation waves outside of the normal frequency range.

THE UNIVERSAL FREQUENCY RANGE

The breakthrough of quantum physics in the twentieth century has in many ways dissipated into the population at large, and increasing numbers of people now describe their experiences in terms of frequencies and waves with which they resonate. Quantum terms have entered the common language in expressions such as "I like his vibes," "We were at completely different wavelengths," and "It all depends on the frequency." Some have also come to ask the philosophical question regarding what the ultimate nature of reality is, given that according to quantum physics the world we are living in is not as solid, or real, as was previously thought. Could there then be an underlying wave field that determines not only how the universe evolves but also generates our coherent experience of the world? If so, what would be the nature of such a wave field? It seems that it was an understanding of this for which Einstein was hoping.

From physics we know of a few different forms of waves that may be candidates for creation waves. There are the electromagnetic waves covering a whole spectrum from radio waves to gamma rays (fig 2.3). There are also mechanical waves, such as ocean waves, or acoustic waves propagated through air, which give us different experiences of sounds. In addition there are the recently discovered gravitational waves.[12] One of the properties that characterize waves is that they have frequencies, and we will here study especially the electromagnetic spectrum in this regard.

It is one of the successes of twentieth-century science to have integrated the many different types of electromagnetic radiation within one theoretical framework.[13] Research over the past century has, however, also shown that the part of the spectrum that we may experience through our senses, that is to say light in the visible range, is only a very small portion of this spectrum. There also exists a wider range of the spectrum that we can only measure and detect with the help of technology (fig. 2.3). The frequencies in this technical range form the basis for many inventions, such as the mobile phone, radio, and television. What is much less commonly realized is that the technically accessible range of the electromagnetic spectrum is only a limited portion (about a third) of its full (theoretical) range. In theory electromagnetic wavelengths up to the diameter of the universe as a whole may even exist. This diameter is currently estimated to be in the range of a hundred billion light-years (10^{27} m),[14] but at the time

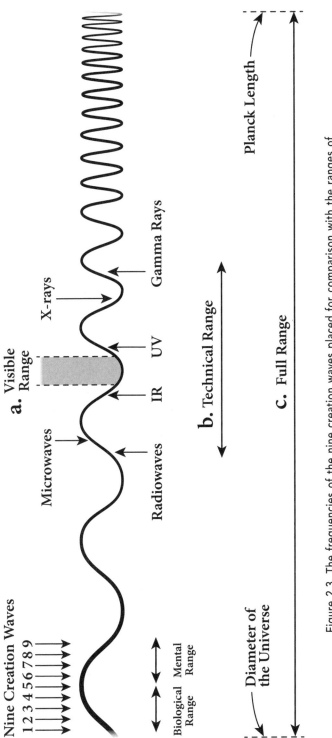

Figure 2.3. The frequencies of the nine creation waves placed for comparison with the ranges of visible, technically measurable, and full ranges of the electromagnetic spectrum. Depending on the frequency, creation waves may belong either to the morphogenetic (biological) or mental range. (Diagram by the author, design courtesy of Bengt Sundin)

shortly after the Big Bang, the Cosmic Axis had a length in the range of a billion light-years.[15]

Hence, the general rule is that you can only measure a wave if it has a wavelength in the range of the object, such as for instance an antenna,[16] that you are using to detect it. Because it is impractical (at least on our present technological level) to build antennas the size of the solar system or the galaxy, we simply do not know anything about the nature of waves with very high wavelengths or what roles these may be playing for the organization of the universe.

We will soon study the frequencies of the creation waves, but it is already important to note the fact that they are way outside of the range that humans may directly detect (or manipulate). This is very consequential and in itself provides an explanation to why they have not been discovered through the use of instruments. In the next chapter we will look at these nine waves one by one, and we will then find that they may be subclassified into a morphogenetic (or biological) as well as a mental range.

Considering how our detection of the electromagnetic spectrum has expanded our knowledge of the universe and increased our technological prowess, it stands to reason that the frequencies we cannot yet detect likely play crucial roles in how the universe functions. The alignments of the large-scale astronomical structures and the Cosmic Tree of Life may in fact depend on interactions mediated by such very long wavelengths. The theoretical frequency range of electromagnetic radiation is much larger than what we can directly experience with our senses or even measure with our current technology.

THE FIRST WAVE OF CREATION

None of the abovementioned types of waves, however, including electromagnetic, would be likely to generate coherence in the universe. What I instead suggest is that the structure of the universe fundamentally is a result of resonance with the creation waves. Creation waves are carrier waves for vibrational holograms, structuring reality by means of straight and perpendicular lines emanating from the Cosmic Tree of Life. These waves have been placed in figure 2.3 together with the waves of the electromagnetic spectrum to facilitate the comparison of their frequencies and presumed wavelengths with those of electromagnetic waves, but this is not to say that by themselves they are electromagnetic in nature.

Hence, there are gaps in our knowledge regarding the creation waves. What we do know about them are their frequencies as well as their polarities, and this is undeniably a strong foundation for further study. Yet, we do not know in what kind of medium these waves travel (if any) or with what speed they propagate (even if I have assumed that they propagate with the speed of light). Although creation waves may have significant properties in common, for instance with acoustic or electromagnetic waves, I believe the creation waves form a distinct class of waves that is more basic for organizing the universe than other types of waves. Serving this end, they provide pure geometries at all levels of the universe. I feel confident that future research will more clearly be able to describe these waves in physical and mathematical terms. Yet, I believe that what is critical at the current time is to convey the knowledge that these waves really exist and indeed are the most meaningful waves for human beings to study when it comes to understanding why we are here and where we are going.

The reader may then ask, what is the evidence for the existence of waves, with periods in the range of a billion light-years, if there is no way that we can directly measure them? The answer is, as we will see in the following chapters, that it is still possible to measure some of their effects, and while this is mostly based on the modern database of knowledge, we have been profoundly helped by some ancient peoples who identified nine levels of the universe or even the nine waves of creation.

Hence, the First Wave (fig. 2.4, p. 38) of the Mayan calendar system,[17] with the lowest frequency, started at the time of the emergence

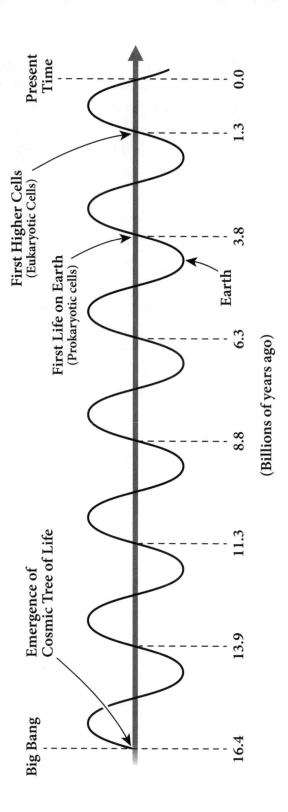

Figure 2.4. The First Wave going from the Big Bang to the emergence of life on our planet. (*Diagram by the author, design courtesy of Bengt Sundin*)

of the Tree of Life (the Big Bang), some 16.4 billion years ago, and has since completed thirteen *hablatuns,* each lasting 1.26 billion years. This wave is a sine function that alternates between peaks and valleys (also called DAYS and NIGHTS), and a full wave period lasts for 2 × 1.26 = 2.52 billion years, and if this wave is propagated with the speed of light this would mean a wavelength of 2.52 billion light-years. The wavelength of the First Wave is thus in the range of the size of the Cosmic Axis around the time of the CMBR, estimated by Dr. Longo to about 0.5 billion light-years.[18] There is thus a reasonable concordance between the wavelength of the First Wave and the diameter of the Cosmic Axis, which indicates that the latter may indeed have been the "antenna" from which this wave has been broadcast.

As we can see in figure 2.4, the beginning points of the last two DAYS gave rise to the first simple life-forms on our planet, prokaryotic cells (3.8 BYA),[19] followed by eukaryotic cells (1.5 BYA), which amounted to some of the greatest jumps known in all of biological evolution. It should also be noted that the neo-Darwinist model upheld by official science has never provided any kind of explanation for how this kind of a jump could take place. Is it then really an accident that the most significant steps in the evolution of cellular life on our planet (upon which all further biological evolution is based) occur at significant shift points (when DAYS begin) in this First Wave? What I instead suggest is that the hologram defining the limits of a cell (its spherical halo) is what brought life to manifest on Earth exactly as the sixth peak of the First Wave began and that this was followed by a considerably more advanced cell form as the seventh peak began. The holograms creating these entities may very well have existed from the very beginning of the wave as the Cosmic Tree of Life came forth, but it was only as planets with the right physico-chemical conditions, such as our own Earth, emerged 4.5 billion years ago that the hologram could manifest as biological life.

All nine creation waves in this calendar system have wavelengths that are considerably longer than what we can possibly measure directly.

Yet, because of the extensive knowledge that we currently possess about the dating of events in the evolution of the universe it is still possible to verify the existence of the creation waves. This will become much more evident in chapters 6 and 7 as we make a more detailed study of recent history.

If the First Wave of creation actually goes back to the Big Bang then there is truly a meaning to the phrase "In the Beginning was the Word," or in other words that a vibration, or a set of vibratory waves with distinct frequencies, began the process of evolution of the universe all the way to the present time and beyond. If this is true, we should recognize that we have an origin already in the birth of the universe and that we could look upon the world as it is now not as a product of random processes but as a result of a directed, purposeful process. I thus suggest that the universe was meant and designed to go through a number of stages to what it is now, and the stage created by the First Wave was the first one of these. Before we go on to study the other eight waves, it is prudent to survey the special role the number nine has played in ancient traditions.

THE HOLY NUMBER NINE

*Even if we know more about the universe than the ancients,
it seems as if they knew something more essential about it
than we do.*

VACLAV HAVEL

Part of our basic knowledge about the creation waves is that they number nine. This is really information gained from ancient cosmologies in which the number nine played a central role. In various spiritual and religious traditions, nine has often been seen as a number signifying completion, and in the decimal system currently used all over the world, the number nine is the completing single-digit number. The origin of the number nine as a base for our counting system can be found in the early Indus Valley culture,[20] which, circa 3100 BCE, was one of the first civilizations to appear on our planet and develop a mathematical system of measurements. Still today, the number nine is revered in Hinduism and is considered to be a complete, perfected, and divine number. In both Hinduism and Buddhism, and various other Eastern spiritual traditions as well, the number 108 (9 × 12) is also the most sacred number.[21]

In ancient China as well, the number nine was deemed special, as it is the highest possible single digit. In China, the number was frequently connected with dragons, the main spiritual powers of Chinese mythology.[22] A Chinese dragon normally has 9 attributes and 117 (9 × 13) scales out of which 81 (9 × 9) are yang and 36 (9 × 4) are yin.[23] (Remarkably, this gives a proportion between yang and yin, 81/36 = 2.25, which is practically identical to the proportion between quasars, 33/15 = 2.2, counted on the two sides of the Cosmic Axis as

Figure 2.5. The nine-story Buddhist temple Hwangnyongsa in Korea (a miniature replica is shown here) was once the tallest building in East Asia and the tallest wooden structure in the world until the Mongols burned it down in 1238 CE. This restoration image of the nine-story pagoda of Hwangnyongsa was made by the National Museum of Korea. (*Photograph by Historiographer*)

mentioned in chapter 1.[24]) Further there are nine forms of dragons, and notably, in our context of studying waves, nine sons of the cosmic dragon. Nine was also recognized as the number of the emperor, the representative of heaven on Earth. The Chinese developed a hierarchical system for determining how many dragons an official could display on his robe. The emperor himself wore his dragon robe with only eight of the nine dragons visible. High-ranking officials underneath him must, however, have all nine dragons hidden, while lower-ranking officials were only allowed to wear robes with five or eight dragons, all of them covered by surcoats. This tells us that in ancient Chinese mythology, the ninth dragon (wave) had a special connection to heaven. There were also nine great social laws, nine classes of officials, nine sacred rites, and nine-story pagodas,[25] all adding to the picture that the nine-level cosmology was very deeply ingrained in ancient China.

In ancient Egypt, the Ennead,[26] a group of nine gods—Atum, Shu, Tefnut, Geb, Nut, Osiris, Isis, Set, and Nephthys—were worshipped in the city of Heliopolis. Among the Ennead, the self-begotten deity Atum, who is also identified with Ra, stands out. Before the gods were separated into genders, Atum masturbated to produce Shu, air, and Tefnut, moisture. Shu and Tefnut then mated, and Geb, representing Earth, was born as well as Nut, of the nighttime sky. The children of Geb and Nut, the brothers Osiris and Set and their sisters Isis and Nephthys, in turn formed couples. The Ennead embodies a creation story, with different aspects of the universe sequentially coming into existence through the activation (or birth) of the nine different gods.

We may then travel from China and Egypt to another part of the world, to Scandinavia, only to find that my Viking ancestors also had a view of nine "worlds" to which the branches of Yggdrasil, the Tree of Life, stretched.[27] The universe was divided into three levels, each with three worlds, totaling nine worlds. At the highest level were the worlds of Asgard, the home of the Aesir, the gods; Vanaheim, the home

of the Vanir, an ancient group of gods; and Alfheim, the home of the
light elves. At the midlevel were Midgard, the home of the humans;
Jotunheim, the home of the giants; and Svartalfheim, the home of the
dark elves. At the lowest level were Nidavellir, the home of the dwarfs;
Helheim, the home of the dead; and Muspelheim, the home of the fire
giants and demons. This cosmology may sound like something taken
from a fantasy novel (and, indeed, it has formed the basis of many stories in that genre), and for this reason it is often not taken seriously.
Nonetheless, it is just another expression of the theme that the universe
is constituted of nine levels, or worlds, all connected to the Tree of Life.
I suggest that these "worlds" are echoes of various holograms broadcast
by the Cosmic Axis and that the four cosmic directions in figure 2.6
(p. 44) are related to the cosmic directions that we now, as discussed in
chapter 1, know to exist.

In the following chapters I will try to explain these worlds in
ancient mythologies in terms that are understandable to modern people. It should, however, already be clear that the notion of nine levels,
or nine waves of creation, was very widespread in the ancient world.
To give some further examples, in the Celtic tradition the number
nine was the central number, and the existence of nine waves was
explicitly recognized.[28] The Aztecs counted nine underworlds,[29] and
the Hopi had nine universes.[30] The number nine is also a holy number in many current world religions. In Judaism, nine doors opened
to the holiest part of the Temple in Jerusalem, and in the Hanukkah
ceremony[31] there are nine candles in the menorah, one used to light
the other eight. In Christianity there is a hierarchy of nine choirs of
angels, while in the Muslim calendar Ramadan is the ninth month.
Based on this concordance around the number nine, it is hard to
believe that this number does not play some fundamental role in how
the universe is designed.

When considering such a role, we should also take note that many
of the cultures that conceived the universe as organized into nine
different levels or structures had no contact with one another, and

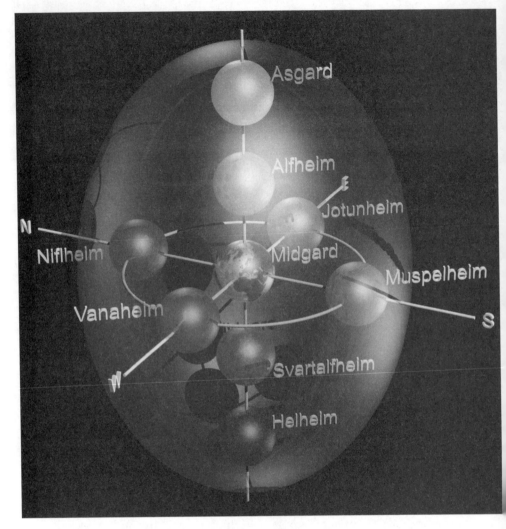

Figure 2.6. Yggdrasil with its nine worlds and four cosmic directions.
(*Nine Worlds of Norse Religion, courtesy of Cush*)

so their cosmologies must have arisen independently. This suggests that the nine-level cosmology has an essence of truth that was experienced by humans living all over the planet—from China in the East to the Maya in the West, with Europe, India, and many other places in between. What I am suggesting is that peoples all over the planet downloaded global holograms created by waves emanating from the

Cosmic Tree of Life, which made them aware of the nine levels of the universe.

Despite this concordance, these nine-level cosmologies from different traditions naturally display some variation as the holograms were subject to cultural and individual differences among the people who downloaded them, resulting in varied interpretations. Yet, it is indisputable that a common theme runs through all of these ancient traditions: the universe was perceived as hierarchically organized into nine worlds, underworlds, or levels, created by dragons or serpents. Especially in the Chinese and Nordic traditions, the nine waves were also valued differently, and not even the Chinese emperor had permission to associate himself with the Ninth Wave. This of course evokes curiosity regarding what kind of information the nine waves, and especially the ninth one, were carrying. What holograms were the waves engendering that led humans to create what they referred to as different "worlds"?

The view I'm presenting here is not that these ancient myths are literally true, as some members of certain traditions may assert. Some aspects of these myths may indeed just be fairy tales. But neither is it my view that these myths are silly false ideas without any foundation, which is the usual modern viewpoint. My view is, on the one hand, that much common ground can be found between reality as we ourselves conceive it based on modern measurements and, on the other hand, the reality as the ancients saw it based on their "intuitions" and direct experiences of higher worlds. I believe the commonalities among these different mythologies are so striking that it suggests the existence of an underlying truth that has now been forgotten.

The ancients lived in a different world from modern peoples and experienced reality through a different hologram than we do now, one that was more conducive to understanding reality through dreams and visions. Regardless, it seems as if a unification of perspectives may now take place between ancients and moderns as modern technology has verified the existence of the Tree of Life that played such a central role in the ancient cosmologies. As we move further into this worldview I think it will become clear that today this truth is something that we badly need to recover.

THE MAYAN CALENDAR WAVES

An ancient culture that we may learn much from about the number nine and the nine waves is the Mayan. As we have seen, this was far from the only ancient culture on our planet to recognize nine levels of evolution in the universe, which more or less all of them did. Yet, the Maya were the only people on our planet who developed an explicit calendar system to chart the nine waves that create these levels. Hence, it is a remarkable fact that the ability of modern man to create a cosmology that is whole and unifies science and spirituality depends directly on knowledge passed down to us from an ancient Native American people. No other people on our planet developed calendars that described wave movements of progressively higher frequencies. Unlike all other calendars, these waves were not based on astronomical observations in our local solar system but on a cosmic creation scheme on a much larger scale.

Very importantly in this context, *the Maya clearly stated that the calendrical waves they followed emanated from the Tree of Life*[32] and that they carried energies that influenced the qualities of different eras.[33] We can immediately see this connection in figure 2.4 where the First Wave starts at the Big Bang with the birth of the Cosmic Axis, or Tree of Life. The connection to the Tree of Life was also directly spelled out in the inscription from Palenque describing the event that initiated the Sixth Wave (the Long Count): "the First Father erected the World Tree," so that "the light could enter. It was made proper, the Raised-up Sky-Place, the Eight-House-Partition, is its holy name, the House in the North."[34] The sixth of the nine waves thus in their view emanated from the Tree of Life (or World Tree) and generated an eight-partitioned hologram on a global scale. It was through the effects of this hologram with straight and perpendicular lines that humans in resonance with it started to create a new reality for themselves at the beginning of the Sixth Wave, as was discussed in *The Global Mind and the Rise of Civilization*. It was the geometric structure of this Sixth Wave hologram that created the rational mind, which in turn gave rise to civilization. The inscription from Palenque is, however, by no means the only example connecting the Mayan calendar to the Tree of Life, and the theme recurs in the surviving Mayan codices.

Even if the Maya used one particular calendar wave (the Long Count or Sixth Wave) to date their pyramids, as well as the events taking place in their political history, they looked at the nine waves very much as a whole—as nine levels belonging to one and the same hierarchical structure. We see this very clearly in that the most significant pyramids they built—at the central plazas of Chichén Itzá (fig. 2.7),

Figure 2.7. The descent of the Plumed Serpent at the nine-story pyramid in Chichén Itzá at spring equinox. (*Photograph by the author*)

Palenque, and Tikal—had nine stories. These pyramids were cosmologies cut in stone that placed the waves in a common context
that connected them with many other aspects of the nine-level
cosmology.

The terrace-formed pyramids, with a staircase in the center, symbolized that the evolution of the universe was like a climb to higher
and higher levels. Each level was developed by a wave movement,
which was symbolized by the Plumed Serpent (called Quetzalcoatl by
the Aztecs and Kukulcán by the Maya). At the equinoxes, the Plumed
Serpent appeared to descend from the pyramid at Chichén Itzá by
forming a wave pattern of seven triangles of light and six of darkness
(compare also the seven peaks and six valleys in fig. 2.4). This incidentally also reflected the wave movement that the Book of Genesis refers
to as the seven DAYS and six NIGHTS of God's creation. The Plumed
Serpent was a symbol of any divine wave of creation and as such was
heralded as a bringer of civilization,[35] the calendar, and many other
things. He also went by the name of Nine Winds (presumably as the
nine wave movements were experienced as spiritual winds). In Mayan
cosmology nine wave movements thus developed the nine levels of
creation, and the Plumed Serpent was a symbol for each one of these
waves. The pyramid at Chichén Itzá was built for the worship of the
nine waves (or winds) of Kukulcán, all emanating from the center of
the universe (symbolized by the house at the top). Much like in other
ancient traditions, these waves were looked upon as living forces: serpents, dragons, or "gods."

Like the Maya, other ancient peoples looked upon the nine different levels (or waves that had created them) as connected and as
parts of a whole. The nine dragons in Chinese cosmology were, for
instance, all connected to the cosmic dragon, and the nine worlds of
the Vikings were all connected to the Tree of Life as were the nine
great gods in Assyria. In their cosmology, the Mayan nine underworlds were looked upon as a totality identified with a creation

god called Bolon Yookte K'uh.[36] Translated to English, this name means the "Nine-Support-Deity," or the "Nine-Step-Temple." This tells us that we are looking at an interconnected system of nine creation waves.

Remarkably, some thirteen hundred years ago the Maya wrote an inscription at the site of Tortuguero to describe what would happen as the thirteenth *baktun* of the Long Count was completed in our own time. It stated that Bolon Yookte K'uh would then "be witnessed" in "his full regalia."[37] This, with little doubt, should be taken to mean that after October 28, 2011, all possibilities of the nine waves ("the full regalia") should be available to us, since Bolon Yookte K'uh was the god of the totality of the nine waves. At the current time there are, in other words, no longer any limits to the interference patterns that may be created from the nine waves.

The shift in 2011 described by the Tortuguero Monument was a game changer of sorts as an evolution that has taken 16.4 billion years was completed. Because we are now beyond this shift, science and spirituality can be unified on a much deeper level than before. We have come to a place where all the possibilities of this creation can come into being, and it is now up to a somewhat confused humanity to manifest its destiny based on the potentialities of the nine waves. A significant aspect of accomplishing this, I assert, is for us to understand the nine-level cosmology of the ancients and learn how to create resonance especially with the Ninth and completing Wave, toward which all of creation has been aiming. This is a possibility that so far very few have realized, partly because of the lack of knowledge and partly because the Ninth Wave has only been accessible for a very short time (since 2011). Yet, the more we develop such a resonance, the greater the possibility will be for us to create lasting peace and prosperity on our planet.

THE NINE FREQUENCIES
OF CHANGE

In later chapters we will study, one by one, some of the effects that the different waves have had on human life. We will then use their frequencies and wavelengths as tools for deepening our understanding of the fractal-holographic model and the cosmic time plan. To facilitate this, I will provide some concrete information about the nine worlds that seems to have been a part of the worldviews of many, if not all, ancient cultures. As a starting point, the nine waves of the Mayan calendar system have been listed in figure 2.8, together with their respective durations, wavelengths, frequencies, and times of activation on our planet.

The First Wave (fig. 2.4), which was activated already at the Big Bang, generated the fundament for the eight higher levels of the pyramid. New and higher waves, *each with a frequency twenty times higher than at the previous step,* have subsequently become accessible at the time points shown in the right-hand column, until we reach the Ninth Wave at the top of the pyramid (fig. 2.8). This means that all nine waves were not accessible at the beginning of creation. Only now, at our present time, after March 9, 2011, *are all nine waves accessible and running in parallel.* In figure 2.9 (on p. 51) some basic keywords are given to describe the kind of phenomena that are created by each of the nine levels listed in figure 2.8.

In column two in figure 2.8, we find the Mayan names for the various half-wave periods of the respective waves—the *baktuns, katuns, tuns,* and so on. The Maya recognized that the different phases of a wave—their peaks or valleys, corresponding to DAYS or NIGHTS—affected their lives differently. Thus, the Maya did not have names for the full wave periods but only for the half-wave periods (fig. 2.10, p. 52). In previous books of mine, where the consequences of shifts between DAYS and NIGHTS have been detailed on several levels, I have used this ancient Mayan terminology.

Wave	Name and Duration of Half Wave (DAY or NIGHT)	Full Wavelength (Light-Years)	Frequency	Time of Activation
9th	Uaxaclahunkin = 18 days	0.1	0.32×10^{-6} Hz	Mar 9, 2011
8th	Tun = 360 days	2	16×10^{-9} Hz	Jan 5, 1999
7th	Katun = 19.7 Y	39.4	0.8×10^{-9} Hz	1755 CE
6th	Baktun = 394.3 Y	788.6	40×10^{-12} Hz	3115 BCE
5th	Pictun = 7,900 Y	15,772	2×10^{-12} Hz	103,000 YA
4th	Kalabtun = 158,000 Y	315,440	0.1×10^{-12} Hz	2.05 MYA
3rd	Kinchiltun = 3.15 MY	6.3 M	5×10^{-15} Hz	41 MYA
2nd	Alautun = 63 MY	126 M	0.25×10^{-15} Hz	820 MYA
1st	Hablatun = 1.26 BY	2.5 B	12.5×10^{-18} Hz	16.4 BYA

Figure 2.8. The nine waves with the respective durations of their time periods, wavelengths, frequencies, and points of activation (Y = year, M = million, B = billion, A = ago). (*Diagram by the author*)

Wave (or Underworld)	Basic Time Period	Phenomena Evolved
9th (Universal)	Uaxaclahunkin	"Multi-D," unity consciousness
8th (Galactic)	Tun	"3-D," smart technologies, female energies, Asian economies
7th (Planetary)	Katun	"3-D," materialism, Americanism, industrialism, democracy
6th (National)	Baktun	Mind, "3-D," civilizations, constructions, nations, writing, science, religions
5th (Regional)	Pictun	Soul, tribal cultures, diversified tools, art, spirituality
4th (Human)	Kalabtun	*Homo*, brain development, fire, tool-making
3rd (Anthropoid)	Kinchiltun	Erect postures, bipedalism, tool-using
2nd (Mammalian)	Alautun	Lateralized multicellular animals, plants to support higher life
1st (Cellular)	Hablatun	Cells, galaxies, stars, planets

Figure 2.9. Keywords for the different realities created by the nine waves. (*Diagram by the author, from* The Global Mind and the Rise of Civilization)

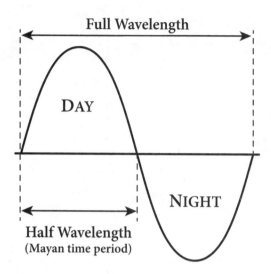

Figure 2.10. Full-wave period in any of the nine waves with its DAYS and NIGHTS. (*Diagram by the author, design courtesy of Bengt Sundin*)

Because of the wave perspective presented here, I will now instead use the terminology of wavelengths and frequencies. The Mayan calendrical time units in column two of figure 2.8 thus represent half wavelengths, while the full wavelengths are given in column three in terms of the astronomical unit of light-years. I would then also like to repeat that the range of wavelengths of these nine waves, as we can also see at the extreme left in figure 2.3, are not on an ordinary scale. Hence, even the shortest of them, the wave period of 0.1 light-years of the Ninth Wave (fig. 2.8), is on a scale equal to the diameter of our entire solar system.[38] This is all assuming that the creation waves, like electromagnetic and gravitational waves, propagate with the speed of light.

The fourth column in figure 2.8 simply provides the inverted values of the wavelengths and thus gives the various frequencies of the nine waves of creation. What we can see from this column is that each wave has a frequency twenty times higher (and a wavelength twenty times shorter) than the wave below it. As we climb (metaphorically speaking) to higher levels of the pagoda or pyramid, the frequencies increase. This hierarchical system, where new higher frequencies are activated according to an exact, mathematically determined schedule, has created an apparent acceleration of the evolution of the universe up until the present time. Consequently, up until the present time, the creative processes in the universe have been accelerating, and we humans have had the experience of time speeding up.

THE INTERFERENCE OF SENSORY INFORMATION WITH THE CREATION WAVES

The waves in figures 2.8 and 2.9 also form interference patterns with one another. Especially today, after all the different waves have become accessible, it seems highly unlikely that any human resonates exclusively with only one of the waves. Any one human being is created by an interference pattern of the different waves, and as we will see in chapter 4, his or her mind is created by composites, or hybrids, of the different holograms these waves give rise to. Even if we can identify the specific phenomena that a particular wave develops (as hinted at in fig. 2.9) and follow those as a result of the unfolding of a wave, it is the multiple possible interference patterns that produce the variation in creation. These interference patterns create the great variety of biological species and also, as we will see later, mental and spiritual variations among human individuals and cultures.

In addition to the interference patterns among the different nine waves, we humans are also exposed to an enormous amount of information carried in waveform, especially in the form of visible light, from our immediate environment. The light that shines on you at this moment from the sun or from the lamps in your house are quanta that contribute to shaping your inner experience together with the electrical signals generated in your brain by the sound waves your ears sense. People are most aware of these frequencies detected by their sensory organs. Superficially, information gained through our senses may seem to comprise the main content of our lives. Some people will say that these frequencies are all that we can experience and so deny everything else.

And yet, I propose that the nine waves of creation create a more fundamental context for our lives, and it is through them that we are connected with Source. These major waves create the framework in which the everyday frequencies in the visible and audible range gain their meaning. A quantum of visible light by itself has no meaning. Meaning is gained from the nine waves and the holograms these give rise to, the reason being that these waves emanate from the Source and so these holograms provide a context and foundation for interpretation of the information we gain through our senses. Hence, even if the nine waves have frequencies in a range that cannot be experienced through our five senses, our whole beings resonate with them, and they may still create our true nature as expressions of the Divine. Because of their very low frequencies, I believe that we at least subconsciously know that they originate from the Source, the Cosmic Axis. Presumably, the sense that many may have of these waves as communicated by the Source will create an experience in them of being divinely guided and compelled to move in a certain direction in life through their influence. I also suggest that our resonance with different waves may play a decisive role in determining the quality of our lives; after all, the nine creation waves create the nature of our beings, our lives, and our connection to the Source.

These nine waves may also explain the mystery of synchronicities,[39] phenomena described by Swiss psychologist Carl Jung to denote remarkable, meaningful coincidences. Such experiences, sometimes of a seemingly magical nature, would likely not result from frequencies in the normal range originating in our immediate environment. Yet, they can be explained by the interference between the waves carrying an experience of deeper meaning. Synchronicities often involve several different people who may be resonating with the same frequency from one of the nine creation waves. Hence, the nine waves may contribute significantly to explaining not only synchronicities but also a host of paranormal phenomena that have defied our understanding of the world based only on the five senses. This may not be so surprising after all, since we are studying a wave field that underlies the evolution of this creation.

3

Waves and Serpents

UNIVERSAL EVOLUTION AND CREATION

The world at first was endless space in which existed only the Creator, Taiowa. This world had no time, no shape, and no life, except in the mind of the Creator. Eventually the infinite Creator created the finite in Sotuknang, whom he called his nephew and whom he created as his agent to establish nine universes.

HOPI CREATION STORY[1]

In the previous chapter we saw that the nine creation waves have different frequencies, which has significant consequences for the roles they are playing in creation. The four lowest waves are in a frequency range that we may refer to as morphogenetic, or biological, as this serves to create the morphology (shape and form) of biological organisms. The four highest waves, on the other hand, are in a frequency range that we may refer to as mental. The Fifth Wave is located at the boundary between these two major frequencies ranges (fig. 2.3, p. 35) and has qualities typical of both. Hence, similarly to how there are qualitative differences in the effects of other frequency ranges, for instance in the electromagnetic spectrum, such as microwaves, UV light, visible light, and so on, there are qualitative differences between the frequency ranges of the four lowest and the four highest of the nine waves. Although biological and mental waves belong to different frequency ranges, it is meaningful to study them in a common context as these waves are sequentially activated according to a strict schedule.

I will in this chapter summarize, one by one, the roles that the six lower waves play. A brief survey will be made of these waves to explain step-by-step how they have brought life from the Big Bang to the dawn of civilization. In later chapters I will more extensively discuss each of the three highest frequency waves and how these waves brought us to our present time and beyond. This approach to study history in a more complete universal context is sometimes called "big history." It is based on the premise that all the different forms of evolution are part of a unified process, although these forms in the past have been studied by different disciplines. The discussion about the six lower waves is given only in abbreviated form here, because these waves are extensively treated in *The Purposeful Universe* (First through Fourth Waves) and *The Global Mind and the Rise of Civilization* (Fifth through Sixth Waves), to which I refer the reader seeking more detailed knowledge.

The large-scale evolution of the universe began, as I understand it, as the Cosmic Axis of pure geometry emerged from the Cosmic Egg and so gave rise to the Big Bang. The sudden appearance of the axes of the Tree of Life led to inflation and later continued the expansion of the universe. The emergence of the Cosmic Axis is thus primary and the Big Bang secondary; the former event then became the beginning point for the activation of a sequence of waves, which have emanated from the axis, according to a set schedule. This version of the birth and continued evolution of the universe clearly differs from the standard scientific model, where everything starts with an explosion, which happens for no reason, and is followed by a remarkable series of "accidents" that eventually culminate in the current life-forms on our planet. This established model lacks any coherent explanation for how and why the evolution of the universe started and how distinct systems of life could have emerged. It also implies that the evolution of life would be a strictly local phenomenon, rather than as in my view a universal phenomenon.

The majority of today's scientists differ from most ancient views of creation. The latter mostly begin with a creator or some kind of formless, all-encompassing water, vapor, or endless space, but there is always a point when creation takes place through the introduction of a separation, often resulting in a polarization into genders, and it is from this that the world as we know it was born. The Egyptian story about the Ennead is an example of such a creation: first there was only the self-begotten Amun-Ra, but then he created Shu (air) and Tefnut (moisture), who separated into the two genders, and from these what was originally one became many. What is implied in this creation story is the introduction of a duality, much like the Tree of Life acts in the Big Bang as pointed out previously.

Such an introduction of a separation of one into two, or the creation of something finite where there was none before, may be incomprehensible to our minds. Yet, I think we have to recognize that this is exactly what happened, and also that without it there can never be any satisfactory explanation to the emergence and evolution of life. That one becomes two as time "begins" may be the ultimate paradox and maybe it is for this reason that our existence will always have aspects that we find mysterious and cannot grasp. Yet, the emergence of duality from unity is a necessary step whenever something new is created. Today's physicists have tried to simply ignore this paradox, and the fact that an initial separation or act of creation is missing in the current formulation of the Big Bang theory may be why this cannot explain the continued evolution of the universe to the structure that it has today, except for in a very fragmented and discontinuous manner.

THE COSMIC WAVE GENERATOR
AND THE FIRST WAVE

The emergence of a Cosmic Axis of pure geometry in a formless sea of energy would, however, satisfactorily account for the emergence of distinct and separate phenomena. The continued evolution of these phenomena can be explained if it were driven by the waves that emanated from the axis. Given that the Cosmic Axis seems to have given rise to a duality on a cosmic scale, this is a conceivable origin to the tensions that have forced the universe to evolve. This is not mere speculation, because we now know that a polarity does exist in the radio sky between the two hemispheres of the cosmos defined by the Cosmic Axis.[2] If there is no polarity, there would be no tension or forward movement. On the other hand, if polarizations generated by the Cosmic Axis give rise to nine waves, then these, as they are broadcast to the entire universe, may create holograms of duality, which in turn would initiate evolutionary processes on many levels of the universe.

The First Wave has a frequency of 12.5×10^{-18} Hz and a wavelength of about 2.5 billion light-years and generated the first evolutionary process of the universe (fig. 2.8, p. 50). Simple cellular life, initially bacteria and then higher, eukaryotic cells, emerged quite suddenly as the two last peaks (DAYS) in the First Wave began. Parallel to this, galaxies, star systems, and planets that could harbor life emerged. This wave, which was activated 16.4 billion years ago, differs slightly from the estimate of 13.8 billion years for the age of the universe, currently favored by most physicists. When considering why these two time points diverge, it is important to keep in mind that estimates do not only depend on the accuracy of the measurements but also on the underlying assumptions of the mathematical models used. Although 13.8 billion years is the favored age of the universe based on WMAP data, both 16.3 and 16.5 billion years have been given as alternatives based on other assumptions.[3] A fundamental paradigm shift in physics may not be so far away, and the correct age of the universe may very well indeed be 16.4 billion years. As long as scientists operate under unproven assumptions such as dark matter or dark energy, I believe that any calculations based on such need to be taken with a large grain of salt.

The theory I am developing here looks at the universe primarily from the perspective of the evolution of life and sees the emergence of astronomical objects as part of the same process. The basic premise is that the existence of life is not an accident but the very reason that the universe exists in the first place. This premise directly conflicts with today's physics, which aims to develop equations to describe the behavior of dead matter and then, not very successfully, tries to fit the phenomenon of life into these. In contrast, the focus of the continued study of the waves here will be on how well their activation and shift points conform to significant steps in the evolution of biological life and its development into the mental sphere.

THE SECOND WAVE
AND BIOLOGICAL EVOLUTION

The Second Wave, with a frequency twenty times higher than that of the First Wave, was activated on or, maybe better, reached our Earth 820 million years ago. This Second Wave transformed single cells into multicellular organisms, such as animals and plants. Its full wavelength is 126 million years; in figure 3.1 we can see how the emergence of the major classes of biological species are related to the peaks of this Second Wave.

　　Based on this figure, I think it is fair to say that the emergence of new classes of species coincides very well with the beginnings of the DAYS (peaks) in this wave. It thus seems warranted to conclude that the Second Wave is behind the evolution of the animals of our planet (plants, too, even though these have not been included in the figure). Unlike Darwinism, this wave model perfectly explains the many sudden large jumps in evolution, such as, for instance, the Cambrian explosion (fig. 3.1), when a host of new classes of species suddenly emerged. The reality—and this has been recognized for a long time even by fundamentalist Darwinists—is that biological evolution proceeds in sudden jumps, bringing major changes, and the wave function explains this. What we can see here is that these jumps conform

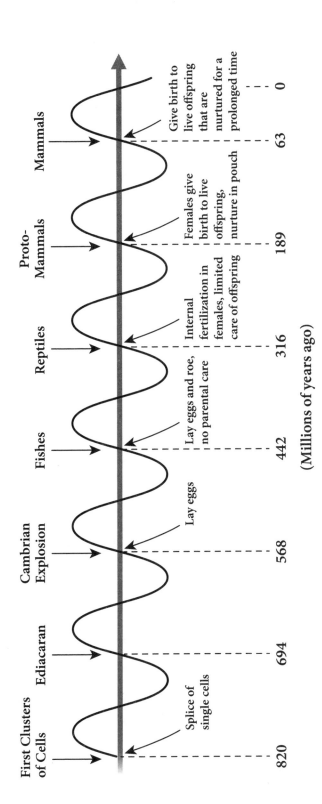

Figure 3.1. The Second Wave and the evolution of significant classes of biological organisms. At the top are the names of the classes and estimates of their time of emergence; at the bottom are some of the characteristics of their modes of reproduction. (*Source: Whitfield, From So Simple a Beginning. Diagram by the author, design courtesy of Bengt Sundin*)

almost perfectly to the beginning of the peaks of the Second Wave, in contrast to the neo-Darwinist idea that species are created through random, undirected mutations in the DNA. (This view would suggest that species should emerge at random points in time, which obviously they do not.) The view of fundamentalist Christians, who believe that there has been no evolution and that all species were created "as is" some six thousand years ago, is obviously also inconsistent with the wave movement in figure 3.1. In the wave model developed here, there is no conflict between evolution and creation. The biological evolution of the species is seen as an aspect of the ongoing wave-like creation of the universe.

Not only the emergence of new classes of species but also mass extinctions conform to the shifts in the Second Wave. This may be exemplified by the biggest such shift point of all time, the Permian-Triassic extinction, which occurred 250 million years ago as a new NIGHT killed 97 percent of the marine species that had existed previously. The four largest extinctions in fact conform to shift points between DAYS and NIGHTS in this wave.[4] Another well-known extinction, that of the dinosaurs sixty-five million years ago, took place close to the beginning of a DAY and paved the way for the dominance of the emerging higher mammals. This extinction was most likely caused by a meteor impact and would thus seem to be accidental. But just because it was caused by a meteor does not exclude the possibility that this event happened in the wider context of the fractal-holographic model of the universe, a context that served to support the proliferation of mammals.

Figure 3.1 illustrates well how the Second Wave (in fact, all the waves) creates evolution through a spiral movement. Waves are not cycles creating identical phenomena every time a new DAY begins. Such cycles would not be evolution but rather going around and around without any direction. With the spiral movement, every new DAY means a more advanced class of animals appears. As an example of how more advanced species emerge, we may look at how the polarity between the left and right halves of the brain increases with every new DAY. In the first half of the Second Wave, early multicellular animals did not always have a defined left-right polarity in their body plans, and they also had poorly developed nervous systems. However, in the second half of the wave, classes of species, such as fishes, reptilians, and mammals, emerged with bodies and brains with bilateral symmetry, along with an increasing polarity in the functions of the brain halves. This polarity becomes most marked in the higher mammals of the seventh DAY. The purpose of this book is, however, not to present a detailed discussion about biological evolution as this was already done in *The Purposeful Universe* (2009). The point to realize is that there is nothing random about this process, and in this regard figure 3.1 speaks for itself. Because it is known from the science of cymatics that wave frequencies can organize matter in accordance with geometric patterns,[5] we may also understand how the different classes of organisms have emerged with the unfolding of creation waves.

SEXUAL POLARITY AT DIFFERENT LEVELS OF THE UNIVERSE

Another aspect of biological evolution that we should pay attention to in the diagram of the Second Wave (fig. 3.1) is the separation into two different genders. This separation is especially significant as it is a part of many creation stories, and we may wonder how it actually happened. In the First Wave single cells did not reproduce sexually, and so this wave did not create different genders. The emergence of two genders was instead created by the Second Wave, during which an increasingly profound polarity developed between them with every new DAY, as indicated in figure 3.1. This wave-like process generating two different genders is expressed both in terms of their outer appearance and in the roles they play in reproduction and the care for the offspring. In all of these regards, the differences increase stepwise over the course of the Second Wave as new DAYS begin. Eventually, the process leads up to the higher mammals, which have very visible differences in appearance between the genders and also in the roles they have in caring for off-spring, where the mother sometimes cares for the young for a long period of time after birth.

Interestingly, the separation into two genders developed in exact parallel to the separation of the functions of the two brain halves.[6] This suggests that there is an evolutionary background to the differential relationships between brain halves in the two genders. The explanation for these parallel developments in brain halves and sexual biology can probably be found in a polarization created by the Cosmic Axis, which separated the two genders in resonance with it. The whole concept of sexual attraction thus becomes understandable as a desire to bridge this polarity. As a curiosity, we may also understand why serpents are symbols of fertility and sexual power: serpents symbolize the underlying reality of waves, and those waves apparently have something to do with the division into sexes and reproduction.

It seems that separations take place in the beginning of DAYS of the Second Wave on several other levels of the universe as well. There is indeed evidence that the evolution of species on Earth has parallels in larger systems in the universe. In our own galaxy, the stars, including our own solar system, move up and down through the equatorial plane of the galaxy in accordance with a sinusoidal movement with a wavelength of 124 million years (fig. 3.2).[7] This wavelength is within measurement error the same as we know that of the Second Wave to be, and we may assume that this sinusoidal movement of our solar system has its origin in the Second Wave. This movement is most likely created by the polarization of the galaxy into Northern and Southern Hemispheres induced by resonance of its equatorial plane with the Cosmic Axis. Moreover, we should notice that the rotational movement of our solar system around the center of the galaxy in a so-called galactic year of 250 million years[8] coincides roughly with two wave periods of the Second Wave (fig. 3.2). The reason the movements of stars in the galaxy differ from what would be expected from gravity alone is probably partly due to the fact that they are under the influence of the

Sixty-two-million-year-long sine wave movements of the solar system in the galaxy. Four such waves equals approximately a galactic year of 250 million years.

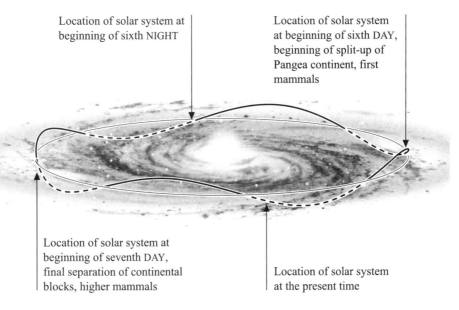

Location of solar system at beginning of sixth NIGHT

Location of solar system at beginning of sixth DAY, beginning of split-up of Pangea continent, first mammals

Location of solar system at beginning of seventh DAY, final separation of continental blocks, higher mammals

Location of solar system at the present time

Figure 3.2. The sinusoidal movement of the solar system around the galactic equator with a 124-million-year wavelength (from Binney and Tremain, *Galactic Dynamics*). Every time a new DAY begins in the Second Wave, a movement of separation between the continents of the East and the West is initiated. At the same time, new species with increased separation of brain hemispheres as well as gender characteristics emerge (fig. 3.1). Note that the amplitude of the wave movement around the galactic equator has been exaggerated for illustrative purposes. (*Diagram by the author, design courtesy of Bengt Sundin*)

Second Wave. Considering that the movement of stars in galaxies was the reason that some physicists postulated the existence of dark matter we may then also realize on what thin ice this hypothesis was created.

A parallel wave movement to this is also apparent in the tectonic plate movements separating the continents of the Western and Eastern Hemispheres on our planet. The final separation between these continental blocks began sixty-five million years ago, as the North Atlantic opened up. This, incidentally, was when the higher mammals emerged, whose brain half functions then "drifted apart" according to an as above, so below scheme in relation to Earth. Polarizations with a 126-million-year-long wavelength thus seem to occur in parallel at several different levels of the universe: the galactic, the planetary, and the organismic. Most likely they also occur exactly in phase with transformations of the DNA code, which is subordinated to the overall changes in the organisms caused by the creation waves.

The wave movement in figure 3.1 very directly reflects a polarization taking place at several different levels of the universe simultaneously at every new DAY. Presumably these movements go back to a polarization caused by the Cosmic Axis, which in accordance with the fractal-holographic model would generate rhythmic pulsations that are in phase with one another on several different levels of the universe. We saw in chapter 1 how a mirroring effect of the Cosmic Axis creates handedness in galaxies.[9] We have here seen that mirror images are also created between the two hemispheres of our galaxy, of our planet, and of the brain halves of its organisms. The Cosmic Axis then clearly plays a significant role in the creation of mirrored symmetry in the universe, but because one of these respective hemispheres is usually dominant, it also creates a polarity: the previously mentioned intrinsic cosmic duality of radio sources. Such polarizations between hemispheres happen on different levels in parallel and serve to synchronize several evolutionary processes with the frequency of the Second Wave.

Accordingly, evolution is not something that proceeds independently, for instance, on the level of the galaxy, Earth, biological species, or their DNA. Instead, in this universe the creation waves have parallel effects on several different levels in accordance with the fractal-holographic model. This means two important things. First, that biological evolution on our planet (or any other planet) is something that originates on a cosmic scale rather than being a process that takes place here in isolation from the rest of the universe. Evolution is a universal process driven and coordinated by waves emanating from the Cosmic Tree of Life. Second, the evolutionary processes at different levels are all parts of a unified process. To create, for instance, a mammal and its habitat, a concordance of wave movements on the universal, galactic, planetary, and organismic levels is needed.

This way of looking at the universe and the evolution of life it generates is in many ways opposite to that of established science, which denies the purposefulness and direction of evolution. In the worldview of today's scientists, the Big Bang was an accident, as was the creation of the moon from an impact, as was the emergence of continents perfect for nonaquatic life, as was the emergence of biological species, and so on, ad absurdum. In the model presented here, the waves emanating from the Cosmic Axis have parallel effects on several different levels, which are synchronized to produce a preset direction for evolution, and there is nothing random or accidental in this process. As we will see shortly, the universe was designed to create humans (or some similar species).

THE THIRD WAVE AND
ERECT PRIMATES

The Second Wave developed biological species in accordance with a clear wave-like pattern, generating increasingly larger brains (compared to body size) and deeper polarization between the left and right sides of the brain (presumably reflecting the inherent yin-yang duality of the universe mentioned in chapter 1) as well as separation into two genders. On top of this, the Third Wave, which on our planet was activated 41 million years ago and has a wavelength of 6.4 million years, created a significant change: it transformed a four-legged mammal created by the Second Wave into a two-legged erect being. From this change, where the Third Wave brought a new geometry into existence, the first monkeys emerged.[10]

As we can see from figure 3.3 on page 68, this level of biological evolution developed according to a wave-like pattern during which species that are more markedly erect emerged on new DAYS. The fossil record for the species developed by the Third Wave is, however, very

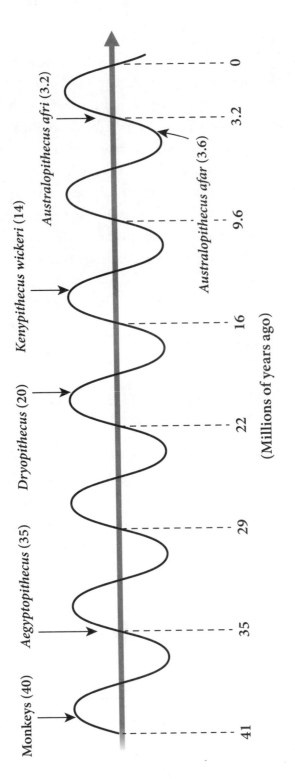

Figure 3.3. The Third Wave reflecting the evolution of anthropoid species increasingly walking upright with hands free. (Diagram by the author, design courtesy of Bengt Sundin)

incomplete, so the various species are more difficult to track than for the other waves. The evolutionary process that the Third Wave covers, as can be seen in figure 3.3, not only has gaps, but some of the fossils have only been found well into the corresponding DAYS. Although this is not a perfect fit to the wave, the insufficient fossil record creates problems for any theory of biological evolution—not just the one presented here.

The Third Wave thus drives evolution to an advanced ape that walks upright and has its hands free and so, unlike its predecessors, is able to use tools. These are very significant steps toward the human species. It can be said that the evolution to australopithecines, an example of which is the famous Lucy discovered by Donald Johanson,[11] is a necessary step toward a species such as our own, one able to develop a technological civilization. Australopithecines, the highest expression of the Third Wave, have, however, long since gone extinct but are considered to have been more humanlike than today's bonobos, chimpanzees, or gorillas.

THE FOURTH WAVE AND THE FIRST HUMANS

The Fourth Wave, the highest in the morphogenetic frequency range, transformed australopithecines to species of the genus *Homo*. This wave was activated on our planet 2.05 million years ago, and its wavelength is 320,000 years. This Fourth Wave serves to develop species that are not only able to use but also make tools, an ability that is considered to be the main distinguishing feature of human beings. The wave's evolutionary process begins with the earliest toolmaker created by this wave, *Homo habilis*,[12] the earliest human species, which was discovered by the famous Leakeys in Kenya. In a series of steps, the process then continued to the species we ourselves belong to, *Homo sapiens* (fig. 3.4 on p. 70), whose earliest known members have been dated to 160,000 years ago.[13] This fits markedly well with the beginning of the seventh peak

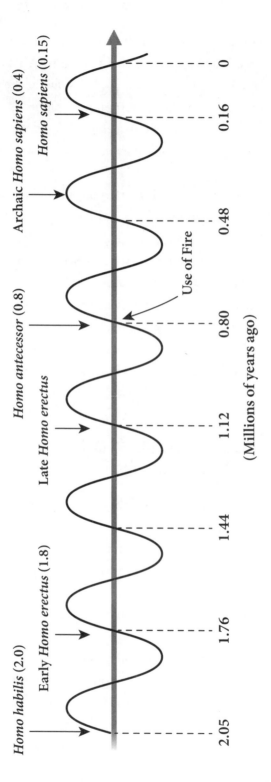

Figure 3.4. The Fourth Wave developing different species of the genus *Homo* with increasingly larger brains (dates from Parker, *Dawn of Man*). (*Diagram by the author, design courtesy of Bengt Sundin*)

of the Fourth Wave. Overall, the emergence of the different species of *Homo* matches the peaks of this wave very well.

What more than anything else characterizes this evolution through the different species of *Homo* (fig. 3.4) is the marked increase in brain size. It has often been pointed out that the speed with which the human brain size evolved from *Homo habilis* of 500 cc to the 1,500 cc of *Homo sapiens* was remarkable as it took place in only two million years. This very complex evolutionary process has been contrasted to how the evolution from bacteria to higher cells required two billion years. The rate of human brain evolution is, however, only a dilemma if you are a Darwinist and believe that evolution is driven at a slow pace by random mutations.

In the theory presented here, each wave in accordance with the Mayan system instead has a frequency that is twenty times higher than the one preceding it (fig. 2.8, p. 50), and consequently the frequency of evolution has sped up eight thousand times from the First Wave (which developed single cells) to the Fourth Wave (which developed the human brain). The Fourth Wave creating the human species thus drives biological evolution forward at a much higher rate than the waves creating simpler organisms.

We should also remind ourselves that each of the nine waves is part of a unified system, where each level is a preparation for the next level to be activated. Even though the different waves play distinct roles—bringing in to existence phenomena that have never been activated before (as indicated in fig. 2.9 on p. 51)—they form a whole where a new wave cannot begin its transformation until the basic aim of the previous lower wave has been accomplished. For this reason their frequencies and times of activation have to conform to precise mathematical relationships supporting a unified process of creation.

In figure 3.5 on page 72, the four waves in the morphogenetic range of the spectrum are shown in different scales so that parallels between the seven steps, or DAYS, in the different waves can be recognized. The end result of each wave then becomes the starting point for the next higher wave, which always has a twenty times higher frequency and

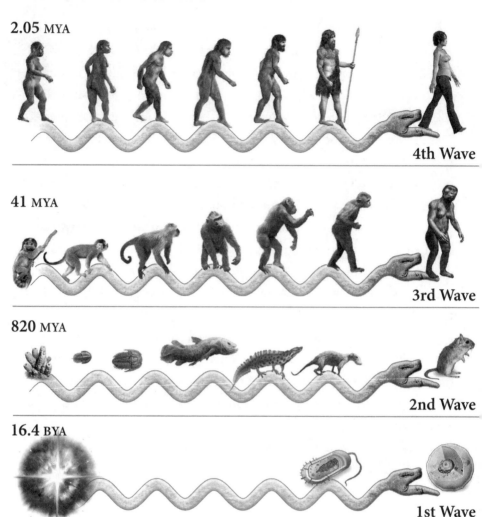

2.05 MYA

4th Wave

41 MYA

3rd Wave

820 MYA

2nd Wave

16.4 BYA

1st Wave

Figure 3.5 The four waves of creation in the morphogenetic frequency range. Note here that these four lowest waves are presented in different scales so that their seven peaks appear in parallel. The end result of each wave becomes the starting point for the next higher wave. (*Diagram by the author, from* The Global Mind and the Rise of Civilization, *design courtesy of Bengt Sundin*)

develops a new aspect of the geometry of the biological species. For instance, the Second Wave could not start to develop multicellular animals eight hundred million years ago until the First Wave had created higher monocellular life on Earth about 1.5 billion years ago (see also fig. 2.4 on p. 38), because these single cells were the necessary starting points for the evolution of the multicellular organisms by the Second Wave. During the Third Wave, primates came into being about forty-one million years ago, but this could not have occurred until the Second Wave had first led to the creation of higher mammals sixty-three million years ago. The process of biological evolution is completed by the emergence of human beings in the Fourth Wave, which then the universe is meant to create in accordance with a directed "plan."

As we will now continue to the mental and spiritual transformations that the higher waves have created in humans, we can see that they proceed in principle in the same way as in figure 3.5. Hence, the manifestation of the destiny of humanity takes the form of a climb to the top of the pyramid created by the nine waves, a climb where no step can be jumped over and where the lower frequency waves provide the fundament for the evolution of the mind.

THE FIFTH WAVE AND SYMBOLIC EXPRESSION

We shall now look at the Fifth Wave, which has a frequency between the biological and mental ranges (fig. 2.3, p. 35), which makes it a midpoint in the nine-level cosmology. This wave was activated 102,500 years ago and developed with a wavelength of 15,800 years. It has transformed *Homo sapiens* to a being that can express itself symbolically, which, as far as we know, humans did not do more than 100,000 years ago. As we can see from figure 3.6 on page 74, the activation of the Fifth Wave did create significant steps in this transition, from which we can gather that *Homo sapiens* underwent a significant shift in its perception of itself and became aware of its connection to a spiritual domain at the beginning of this wave.

As an expression of this altered perception, we may note that it is from the beginning of the Fifth Wave that the first human burials are known.[14] This in turn means that a sense of an afterlife might have emerged or possibly even that there was a perception of a soul

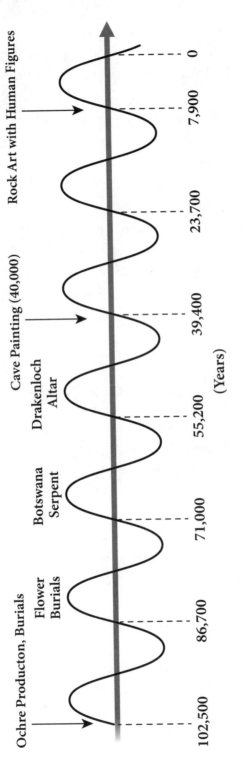

Figure 3.6. The Fifth Wave developing different symbolic expressions of early *Homo sapiens*. (*Diagram by the author, design courtesy of Bengt Sundin*)

separate from the body. Whether such speculations are true we will never know for sure, but at least humans at this time became aware of death. Moreover, the first production of art has been inferred from this time, based on the discovery of an ochre production site in South Africa that is about one hundred thousand years old.[15] No actual objects of art have been found from this period, but the making of ochre indicates that people then started to adorn themselves or express themselves symbolically. Taken together, the findings from the beginning of the Fifth Wave indicate that *Homo sapiens* then became more self-reflective and less animal-like. Even if the human beings in resonance with the Fifth Wave did not have rational minds, indications are that they started to experience a soul, could feel empathy,[16] and possibly started to experience their existence in a larger spiritual context.

Not very long after the beginning of the Fifth Wave, we find the very oldest (70,000 BP) piece of art on our planet, a serpent from Botswana (fig. 3.7 on p. 76) that apparently was part of a ritual site.[17] This earliest finding of ritual art representing a giant python is very noteworthy in the context of our studies of wave movements because of the multitude of markings that have been made on the python's scales, reminiscent of the Chinese and Mayan preoccupation with scales on dragons or on the Plumed Serpent at Chichén Itzá (see fig. 2.7, p. 47), respectively. For the Chinese and Maya, the scales represented shifts between the different time periods of the waves—DAYS and NIGHTS—and thus had prophetic significance. It's remarkable that a people in Botswana as far back as maybe seventy thousand years had already become aware of wave-like shifts in time and used the same symbolism: scales on a serpent.

Long before people started to consider the existence of a god or gods, or a path to enlightenment, it thus seems they created rituals with serpents. The San Bushmen, arguably the oldest culture on our planet, whose ancestors created this serpent, say they descend from a giant python, which in their universe was a creator god.[18] People in the Amazon likewise hold a view in which human beings were created by the great Anaconda. At first this may seem difficult to embrace, but if we recognize that the serpent, giant python or anaconda, is a representation of how they experienced the Fifth Wave, it makes very good sense. As we have seen here, we all, along with the Bushmen, *do* descend from waves, and the only possible way for ancient peoples to concretize the power of a sine wave was by using the symbol of the serpent.

Another important parallel to this giant python can be found in one of the world's oldest cultures—that of the Aborigines—who populated Australia about fifty thousand years ago. With some variation, groups of this people looked upon the Rainbow Serpent[19] as the

Figure 3.7. The great python from the Rhino Cave in Botswana dated to 70,000 BP. (*Photograph by Sheila Coulson, University of Oslo, Norway*)

creator god. The idea of following a wave and recognizing its spiritual powers, as we will do especially in chapter 9, is thus not something new but goes back very far in time. The serpent might have been experienced as the main creator god, because, after all, the wave-like shifts might have been the only things of an otherworldly nature that humans had yet experienced. We can say that they resonated with the waves that underlie our existence.

The somewhat more recent Drachenloch Altar (fig. 3.6), discovered in current-day Switzerland, confirms that people at a very early point in the Fifth Wave (50,000 BP) had an awareness of wave-like movements between DAYS and NIGHTS. On the altar, seven bear skulls were placed facing the opening of the cave, and hence the light, while six niches had been carved in the back of the cave where bear skulls were placed in the dark.[20] This fits very well with a wave movement of seven DAYS and six NIGHTS up until the present time, as shown in figure 3.6.

Admittedly, singular finds like these do not present a closed case based on the evidence even though these are the oldest ritual sites of which we know. Yet, it is possible that they reflect symbologies that were then more widespread, and I am suggesting that the role of waveforms and their ancient symbols in the form of dragons and serpents have been completely misunderstood and their importance totally underestimated by modern man. I believe that the earliest ethics of humankind, as well as the earliest wisdom, was inspired by the creation waves, and so we should not be surprised if people looked upon serpents as gods.

The real breakthrough in artistic self-expression on a broader scale in the Fifth Wave came only with the fifth DAY (fig. 3.6) in the form of cave paintings, mostly with animals as motifs, which appeared for the first time about forty thousand years ago, notably in Europe but also in Australia. The apparent lack of novelty in the following sixth DAY may be related to the Ice Age, which might have blocked artistic creativity or destroyed its results. After this break, cliff paintings with humans as motifs appear in the seventh DAY, which can then be looked upon as the highest expression of this wave. Soon, however, a new wave would start to interfere with their spirituality, as well as with the artistic expressions of Neolithic man.

THE SIXTH WAVE AND THE RATIONAL MIND

The Sixth Wave is the first in the mental frequency range (fig. 2.3, p. 35) to be activated. It was activated in 3115 BCE and has a wavelength of 788 years. Arguably its activation meant the most significant shift in human history. The Sixth Wave transformed Fifth Wave humans who had begun to express themselves symbolically to beings with rational minds. Only after the mind of the Sixth Wave was downloaded did people start to create civilizations. To demonstrate the concordance of the rise of civilization with the activation of the Sixth Wave, datings of the first emergence of various phenomena associated with civilization have been summarized in figure 3.8. Even though some of these dates can be discussed, the overall picture is fairly clear that the emergence of civilization coincided very well with the beginning date of the Sixth Wave in 3115 BCE.

Although the dates at which these expressions of civilization first appear vary slightly, what is most striking is their overall concordance.

First cities	(Sumer, 3200 BCE)
First pyramids	(Egypt and Sumer, 3100 BCE)
First monarchy	(Egypt, 3150 BCE)
First numerals	(Sumer, 3100, Egypt 3000 BCE)
First measures	(Indus Valley, 3250 BCE)
First writing	(Indus Valley, 3250, Sumer 3200, Egypt 3200 BCE)
First money	(Sumer, 3000 BCE)
First calendars	(Egypt, Sumer 3000 BCE)
First wheel	(current-day Slovenia, 3200 BCE)
First bronze	(Anatolia, Crete, and Sumer, 3000 BCE)

Figure 3.8. Phenomena associated with civilization emerging around the beginning of the Sixth Wave in 3115 BCE. (*Diagram by the author*)

Civilizations, which here are taken to mean cultures based on city life with a system of writing, for the first time appeared on our planet, in Egypt, Mesopotamia, and the Indus Valley. By all accounts these different civilizations emerged independently; it is known, for instance, that their systems of writing were not derived from one another.[21] Pyramids also appear at this time almost simultaneously[22] in different parts of the world. Even though the cultures that created the pyramids in Peru and Mongolia or the megalithic monuments in the British Isles[23] did not develop into lasting civilizations, it is obvious that something changed radically in these places at the beginning of the Sixth Wave. Maybe it is not an accident that both the Maya and the Hindus[24] have calendars that start close to this point in time.

The fact that civilization emerged on our own planet so suddenly and with so few preparatory forms has long been an enigma to historians. Within the framework of the old materialist paradigm, its sudden appearance is indeed difficult to explain. Many alternative researchers have come to believe that there must have been some earlier civilization before the ones we actually know of. But if we recognize civilization as a result of a shift in consciousness induced by the Sixth Wave there is no reason to assume that any earlier civilization existed. The activation of the Sixth Wave would also explain why people in such widely disparate locations as Peru, Egypt, Mongolia, and Mesopotamia suddenly began to build pyramids.

The most straightforward explanation for this sudden emergence of civilizations is that people rather suddenly started to download a new hologram that created a rational mind (see fig. 3.9 on p. 80) as part of the fractal-holographic model of the universe. A whole range of different phenomena that emerged in these different cultures at approximately the same time can be attributed to a new perception of reality, a new structuring of reality through the influence of this hologram, which unlike that of the Fifth Wave was defined by straight and perpendicular lines. The nature of this hologram, mediated to us through our resonance with the Earth (fig. 3.9), is discussed extensively in *The*

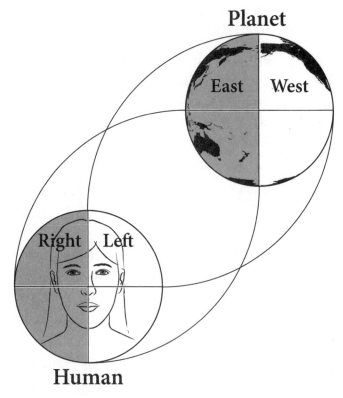

Figure 3.9. Sixth Wave hologram on human being in resonance with Earth.
(*Diagram by the author, design courtesy of Bengt Sundin*)

Global Mind and the Rise of Civilization. In the same way as the waves of lower frequency created sudden jumps in biological evolution, a wave with a higher frequency suddenly activated the rational mind. The global nature of this new hologram is the reason that civilization began independently and almost simultaneously in three different regions of the world. Civilization did not create the mind; rather the activation of the rational mind through the Sixth Wave created civilization.

The downloading of the new hologram was only the beginning of a process of spreading and deepening civilization across the globe by the Sixth Wave. *The Global Mind and the Rise of Civilization* discusses many examples of how the Sixth Wave step-by-step developed different aspects of the human mind. Figure 3.10 shows how the peaks of

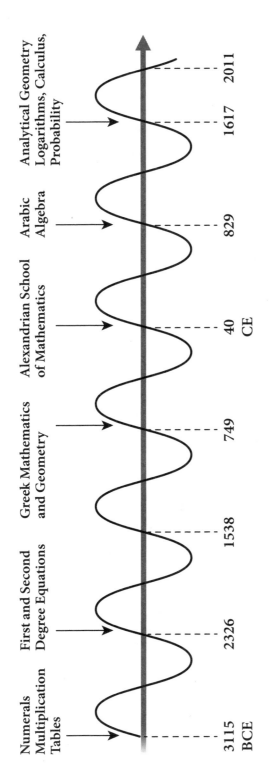

Figure 3.10. Evolution of mathematics and geometry under the influence of the Sixth Wave. (*Diagram by the author, design courtesy of Bengt Sundin*)

the Sixth Wave developed the sciences of geometry and mathematics.[25] This evolution started with the first use of numbers and multiplication tables in Mesopotamia, Egypt, and the Indus Valley, with the perfect geometry of the pyramids being a visible embodiment.

Through a series of steps, this evolutionary process continued in Europe with an explosion of mathematical creativity during the early seventeenth century as a result of the beginning of the seventh peak of the Sixth Wave. In this final step the rational mind, through the new left-brain straight-line hologram that it was carrying (fig. 3.9), created a very dramatic paradigm shift, that of the scientific revolution (fig. 3.10). After the shift point in 1617, the first mathematical laws of physics were formulated in the works of Galileo and Kepler. It is hard to imagine what the world would look like today if no one had come up with the idea that there are mathematical laws of nature.

What is suggested here is that the emergence of civilization was caused by a particular creation wave emanating from the Cosmic Tree of Life, the Sixth Wave, which carried a new hologram, which in turn created a new relationship to our external reality. Consequently, the mind did not have its origin on our own planet and may very well have been experienced as coming from the sky or as extraterrestrial. This does not imply any direct participation in the process by actual extraterrestrial beings. Instead, in accordance with the nine-level cosmology and the ancients' frequent perception that humans originated in the "heavens," I assert that a wave of transformation emanating from the Cosmic Axis is the best explanation for the sudden emergence of civilization on our planet.

SERPENTS IN ANCIENT CULTURES

So there were three of them, as Heart of Sky, who came to the Sovereign Plumed Serpent, when the dawn of life was conceived: How shall it be sown, how should it dawn? Who is to be the provider, the nurturer?[26]

For a long time it has posed a dilemma to anthropologists and students of mythology why the serpent has played such a prominent role in the rituals and belief systems of ancient cultures. As indicated by the finding of a serpent ritual site in Botswana, this role goes back to the earliest time of human culture. I believe there are two reasons why this prominent role of the serpent has been seen as an enigma. One is that, looked upon with our modern eyes, a snake does not appear to be "the craftiest of the animals" or as one that harbors wisdom and knowledge. It is a reptile acting mostly on its instincts and does not have the playfulness or intelligence of a mammal.

The second reason is that modern people are only now becoming aware, partly through quantum physics, that we are living in a sea of waves creating what we experience as a holographic reality. These waves emanate from the Source, the Tree of Life, and even if we do not see them with our senses, we may at least subconsciously recognize their power and sacred origin. *What has been demonstrated in this chapter is that waves with frequencies that are outside the normal range do exist and play a decisive role for the evolution of the universe.* The ancients obviously did not understand the waves in terms of physics but rather as serpents that were sacred symbols of divine power. They experienced reality differently, and in a sense more intelligently, as they were dominated by other mental holograms than we are now.

Nonetheless, it is a fact that the serpent was a very significant symbol of power and prophecy in ancient cultures. It is associated with fertility, sexual magic, duality, wisdom, knowledge, and vengefulness, none of which we would immediately associate with a snake. As we have noted, despite the unassuming nature of the snake, San Bushmen believe that they descended from a giant python, who was also a creator god. Similarly, among the Aborigines in Australia, the Rainbow Serpent is the main creator god. (The word *rainbow* presumably refers to the serpent coming from the sky, as creation waves do.)

The serpent is one of the oldest and most prevalent mythological entities and has played a role much larger than what we would normally associate with the snake as an animal. I believe that we have here finally found the reason for the mythological importance of the serpent, which is that, as I have already pointed out, the serpent is the most natural way to symbolize or represent the movement of a sine wave. It is hard to understand otherwise why the Bushmen and the Australian Aborigines would see their supreme deity, the creator god, as a serpent. It seems clear that already in the Fifth Wave people became aware that there were waves, which they conceptualized and experienced as serpents.

This worship of the serpent/creation wave presumably became even more pronounced with the Sixth Wave. As is apparent from the quote on page 82 from the Popol Vuh, the so-called bible of the Maya, the Plumed Serpent was looked upon by them as the sovereign deity. ("Plumed" or "feathered" presumably refers to something flying in the sky, as waves do.) The Plumed Serpent—Quetzalcoatl to the Aztecs and Kukulcán to the Maya—was seen as the bringer of civilization and the calendar.[27] For these reasons, this deity was likely a symbol of the Sixth Wave rather than the Fifth. Based on their experiences of its wave movements, the Mesoamerican peoples would see civilizations come and go with the Plumed Serpent. To modern people the "disappearance" of the Maya or the Toltecs may be mysterious, but to those peoples who were fully aware of the power of the waves, the disappearance of cultures was merely a matter of the Plumed Serpent molting his skin and moving on. As we will see later, the ancient Mesoamericans were right about this.

In ancient China, there is a very interesting parallel to this role of Quetzalcoatl as a bringer of civilization. The legendary hero, or god, Fuxi together with his twin sister Nuwa (fig. 3.11) are there credited with having brought civilization to humanity.[28] Fuxi brought the square and Nuwa the compass, tools that are very much related to the rectilinear hologram of the Sixth Wave (fig. 3.9).[29] These tools would incidentally also be very useful for the building of pyramids, which began at the time of appearance of Fuxi and Nuwa at the beginning of the Sixth Wave. Fuxi and Nuwa came with a wave that not only brought

Figure 3.11. Ancient painting of Nuwa (left) and Fuxi (right) unearthed in Xinjiang, China. Currently housed in the Xinjiang Uighur Autonomous Region Museum.

technology but also a polarity between the genders. The most interesting part of the mythology of this couple may, however, be that the lower parts of their bodies were serpentlike. Hence, the role of this couple is identical to that of Quetzalcoatl. They symbolized that the Sixth Wave, which creates rectilinear holograms, brought civilization. While modern people may need quantum physics to have a language for these changes, the ancients were so in tune with the waves that they directly experienced their effects.

In most ancient cultures, the serpent had a prominent mythological role. The Egyptian pharaohs, for instance, had a serpent at the front of their crown, presumably for spiritual guidance, and the high priestess of the Oracle of Delphi went by the name of Pythia,[30] presumably because the prophetic art required knowledge of the shifting energies of the cosmic waves. Rather than reviewing all of the many cultures that considered serpents significant, it may be more relevant to ask if any cultures existed that did not see the serpent as having a special spiritual power.

INTERFERENCE PATTERNS
BETWEEN WAVES

Humans have not, however, been in resonance with merely one wave at a time but with several as the creation waves were running in parallel. The activation of the Sixth Wave in 3115 BCE, for instance, did not mean that people stopped being in resonance with the Fifth Wave. Instead, *people started to resonate with the interference pattern between the Fifth and the Sixth Waves.* Step-by-step, as people resonated with the different peaks of the Sixth Wave, this new and higher wave became predominant, and the influence of the Fifth Wave decreased. As this happened, and the human mind became stronger, over time, and especially with each new peak of the Sixth Wave, most expressions of animal mythology inherited from the Fifth Wave disappeared—including worship of the serpent.

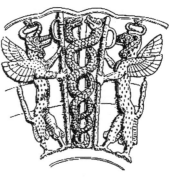

Figure 3.12. The Sumerian deity Ningizzida, "lord of the good tree," is accompanied by two intertwined serpents. It is the oldest known image of two snakes coiling around an axial rod, dating from before 2000 BCE.

The ancients were not unaware that they were in resonance with the interference pattern between two waves. The oldest known representation of two entangled serpents, symbolizing the interference between the two waves, is from Sumer (fig. 3.12). The name of the entity depicted, Ningizzida,[31] meant "lord of the good tree," which implies that this early civilization looked upon the Tree of Life not only as good but also as a ruler. The caduceus, a symbol of an interference pattern of waves emanating from the Cosmic Axis, or Tree of Life, has remained a symbol of healing well into modern times.

It has been suggested that the caduceus or symbols such as the one in figure 3.12 could be representations of the double helix of the DNA, but there is no reason to believe that the ancients knew anything about that. Besides, the double helix does not have a "staff" or "good tree" at its center, which is a centerpiece in many ancient representations of the double helix symbol. We have reasons to believe, however, that the ancients were aware of the waves of creation and hence the symbol of the serpent was widely spread for these waves. The connection of the staff to the serpent is common in ancient cultures. The staffs of Moses and Aaron,[32] which could be transformed to serpents and perform miracles, are examples of this connection. I thus think that the true origin of the caduceus, or serpents around the pole, is as a symbol of the waves that emanate from the Cosmic Axis. Someone who had a strong contact with the Cosmic Axis (which, as we saw in chapter 1, is the Creator) would also be able to send out waves of creation, symbolized by the serpent. So even if the ancients did not know about the DNA, they may have known much better than modern people the basic relationships according to which the universe was created.

Yet, it is natural if we ask why a symbol for the interference of two different waves would become a symbol for healing throughout the ages, even long after its original meaning had been lost. Assuming that the Mesopotamians who created it experienced the interference of the Fifth and the Sixth Waves, I think we should realize that the transformation people went through when they started to download the Sixth Wave must have been very challenging and pulled them in different directions. The previous balance disappeared, and people were most likely torn between the earlier more natural way of being in the Fifth Wave on the one hand and on the other hand that of the rational mind, which came with the new hologram from the Sixth Wave. The latter, as we will see in the next chapter, may also have had some very negative consequences for many of them. I suspect the reason that the interference pattern of the two waves has become a symbol of healing is that people at the time came to realize that resisting either the influence of the Fifth or the Sixth Waves would not lead to harmony. Such an attitude would only create conflicts between the two ways of being in an individual. Harmony and healing would instead have to be created by integrating the two waves and their interference patterns, which the caduceus symbolized.

To summarize, based on what we know from prehistory, the experience of the serpent, or wave, was the first conscious human experience of an otherworldly force. We can track this experience back to early in the Fifth Wave, when humans were emerging from the essentially animallike state they had been in under the influence of the Fourth Wave. It is reasonable then to assume that this relationship to the serpent, what in fact was a wave originating in the Tree of Life, was the first basis for ethics. It presumably was also the first wisdom to transcend the everyday life of fight or flight that otherwise dominated.

Just as the ancients learned to create resonance with the Fifth and Sixth Waves, we must gain knowledge about the nine waves of creation and create resonance with them in our own time. Creating resonance is a phenomenon that goes back to the earliest cultured human beings and was widespread among the ancients until they were overshadowed by the modern mentality.

4

The Hologram of
Good and Evil

THE TREE OF LIFE IN ANCIENT
REPRESENTATIONS

The cosmology of nine levels is, as we have seen, practically ubiquitous among the traditional cultures of our planet, and the same can be said about serpents and dragons symbolizing spiritual wave movements. Our inquiry, however, began with the recent discovery of the Cosmic Tree of Life, and we have continued to verify that the universe is created by a series of waves emanating from this Tree of Life. Yet, only a few examples have been given of how the ancient cultures looked upon the Tree of Life, which is another such ubiquitous "myth" that, in one form or another, can be found almost everywhere on our planet. Naturally, our interest in the Tree of Life becomes greater when we know that it is not a fantasy, and this is a reason to explore what additional hints about its role and function we may gain from such ancient traditions.

The oldest representations of the Tree of Life are found from Mesopotamia from the early third millennium BCE.[1] In the previous chapter we saw one of the forms (fig. 3.12, p. 87) in which this culture represented the sacred tree as an axis, often called axis mundi,[2] with two serpents intertwined around it. In this depiction the axis also defines a left and right side, which are mirror images of one another. This is typical of ancient representations of the Tree of Life (see also fig. 4.1c on p. 95 and fig. 5.1 on p. 122), and has its background in the large-scale evolution of the universe. On lower levels in the fractal-holographic model, we have seen how hemispheric mirror images have been created on the level of our galaxy, our planet, and biological organisms. Hence, the mirroring effect of the Tree of Life is apparent both in ancient myth and from empirical evidence about how the universe is created.

Another aspect of the Tree of Life in the Sumerian relief is the existence of waves, symbolized by serpents emanating from the tree. These waves began with the First Wave, which has a wavelength of a billion light-years, a scale that is in reasonable agreement with the Cosmic Axis at an early point in the evolution of the universe. On top of this First Wave, a series of waves, each with a twentyfold higher frequency than the one preceding it, have been activated and from these transformative interference patterns have been created. In the following chapters we will continue our climb to higher levels of creation, eventually leading up to the wave that is most relevant for us today, the Ninth Wave. Before doing so, we will first need to understand more about how interference patterns are formed and, most importantly, what kind of holograms are produced in people in resonance with the different waves.

If we continue on the course of history, we find from the second millennium BCE representations of the Tree of Life in the entire region of the ancient civilizations spanning from the Indus Valley to Egypt (fig. 4.1, p. 93) to Greece.[3] Kings were commonly shown not only tending the Tree of Life but also carrying around a branch from it to symbolize that they had part in it and that their kingship through this tree had a divine origin. The oldest name of Babylon, Tin-tir-ki, meant "the place of the tree of life." The Egyptians also had an elaborate story about the Tree of Life, which had its center in the city of Heliopolis. According to them, the tree represented the world pillar, or axis mundi,[4] the center of the universe around which the heavens appeared to revolve—a concept similar to the axis of evil from modern science. Moreover, the earlier mentioned Ennead (nine gods) were said to have emerged from the Tree of Life. What may be the most important element to this Egyptian construction of the universe, in our present context, is that *the Tree of Life was seen as holding the knowledge of the divine plan.*[5] This amounted to a map of destiny, which has existed since the world was created. The information in the previous chapter—showing that all aspects of creation can be attributed to waves of evolution emanating from the Tree of Life, seems to corroborate this view of the ancient Egyptians.

A particular representation of the Tree of Life, with an additional Tree of Knowledge of Good and Evil, which became tremendously influential through its later incorporation into the religions of Christianity and Islam, is that of the Jewish creation story, which will be discussed in the next chapter. There were also real-life symbols of the Tree of Life, such as in Scandinavia, where ash trees were honored as living embodiments of Yggdrasil,[6] but other examples can be found across the world from the Maori to the Maya (fig. 4.1a–c). Often trees with certain impressive characteristics, such as the kauri tree and the ceiba tree, serve as symbols of the Cosmic Tree of Life. The kauri tree[7] (fig. 4.1a) has an impressive trunk, and the ceiba tree[8] (fig. 4.1b on p. 94) has the distinction of sometimes having roots in four directions and branches that are perpendicular to the trunk.[9] Even today, Mayan lumber workers will spare the ceiba trees when cutting down a forest.

Given the wide range of cultures, sometimes separated by oceans, worshipping Trees of Life, it seems obvious that the symbol of a sacred tree was not spread through interpersonal contact. Rather, people in all parts of the world in this era had a direct experience of the Tree of Life, and based on this they portrayed it in their art and sometimes written texts. As is usual with ancient symbolism, there is some variation in how it was represented. Unlike in our own time, it was not possible to send out a satellite that created a picture of the Cosmic Axis. Instead, the different cultures became aware of various facets of the Tree of Life through their direct resonance with it. But, as noted with the symbol of the serpent, the truth would be somewhat distorted depending on the frame of mind of the person downloading the information.

Figure 4.1a. Kauri tree worshipped by the Maori as the Tree of Life. (*Kauri,* Agathis australis, *Waipoua Forest, New Zealand*)

Figure 4.1b. Ceiba tree worshipped by the Maya as the Tree of Life.
(*Photograph by the author*)

Figure 4.1c. Temple relief of Tree of Life with Ramses II in Egypt. (*Courtesy of River Tay*)

The Tree of Life, the serpent, and the number nine were thus ubiquitous parts of the worldviews of ancient societies. The main components of this shared cosmology are now being retrieved and finally understood because they are consistent with the facts of modern science. If we look upon them in an appropriate way, as aspects of a quantum-holographic theory of physics, the existence of these phenomena make sense and, as we will see later, have the capacity to explain what is happening in our own time. As this model presents a coherent picture from the ancient cosmologies, it is thus meaningful to continue the inquiry based on the Egyptian belief that the Tree of Life held the knowledge of the divine plan[10] and amounted to a chart of destiny.

THE DESTINY CHART OF HUMANITY

Among the nine waves of creation emanating from the Tree of Life, the four higher waves (sixth through ninth) differ from one another in two significant respects, which explains why they each create such a different reality and experience of reality, as we saw examples of in the previous chapter. One respect, summarized in figure 2.8 on page 50, is the frequency of the waves, which played an important role in the acceleration of biological evolution toward higher species and which also has generated an experience of a speedup of time in more recent times. Another respect is the geometry and especially the polarities of the holograms of the higher waves (fig. 4.2). Every time a new wave in the mental frequency range has been activated on our planet, humans have begun to download a new hologram of the mind. Each wave creates a distinct hologram, which in turn creates a framework from which to experience reality. Such holograms downloaded from the Source, the Tree of Life, generate our fundamental attitudes toward life. Remarkably then, these shifting polarities ultimately seem to go back, not to some metaphysi-

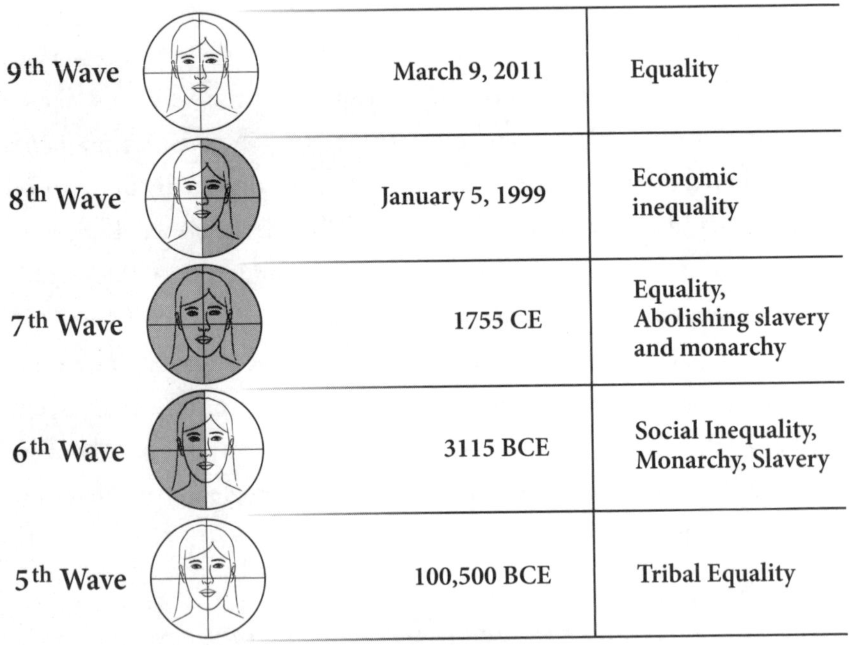

9th Wave		March 9, 2011	Equality
8th Wave		January 5, 1999	Economic inequality
7th Wave		1755 CE	Equality, Abolishing slavery and monarchy
6th Wave		3115 BCE	Social Inequality, Monarchy, Slavery
5th Wave		100,500 BCE	Tribal Equality

Figure 4.2. The Destiny Chart of Humanity: The holograms of the higher waves and their basic impacts on social relationships. (*Diagram by the author, design courtesy of Bengt Sundin*)

cal phenomenon, but to the inherent duality, or "inherent anisotropy," recently discovered in the universe (see chapter 1). The four different polarities of the mind shown in figure 4.2 then would correspond to each of the "four cosmic directions" (which are not the same as the four directions on our own planet) shown in the Tree of Life in figure 2.6. At the times of activation of new waves with higher frequencies, new holograms based on each of the four cosmic directions would be created along with new realities for the human beings.

The effects of the different holograms in figure 4.2 will be thoroughly studied in the following chapters, but in short, depending on which wave you are in resonance with, a particular hologram will structure your mind and perception of reality. As a consequence, how we experience and create our external world will depend on which wave(s) we are in resonance with. The different holograms, for instance, provide an explanation for why the worldview of the ancients (Sixth Wave) was not the same as our own (for most people Seventh and Eighth Waves) and also why modern people have created a very different world. Human beings understand their world based on the information they receive through the particular filter the hologram provides for them. Moreover, if we resonate with a particular wave and a corresponding hologram, we will attract people and circumstances that are consistent with these. We then together tend to create a reality consistent with a particular hologram and often resist anything that seems inconsistent with this. Our external reality is thus created in accordance with the principle of as inside, so outside.

Among many other things, these holograms, each associated with a particular wave with a particular frequency, also provide an explanation for how basic social relationships have changed over the course of human history: people have projected the polarities of the holograms onto the world and then created social realities consistent with these. Figure 4.2 shows in a simple form the times of activation of the different holograms dominating the human mind, as well as very broadly the social consequences of these holograms. The holograms of the Fifth, Seventh, and Ninth Waves tend to create egalitarian societies, whereas those of the Sixth and Eighth Waves, where reality is perceived through a left-right polarity, tend to create unequal social realities. More broadly, all of human history can be understood from the shifts between the different polarities of the holograms in figure 4.2. In several previous books I have described how the shifting polarities of the human mind determine history. Thus, the most fundamental shifts in the human mind take place as a result of the activation of new waves.

In my view, figure 4.2 is the most important chart in this book: from it we can broadly understand how the human mind has been shifting over time as well as which holograms are available for us to resonate with at the present time. Interestingly, if we look at the sequence of holograms in this figure, we can see that *in the course of the climb to higher waves, humanity has gone from a phase of unity in the Fifth Wave to separation created by the introduction of the dark filters of the Sixth, Seventh, and Eighth Waves, followed by a return to unity with the Ninth Wave.* This idea of a return to unity is prevalent in several religions (including all the Abrahamic) and spiritual traditions, and perhaps the waves can now, for the first time, provide a rational explanation to this.

We can furthermore see that *the filters of the holograms, even though they appear polarized when viewed separately, even out over time so that both the left and right hemispheres of the brain receive the same amount of light from the holograms.* Some would call the mental change that this ascent through the waves engenders as "raising our vibrations" or "entering a higher state of consciousness." The spiral movement through the polarities that are part of this ascent may also be referred to as the Kundalini energy rising. This notion from India refers to a serpent-like activation of a coil along the spine. In line with the ancient Egyptian view of the Tree of Life, I call figure 4.2 the Destiny Chart of Humanity. Climbing to the Ninth Wave and downloading a hologram with no filters or duality amounts to the fulfillment of humanity's destiny.

Because there is a correspondence between the holograms in figure 4.2 and their frequencies, we can now begin to understand the origin of everyday expressions such as "being on the same wavelength" or "resonating with someone" to denote getting along well. The frequencies talked about in such expressions obviously do not refer to visible light or sounds but to the much more profound similarities between two persons who download the same hologram. In general, people whose minds are shaped by the same holograms are, literally, on the same wavelength and resonate with each other because they see the world through the same filter. Such resonances with the same wave generate synchronicities. People in resonance with the same wave or specific interference patterns between different waves may unknowingly be involved in the same processes and so experience synchronicities.

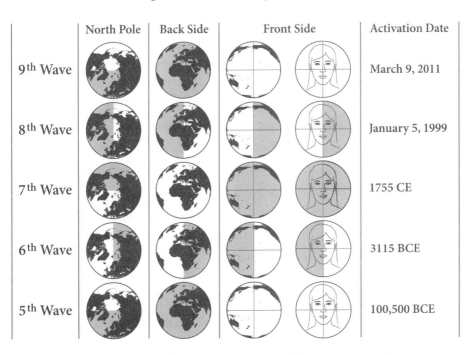

	North Pole	Back Side	Front Side		Activation Date
9th Wave					March 9, 2011
8th Wave					January 5, 1999
7th Wave					1755 CE
6th Wave					3115 BCE
5th Wave					100,500 BCE

Figure 4.3. The polarities of the planetary round of light as they manifest in the five highest waves of the mind as seen from different perspectives. Note that the holograms shown here are the ones that are activated by periods that are DAYS in the respective waves. NIGHTS mean that the lights of these polarities are deactivated. (*Diagram by the author, design courtesy of Bengt Sundin*)

THE PLANETARY ROUND OF LIGHT

How does the Cosmic Tree of Life generate the different polarities of the holograms in figure 4.2 and why do they shift? To answer this, we need to first be aware that there is a holographic resonance between Earth and human beings: the left-right polarity of the human mind is created through resonance with the west-east polarity of Earth. Hence, the Western Hemisphere in all the waves is primarily in resonance with the left hemisphere of the brain (see fig. 3.9 on p. 80). Similarly the Eastern Hemisphere is primarily in resonance with the right hemisphere of the brain.[11] As is amply discussed in *The Global Mind and the Rise of Civilization*, the human mind does not find its origin in the brain but in the holograms, which are most immediately mediated to us by Earth. Figure 4.3 shows a somewhat more complex diagram of the holograms of the higher waves than figure 4.2, as it also demonstrates the influence of the holograms on Earth.

From different viewpoints, the columns in figure 4.3 show how the polarities of the various holograms affect Earth. If we look at the polarities of the holograms from the perspective of the North Pole (column one), we can see that shifts between them are caused by 90-degree shifts around the polar axis. Hence, every time a new wave has been activated on our planet, the polarity of its hologram from this perspective has shifted 90 degrees, and as can be seen in columns two and three this is reflected on the level of Earth. In turn, these shifts are reflected in the holograms dominating humans (column four) in resonance with Earth. Given that the waves emanate from the Cosmic Axis, these shifts in polarity around Earth's polar axis are thus created through resonance with the Cosmic Axis in accordance with the fractal-holographic model shown in figure 1.5 on page 24. Ultimately, the various polarities of the holograms thus go back to different resonances with the intrinsic duality of the universe upheld by the Cosmic Tree of Life as discussed in chapter 1.

To ask why the Cosmic Tree of Life undergoes this Planetary

Round of Light, however, which is reflected in the global mind and individual human minds, is like asking why there was a Big Bang or why there is a Cosmic Tree of Life. We have already seen (chapter 1) that there is evidence that the Cosmic Axis creates corkscrewing movements[12] and influences the polarities across the universe,[13] and so there is little reason to be surprised that it expresses itself in this way as well. The consequence of undergoing this Planetary Round of Light is, as we will see more of later, not only that human beings will develop different technologies but also that they become increasingly self-aware.

Their common resonance with the Earth is the reason people in so many different parts of the world, as discussed in the previous chapter, came to develop nine-level cosmologies that are very much related. The idea of a return to unity, prevalent in many religions and spiritual traditions seems to result from the same resonance. The global mind creates a common resonance among people from different parts of the world who then receive information filtered by the same hologram. From this they draw similar conclusions about the world and its destiny. The fact that our individual minds have been created through resonance with one and the same global hologram has, in fact, been a very powerful cohesive factor for social life on Earth. Without resonance with a common hologram, our minds would presumably have been so variable that we would not have been able to understand anybody else, and social structures might not have emerged on our planet.

The common resonance with Earth has affected not only human ways of thinking but also the external worlds humans have created. The common resonance with the Sixth Wave is, for instance, the reason that people in widely different parts of the world started to build pyramids at the same time.[14] As mentioned in the previous chapter and as was extensively developed in *The Global Mind and the Rise of Civilization,* the different aspects of civilization (fig. 3.8, p. 78) first appeared simultaneously and independently in several different parts of the world as the Sixth Wave was activated in 3115 BCE. People everywhere then came to be in resonance with the same hologram, which created a rational mind, which in turn created civilization.

POLARITY SHIFTS OF
THE MIND

It should be noted that *the polarities shown in figures 4.2 and 4.3 are those that dominate during the DAYS, while during the NIGHT phases the holograms are not lit up* (fig. 2.10, p. 52). As the waves giving rise to these holograms go through phases of peaks (DAYS, or light) and valleys (NIGHTS, or darkness), human perception of reality is correspondingly altered so that mental shifts take place. It is a general rule of these creation waves that during peaks, or DAYS, the holograms are activated. During this time, the new phenomena being brought to the minds of human beings are expressed with the greatest strength. In the NIGHTS, on the other hand, the holograms are deactivated, and there is less creativity. Examples of how the shifts between DAYS and NIGHTS, and vice versa, follow such a pattern were presented in the previous chapter. In these, steps forward typically occurred at the beginning of the DAYS of the waves.

This model of shifting polarities of the mind has tremendous explanatory power when it comes to human history. For instance, it helps us determine the roles of different brain halves in different eras and different planetary transformations. It also determines if people are in contact with the divine light or separated from it through dark filters. It tells us if people are predominantly inclined to create unity or conflicts and many other things. Yet, overall, people are not aware that their minds are being dominated by these waves and the particular holograms they create. As mentioned in the discussion on quantum physics, the waves are not directly visible to us and present somewhat of a hidden reality. As a result, we take our perception of reality for granted and think that looking at the world through a particular hologram gives us the one and only objective truth. These filters are to us much like water is to fish: it's the only medium we know. If we get stuck with a particular filter and can only see reality through this, our minds will be closed. Creative people are those able to resonate with interference patterns, and maybe such a resonance with an interference pattern was what the Sumerian Tree of Life (fig. 3.12, p. 87) referred to. Over time, however, the relative influences of the different waves change and give rise to different interference patterns, resulting in hybrid holograms.

There is then no such thing as an eternal or unchangeable "human nature." Instead, what human beings are like differs widely between different eras depending on which waves and interference patterns they are predominantly in resonance with. The mental differences among a cave painter from the Upper Paleolithic from forty thousand years ago (Fifth Wave), an early civilized Egyptian from five thousand years ago (Sixth Wave), and a modern urban tweeter (Eighth Wave) cannot be explained by differences in their DNA. Their differences are determined by the holograms and interference patterns from which their minds have been created. Accordingly, each hologram and the interference patterns among the waves creates a particular kind of "human nature."

SYMBOLS OF DUALITY

As already mentioned, the hologram of the Sixth Wave (figures 3.9, 4.2, and 4.3) plays a special role as it is the first one emanating from a wave in the mental frequency range of the spectrum (fig. 2.3, p. 35). For this reason, its geometry will serve as the basic departure point for the continued evolution of the human mind, even when holograms of the higher levels have been added to it. The Sixth Wave hologram thus provides the core of the "rational mind" and so has had a long-lasting power over the course of human history. In contrast, the Fifth Wave (fig. 4.2) produced no filters in human beings, and so those early humans lived in unobstructed contact with nature and the Divine. This reality would dramatically change as the Sixth Wave was activated and a new hologram was downloaded (fig. 3.9, p. 80).

Figure 4.4 shows a few examples of how different ancient peoples symbolized the new hologram created by the Sixth Wave. Although many in modern times have tended to look at these as more or less meaningless symbols made for no reason, we may now begin to understand that the ancients depicted these archetypal symbols as reflections of the new hologram that created their new civilized reality. These geometric symbols were important as they helped clarify the new reality human beings were experiencing.

Despite the variation in their details, these symbols share the same essential features, a light-dark polarity and a partitioning into eight energies by a compass rose geometry. The *hunab-ku* symbol in figure 4.4a is of Aztec origin and is found in the Codex Magliabecchiano.[15] The *dingir* symbol[16] in figure 4.4b is the oldest of the three and can be traced to the late fourth millennium BCE in the Sumerian culture. The Sumerians apparently used this symbol to denote divinity, as in the cuneiform script the dingir symbol was always placed next to the names of gods. Indeed, it is a hologram emanating from the Source, the Tree of Life, as all the symbols are, which originates in the rectilinear geometry of the Cosmic Tree of Life. The Eastern *bagua* symbol[17] finally has become the world's most famous symbol of duality. An extensive

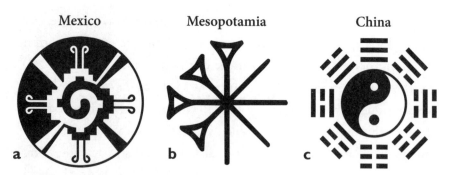

Figure 4.4. Symbols of the duality of the Tree of Life from different parts of the world: a. Aztec, b. Sumerian, and c. Chinese. This duality is also known as the Tree of Knowledge of Good and Evil.

philosophy has also been developed around the yin-yang polarity, and the interpretations of I Ching trigrams surrounding this go back to the earliest times of Chinese civilization.

All three of these symbols, which together prove that the new hologram of the Sixth Wave could be downloaded from the Far East to the Far West, can be looked upon as examples of sacred geometry. What sacred geometry is here taken to mean is geometry that originates in the divine Tree of Life. Because people at the time knew that sacred geometry was part of the holograms that shaped their existence, it was practiced as a means of spiritual elevation. It should be noted that the symbols in figure 4.4 were not the only ways of presenting the sacred geometry of the new hologram. Much more complex aspects, such as the Flower of Life, could be added. The most important aspect of the hologram is expressed as a simple four-directional cross in the midst of a circle.

This may be the time to point out that in this theory there is really no longer any distinction between the physical and metaphysical realms. The symbols in figure 4.4, and in particular the yin-yang symbol, which is the most well known of them, are usually considered to be metaphysical, belonging to a realm other than the physical. The concept of metaphysical now, however, loses its meaning as the yin-yang polarity actually belongs to the same spectrum as physical phenomena; however, it is mediated by a part of the spectrum not visible to our eyes.

THE SACRED GEOMETRY OF THE
SIXTH WAVE MIND

If we dissect the symbols of the Sixth Wave hologram in figure 4.4 we find that all three reflect significant facets of this hologram. The first facet is the existence of a circular enclosure, the second is an eight-partitioned structure (which includes a cross), and the third is the light-dark duality. All three facets of the hologram originate in the Cosmic Tree of Life and have significant consequences for the mind of the person who has downloaded it. The spherical enclosure creates cohesiveness, giving an individual the experience of having only one mind that coherently processes all the information from the frequency realm. We may think of this enclosure as a halo that gives our minds the boundaries and unity that makes us function in the world as distinct individuals. In this way, we experience the continuity of our lives, or in other words, we experience ourselves as the same person today as yesterday.

The second aspect that all three symbols of the hologram have in common is the structured eight-partitioning that separates our perception of reality into different compartments, defined by straight and perpendicular lines. The Chinese bagua symbol may in this respect be the most advanced as its eight trigrams also define the different energies of the compartments. The compartmentalization of reality resulting from this facet is what gives rise to what we call the rational mind, and many examples of how the various capabilities of the mind emanate from this structuring are discussed in *The Global Mind and the Rise of Civilization*. The straight and perpendicular lines that were re-created inside people who downloaded this hologram became the inner reference system for everything they did, including creating art. The rational structuring of reality that this hologram provides forms the basis of civilization.

In *The Global Mind and the Rise of Civilization* several examples are given of the evolution of art as a projection of the Sixth Wave mind. Here only a simple example will demonstrate this effect of the rectilinear geometry: art produced before the Sixth Wave hologram could be downloaded (fig. 4.5a) was fundamentally different from the art that was produced after (fig. 4.5b). Hence, the scene from Egypt's New Kingdom in 1500 BCE[18]—created after the downloading of the new hologram—is much more structured along vertical and horizontal lines than the forty-thousand-year-old cave painting[19] from Altamira (created before the downloading). Straight and perpendicular lines, or symbols like those in figure 4.4, are nowhere to be found in nature (except for in the pure geometry of the Cosmic Tree of Life) nor are they in the Paleolithic art from the earlier era; they do not appear on any scale in art until the beginning of the Sixth Wave, when the shift allowed for resonance with these lines. Not surprisingly then, as we could see in figure 3.10 on page 81, it is only from this point in time that geometry and mathematics would begin to evolve among the early civilizations. There could be no science of geometry until human minds downloaded a hologram with a geometric structure.

The third common facet of the symbols in figure 4.4 is the duality and light-dark polarity between the left and right sides of the

Figure 4.5. a. Art before the downloading of the Sixth Wave mind (Altamira, about 15,000 BCE, drawing by Marcelino Sautuola, 1880), and b. after the downloading of the Sixth Wave mind (weighing of the heart scene from the Book of the Dead of Hunefer, Egypt, New Kingdom, circa 1500 BCE). (*Photograph by Jon Bodsworth*)

hologram. This duality of the Sixth Wave mind almost certainly played a significant role for the emergence of technology in the early civilizations. Seeing the world through such a polarity also allowed people to make distinctions. The dualist mind basically serves to introduce a very marked compartmentalization to our perception of reality, and as a result of this, we have become capable of developing different forms of technology. Without duality the mind would not have had the discernment to isolate metals from ores or make bronze (fig. 3.8, p. 78) from copper and tin. Without this emergence of metallurgy, dependent on the ability of our minds to mentally compartmentalize different elements, we would not today have cars, airplanes, or computers. The reason we do not find any systematic applications of technology or metallurgy before the beginning of the Sixth Wave in 3115 BCE is simply that people before this did not have partitioned dualist minds with the ability to discern and separate different aspects of reality.

On the other hand, the dualist mind was very much behind the basic divisions in the social life and religions of the early civilizations. The emergence of monarchies, and hence centers of governance, coincided with the downloading of a dualist global mind. The kind of inequality this created, for instance by leading people to see the pharaoh as divine and common people as not divine, caused a profound rift in human society, which sometimes took the form of slavery. Through the lens that the new polarized mind provided, some people, such as the king, nobility, and priesthood, would be seen as worth more and placed in the category of "good" (light, yang), whereas others, such as common people, peasants, and slaves, would be considered worth less and categorized as "evil" (dark, yin). The social consequences of this duality constitute the most problematic aspect of the external reality created by this Hologram of Good and Evil. From the social standpoint, this duality had consequences that many of us would today look upon as negative. Notably, there is a direct connection between the polarity of the Hologram of Good and Evil and social and economic inequality (fig. 4.2). As people downloaded this hologram, they would tend to auto-

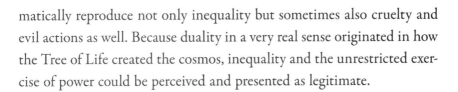

matically reproduce not only inequality but sometimes also cruelty and evil actions as well. Because duality in a very real sense originated in how the Tree of Life created the cosmos, inequality and the unrestricted exercise of power could be perceived and presented as legitimate.

TRANSITING TO CIVILIZATION

As hinted at in the previous chapter, the transition from being in resonance with the Fifth Wave to being in resonance with the Sixth Wave may not have been so easy. It seems that in the areas where the conditions were ripe for it—Egypt, Anatolia, Mesopotamia, and the Indus Valley—people enthusiastically started to create civilizations around 3115 BCE (fig. 3.8, p. 78). After all, they experienced civilization as a gift from the gods, and because this gift had a divine origin, it was incumbent upon them to develop it. Yet, at the same time people in this era shifted from being what the Hopi would call one-hearted to two-hearted, as the duality of the hologram mentally split a person in two.[20] The downloading of the Sixth Wave hologram also meant an experience of a separation from nature as well as from the Divine, which became the beginning of a long-standing perceived conflict between human beings and God.

In *The Global Mind and the Rise of Civilization,* I extensively discussed the more positive aspects of the rise of civilization. Here I will seek to clarify the more negative aspects of civilization. That civilization had both positive and negative qualities was explicitly described by the Sumerians, whose gods Enki and Inanna were thought of as having given out the gifts of civilization called *Me.*[21] The Me also included such characteristics as "falsehood" and "enmity," but because the gifts of civilization were divinely and inscrutably decreed, they were not to be questioned. This is consistent with the new theory about the origin of evil as well as of social injustice that is presented here. This theory entails an entirely new way of approaching the betterment of humanity by becoming aware of the origin of the duality of the human mind and transcending this duality through creating resonance with waves at higher levels.

Because separations were caused by an inner change resulting from the downloading of the Sixth Wave hologram, all human relationships were affected by it. Projecting the duality of this new hologram onto the social networks that had existed for thousands of years in hunter-gatherer societies must have caused pain and in many ways destroyed the old ways of being and the tribal networks that had been created around them. We will most likely never know for sure how people experienced life in the Paleolithic and Neolithic eras, but the closest we may get is to look at some indigenous cultures, such as the San Bushmen or the Australian Aborigines, some of whom are still hunter-gatherers. An inspiring fictional example of such a culture is the Navi people of the *Avatar* movie, who were desperately trying to protect their beloved Tree of Life.[22]

Many ancient cultures talked about a golden age preceding their own, not least the Egyptians, who spoke of an era called Zep Tepi, or "first time."[23] I do not think that this golden age should be understood as being more technologically advanced, as it seems that such advancement requires a dualist mind. Rather, it could have meant a time when people, before the downloading of the Sixth Wave mind, were in a state of unity with the Divine with no experience of separation. In general, hunter-gatherer cultures are more egalitarian and peaceful than those based on city life (which is the definition of civilization), and peace may very well have been the norm before the Hologram of Good and Evil was downloaded.

Before studying the actual changes that took place in human relations as a result of the separation created by the Sixth Wave hologram, I need to point out that the nine creation waves are not the only ones that influence our perception of reality. The frequency realm also includes prewaves, which serve to prepare humans for the change that comes when any of the nine waves proper is activated. Prewaves bring the same holograms as proper waves, but the holograms in them are not as markedly expressed. The most powerful prewave of the Sixth Wave began 10,250 years ago (8240 BCE) and so had twice

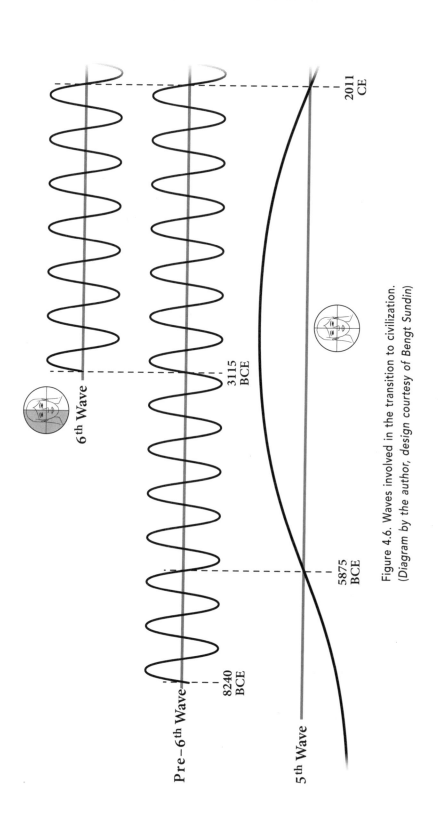

Figure 4.6. Waves involved in the transition to civilization. *(Diagram by the author, design courtesy of Bengt Sundin)*

the duration of the Sixth Wave up until the present time. Other pre-waves of the Sixth Wave began 51,250 years ago and 25,600 years ago, which correspond to a half and a fourth of the Fifth Wave, respectively. While prewaves will only be mentioned in passing here, they do play significant preparatory roles. We may note that 51,250 years ago corresponds with the time when people started to diversify their tools,[24] and this may be looked upon as an early preparatory wave not only for agriculture 10,250 years ago but also for civilization 5,125 years ago.

The beginning of the pre–Sixth Wave thus coincides with the beginning of agriculture and the Neolithic era, whereas civilization does not emerge until the beginning of the Sixth Wave proper. The phenomena that the pre–Sixth Wave and Sixth Wave introduce, however, take their starting points in the Fifth Wave and are created from interference patterns with this. Regardless, what these waves mean is that the Hologram of Good and Evil was downloaded in two steps, which in parallel with the material and technological advances resulted in an increased experience of duality.

THE ORIGIN OF DOMINANCE AND SUBJUGATION IN THE HOLOGRAM OF GOOD AND EVIL

Among the consequences of the Hologram of Good and Evil, as I will henceforth call the hologram of the Sixth Wave, was the emergence of slavery, which is an obvious expression of dominance and subjugation. Slavery is known to have been practiced in all major early civilizations, and the earliest examples of codified laws look upon it as an established institution.[25] As these very civilizations were products of this hologram, it would seem that slavery could have been generated by this hologram as well. Yet, slavery is believed to predate civilization and go back to the early Neolithic,[26] which could mean that it resulted from the download-ing of the preparatory dualist mind of the pre–Sixth Wave (fig. 4.6).

We, admittedly, do not know exactly when slavery began and therefore must consider the hypothesis that slavery was caused by the Hologram of Good and Evil as unproven.

What we do know, however, is that by the time the first monarchies, such as in Egypt, emerged around 3100 BCE, societies became markedly separated into different classes with different privileges, and slaves formed one such class of people. Pharaohs, along with almost all rulers in early civilizations, were considered to be divine and to be expressions of a divine will or order. The common people and slaves were also part of the same divine order. The polarity of the Sixth Wave mind almost automatically created a separation between rulers and ruled, as it was half divine light and half darkness. Projecting this onto the external world resulted in the formation of different classes, among them slaves.

The duality of the Hologram of Good and Evil meant that civilized societies early in the Sixth Wave by necessity would reproduce a profound inequality and a system of governance sharply separating the rulers from the ruled. Since at least early in the wave people recognized that the dualist perception had a divine origin, they would also take this state of affairs as a given. Later, from about 550 BCE, I believe that the hologram had become so deeply integrated in people's minds that the duality had become second nature; people were unaware that it was something distinct from themselves.

The existence of this Hologram of Good and Evil explains the kind of slave mentality that has characterized humanity for most of the 5,100 years of civilization. The legitimacy of the rulers and their dominance was not only propagated by the rulers; the ruled shared the same dualist mind and also thought it natural that the world should be divided into rulers and ruled. Although there were occasional slave revolts in ancient times and peasant revolts in medieval Europe, in the end these revolts always failed, because their goals were not consistent with the Hologram of Good and Evil. At the time, everyone, including the rebellious, was in resonance with the Hologram of Good and Evil and had integrated it. Even when a revolt succeeded, the slaves or

peasants behind it would soon reproduce a new separation between rulers and ruled, because the insurgents were unable to transform or transcend the dualist hologram. Possessed with a dualist mind, they would
always reproduce a class society, with a new face on the throne. What
also might have contributed to the persistence of societies based on
division is the fact that in whatever direction people were looking, they
would see manifested the same separation between rulers and ruled.

What this tells us is that no revolution aiming merely to change
the external manifestations of the mind is likely to be successful, and
more recent world history bears testimony to this. No lasting social
change is possible if it is not promoted by people who have transformed their minds on a deep level and are not ruled by this duality of the Sixth Wave hologram. To put it in other words: the basic
structure and duality of the mind remains unalterable as long as it
is sustained by resonance with a given wave. A hologram carried by
such a wave thus has enormous power in guiding us to create and re-
create a certain reality. If we want to change the external world in a
lasting way, we have to be able to transcend the duality of our minds.
Because our external reality with its social relationships and technology is ultimately a projection of our inner world, the same dualist relations will always tend to be reproduced as long as we are downloading
the same hologram. This also tells us that to the extent that we want
things to change, we will have to understand the Destiny Chart of
Humanity and what we can do to transcend the duality of our minds,
which has had an origin in a resonance with the duality of the universe as a whole. For the most part this is not even recognized as a
problem, and humanity as a whole certainly has not yet become aware
of this.

In addition to the social inequality discussed above, warfare is a
phenomenon that likely had its origin in the inherently conflictual
dualist mind created by the Hologram of Good and Evil. Dominance
is a direct consequence of a dualist mind, and warfare has often been
a tool to establish and maintain this practice. Compared to slavery, its

time of emergence may be easier to ascertain, as it would be expected to leave deeper traces in the archaeological record. To begin with, we may notice that the cave paintings from the Paleolithic—before the downloading of the Hologram of Good and Evil—do not show any signs of warfare.[27] The earliest find that is possibly indicative of warfare is a cemetery on the Sudan-Egypt border, which is about fourteen thousand years old.[28] Nonetheless, even from the Neolithic (that is, after the downloading of the pre–Sixth Wave hologram 10,250 years ago, fig. 4.6), towns were generally unfortified and were built in areas, such as fertile valleys, that would have been difficult to defend if attacked. Moreover, skeletal and burial remains do not generally indicate the presence of warfare during this era. This seems to indicate that even after the activation of the pre–Sixth Wave, warfare remained an unusual phenomenon, if it existed at all. Organized warfare, and certainly that based on weapons made of bronze, emerged only after 3000 BCE, likely resulting from the activation of the Hologram of Good and Evil. The dualist mind that became accessible at that point in time then created a perception that your own ruler and your people were "good" (worth fighting for), whereas other people, the "enemy," were "evil" (worth fighting against and killing). The Hologram of Good and Evil by necessity created conflicts among people, with each group aiming to subjugate others, who were perceived through the dark filter.

In addition, cities and literacy, the hallmarks of civilization, at this time became the basis for marked class distinctions: those living in cities increasingly fed from those toiling in the soil, and those with the ability to read and write would have access to knowledge and power, not available to everyone. Similarly, the priesthoods, which often had such knowledge and were believed to be in closer contact with the gods, would emerge as a superior class within the context provided by the Hologram of Good and Evil. In fact, all social structures that emerged around the phenomena that were created from resonance with the Sixth Wave (fig. 3.8, p. 78) would themselves generate social relationships based on duality, and in many ways these structures have survived to our own time.

WHAT IS THE ORIGIN
OF AUTHORITARIAN RULE?

The question of the origin of authoritarian rule is fortunately currently becoming a topic of discussion. How did an elite originate to begin with, and why has it been so widely accepted? To inquire into the causes of social, political, and economic inequality is one of the most important things we can do at the current time. What is the origin of forced authority, and why do some people dominate others? What is emerging from the present study is that there is no such thing as a "human nature." Social relationships are profoundly influenced by the holograms that humans download at different frequencies (fig. 4.2). In the following chapters, we will look at how these influences have changed over time.

If this is so, and I believe it is, we may gain the insight that there is no such a thing as a force of evil and that the evil acts humans sometimes commit are a consequence of a particular dualist hologram they have downloaded. You may say that there are certain steps in the climb to the ninth level of the pyramid that have negative side effects. The ancient peoples clearly seem to have been aware that this duality was something originating outside themselves, as they grappled with it in their creation stories. In our own time, this awareness has, however, been largely lost, and many have probably come to believe that duality is something that is an inherent part of our nature.

To further ponder the consequences of the duality of the Sixth Wave hologram, we may start by asking ourselves how we perceive reality with this holographic duality filter applied to our inner vision. If the symbols in figure 4.4 indeed are symbols of the mind, then this polarity filter would in fact shape all of our experiences and color all information from the world that surrounds us. If the polarity filter is perceived as having a divine origin, its influence would be even stronger. Even if people shortly after the activation of the Sixth Wave were able to "see" this filter (or at least experience it so clearly that they would make symbols of it), there are reasons to believe that later it became second nature to humans. Human beings would then be inclined to believe that the world really *is* the way it is perceived through this dualist filter.

Sixth Wave duality in its modern form—racism, sexism or the like—is thus not something that pops up for no reason in the mind of someone. Naturally, there may be personal reasons why such attitudes get stuck in a particular individual, but the reason dualist thinking exists among humanity in the first place is as a residue of the resonance with the Sixth Wave, which dominated humanity for a long time. Contrary to what most people would say, I thus do not believe that the division of society into classes of rulers and ruled has its origin primarily in the kind of social training and education people receive. Naturally, social training plays a role, but only inasmuch as it reinforces and codifies the polarity that already exists in the dualist mind. Authoritarian rule thus finds its primary cause in the Hologram of Good and Evil, and there are several reasons that this hologram has had such power. One is that *without this dualist global mind, we would not today be living in a civilization.* Again, the Sumerians, who were maybe the first people to resonate with the Sixth Wave and create a civilization, recognized not only the practical advances but also the enmity that came with it.[29] I believe it is important for us who live today to understand that it was not civilization as such that created the enmity. Instead, it was the Hologram of Good and Evil that created both the technical advances and the negative aspects of civilization. I think we should also recognize that human beings have no power over the design of the holograms (and even less so over the inherent duality of the cosmos). Yet, as we will see later, in the multilevel mind that is currently available to us, we have a choice about which waves to develop resonance with.

Another reason for the hologram's power is that early on people realized that it emanated from the Source of the Tree of Life and therefore could be legitimized as being part of a divine order. Consequently, members of the ruling class could present themselves as the divinely ordained upholders of the external expression of this hologram. Moreover, because people experienced the duality as emanating from the Source, they more easily became fanatical about the righteousness of their own views and upheld religions or social systems based on duality. Through a combination of these factors, a social order was cemented.

Many people have integrated the Hologram of Good and Evil to such a degree that they believe that there is an eternal struggle going on between the forces of good and evil in the universe. Such notions are supported by the media through popular movies such as *Star Wars* and *Lord of the Rings*. Yet, the concept of such an eternal struggle leaves people without hope as it becomes impossible to figure out how this struggle could come to an end. Though such movies are entertaining, they insidiously convey a disempowering message. The same can be said about religious notions, notably in Christianity and Islam, that there is an independent force of evil. Conspiracy theories have also in modern times replaced the devil with notions of reptilians[30] or Anunnaki[31] as the source of evil in humanity. I find such explanations superficial and lacking any real research basis. For the most part these ideas are themselves merely projections of the Hologram of Good and Evil and serve to reproduce exactly the kind of duality that the proponents of the conspiracy theory purport to fight.

I believe such ideas are disempowering and can only serve to make people lose hope. What instead does give hope and a possible direction for the future is the realization that the Hologram of Good and Evil only represents a single step of the climb back to the unifying hologram of the Ninth Wave. By making the climb consciously with full awareness of what changes it involves, it is possible to be part of manifesting the destiny of humanity. The Hologram of Good and Evil, which, after all, has given us our civilization and an awareness of ourselves that would not have existed otherwise, cannot be fought head on, not even with our thoughts. Any hologram of the mind is much more powerful than our thoughts, because the hologram is what selects and organizes our thoughts. A hologram, such as the Hologram of Good and Evil, can, however, be transcended and left behind as we manifest the Destiny Chart of Humanity.

5

Ashur, Yahweh, the Church, and the Ultimate Transcendence of Duality

WOMEN AND THE HOLOGRAM OF GOOD AND EVIL

We have now seen how dominance and subjugation emerged in the social arena as a result of the downloading of the Hologram of Good and Evil produced by the Sixth Wave. A noteworthy thing is that the history of the subjugation of women seems to run in parallel to those of slavery and warfare. There is no archaeological evidence from the Paleolithic, with its nonfiltered Fifth Wave mind (fig. 4.2, p. 96), indicating that women were in an inferior position to men. On the contrary, the many female statuettes found from this era indicate that women may have been held in higher esteem than men. The oldest known representations of humans, Venus from Hohle Fels[1] and Lion Woman,[2] both about forty thousand years old and found in present-day Germany, are both female. But after the downloading of the pre-Sixth Wave (fig. 4.6, p.111) some ten thousand years ago and with the resulting rise of agriculture (see *The Global Mind and the Rise of Civilization*, p. 139), men became dominant. The rest is, as they say, his story, and at least up until the twenty-first century CE, men have been the dominant gender in the political and economic arenas.

How did this shift to a subordinated role for women take place? As I hinted at above, the best explanation seems to be that the Sixth

Wave hologram played the instrumental role for developing a patri-archal society. The fact that the subjugation of women, slavery, and warfare all seem to be correlated with the Sixth Wave (and its pre-wave) indicates that they are all results of its emerging hologram. In his excellent book *The Alphabet versus the Goddess,* Leonard Shlain points out that in the ancient Mediterranean cultures whenever writ-ing comes in, the worship of the Goddess goes out. This by itself is a strong argument that women became subordinated as the Sixth Wave hologram eclipsed that of the Fifth Wave. Because we know that writ-ing came with the Sixth Wave (fig. 3.8, p. 78), this would mean that it was also the Sixth Wave that killed the Mother Goddess, symbolizing the subjugation of women.

We should be aware, however, that the duality between men and women (or among people of different races) is not something that exists "out there" in the external reality. Men and women are simply different kinds of human beings with different spiritual energies, and the only way that an oppressive or conflictual relationship between them could have emerged is through the projections of a dualist mind. Thus, the Hologram of Good and Evil did not change the external reality in itself but only the human perception of it. As a conse-quence, if it were not for the dualist mind there would be no conflicts or oppression in human relationships. The power of the Sixth Wave hologram has, however, been such that women for a long time came to be subjugated by men. What is more, this subjugation has often been legitimized by religious doctrines claiming to embody a higher truth. The story of Adam and Eve in the Garden of Eden is such a doctrine.

THE ASSYRIAN TREE OF LIFE

As mentioned earlier, the oldest representations of the Tree of Life known to us are found in Mesopotamia, and an early Sumerian depic-tion of the "lord of the good tree" (also called the Tree of Truth)[3] was shown in figure 3.12 (p. 87). The Tree of Life seems to have continued to play a significant role in Mesopotamia even as its dominant civilization changed from Sumerian to Akkadian, Babylonian, and Assyrian. It may actually be the Assyrians, militarily the most powerful of the Mesopotamian kingdoms, that developed the most prominent worship of the Tree of Life. Hundreds of reliefs are, for instance, known from this kingdom where a king (often as in fig. 5.1 with a mirror image of himself) tended the Tree of Life. Naturally, this had a political function as the king through his connection to the Tree of Life gained legitimacy for his rule and so wanted everyone to see this. Yet, remarkably, there does not in the Assyrian records exist any explicit explanation as to what this Tree of Life actually is.

This absence of information poses an enigma. It is possible that

Figure 5.1. King Ashurnasirpal II tending the Assyrian Tree of Life together with a mirror image of himself and Ashur, the One God, hovering above the tree, from wall relief at Nimrud, 865 BCE. (*Courtesy of Paul Williams*)

the existence of the Tree of Life was so obvious to the Assyrians that there was no need to give an explanation. It is also possible that the Tree of Life was so sacred that it should not be mentioned in word or text. Yet another possibility, which I consider the most likely, is that the actual knowledge about the Tree of Life was kept secret from people at large. When considering this, we should take into account that the knowledge about the Kabbalistic Tree of Life[4] in the Jewish tradition for the longest time was taught exclusively to married men over forty years of age and was kept secret from most people until somehow it leaked out a few hundred years ago and became part of Hermetic Kabbalism.[5] Possessing knowledge about the Assyrian Tree of Life, which most likely is the origin of the Kabbalistic Tree of Life, may similarly have been seen as so important that it became the prerogative of a few.

To provide a modern understanding of the Assyrian Tree of Life, I would like to quote from an article about it by Benjamin Daniali.

> The Sacred Assyrian Tree of Life is the divine knowledge. The Tree is ancient wisdom. "It is a path for human to become a 'perfect man.'" The Tree is a bridge between the world and God and His Heaven. It is a ladder to be climbed through ascetic life and a device to receive divine powers and knowledge. "Tree generally represents the forces behind Creation on all levels; from microscopic to macrocosmic." The significance of the Tree is seen in the ancient world among Assyrians and Egyptians. Jews later on inherited the concept of the Tree, apparently from Babylon, slightly modified it and formed Sacred Teachings of the Kabbalah, a Jewish mysticism that means "called Ghabel Alahah," in English "Accept God/Receiving."[6]

Many of these statements resonate strongly with what has already been verified in this book. Hence, the Tree of Life is described as a path to becoming a perfect human, and very notably to become this we need to climb a ladder. Also, as has been described in the fractal-holographic model, the tree manifests creation at all levels, from macrocosmic to microscopic. Yet, to scholars, it has been a mystery what the Assyrian Tree of Life, which appears in so many reliefs from Assyria, actually refers to and why it was such a central focus of worship. In this book, I have proposed that the Tree of Life is not a fantasy but something that has existed from the beginning of time, and so much of the mystery disappears. Nonetheless, certain aspects of the role the Tree of Life played in the religion of the ancient Assyrians may still seem mysterious. Fortunately, however, there is circumstantial information about this. Based on such, Professor Simo Parpola, an Assyrologist at the University of Helsinki, has re-created the Assyrian Tree of Life (fig. 5.2a) based on the nine most significant gods[7] of the Assyrians and the qualities and numbers associated with them.

To be able to analyze this composite Assyrian Tree of Life in figure 5.2a, I will use the image of the hologram of the Sixth Wave (fig. 5.2b) for comparison. This hologram, as we know, created civilization through its favoring of the left brain with light and leaving the right brain in the shadow. In figure 5.2b, the right side of the head from our perspective (which is the left brain from the model's perspective) corresponds to the right column in the Tree of Life in figure 5.2a and vice versa for the left side of the head. The central column in figure 5.2a then corresponds to the Cosmic Axis, which is also reflected in the straight vertical line through the face in figure 5.2b. Based on the Assyrian Tree of Life reconstructed in this way, I assert that this is in fact another representation of the Hologram of Good and Evil, which is more elaborate than the one from Sumer/Mesopotamia shown in figure 4.4b (p.104). The parallel to this eight-partitioned dingir symbol becomes clearer if we look upon Ishtar in the center of fig 5.2a as connected to eight other gods.

In the tree in figure 5.2a, the gods in the central column are Anu, the father of the gods and the god of heaven, Ištar (Ishtar), the goddess

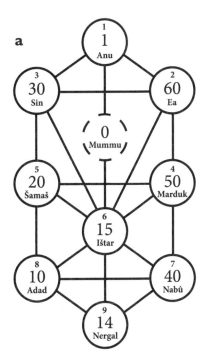

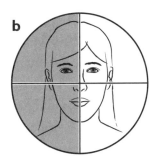

Figure 5.2. a. Reconstruction of the Assyrian Tree of Life with the nine great gods and their associated numbers. [*From* Parpola, Journal Near Eastern Studies *"Assyrian Tree of Life" 52:3 (1993) Figure #9 (pp. 183 to 183). Used by permission of University of Chicago Press.*] b. The hologram of the Sixth Wave.

of love, and Nergal, the god of death, central deities keeping the basic balance of the axis mundi (compare fig. 3.12 on p. 87). What is then interesting to see is that the gods in the right column (which corresponds to the light in fig. 5.2b) consistently have higher numbers than those in the left column, signifying higher values as gods. The gods in the left column are Sin, the god of the moon, Šamaš (Shamash), the god of the sun, and Adad, the weather god, in other words, nature gods. Going back to the right-hand column, we find Ea (called Enki by the Sumerians), Marduk, and Nabu,[8] deities that express left-brained civilization. Ea, at the top, was often portrayed as overtly sexual and is associated with virile masculinity. He also had the significant function as the keeper of the gifts of civilization. On his part, Marduk, who later became the most prominent god in the Babylonian pantheon, may be best known for having killed Tiamat, a primal goddess or Earth mother. Tiamat was also sometimes seen as a serpent,[9] and we might see this victory of Marduk as a parallel to Yahweh cursing the serpent in the

Garden of Eden story. Nabu became the god of writing, progressively taking over this function from the goddess Nidaba. Initially, he was a minister of Marduk but later became his coregent as the head of the pantheon.

This is the Assyrian understanding of the Tree of Life, and it tells us things about how the Tree of Life was perceived in the Sixth Wave that the symbols in figure 4.4 (p. 104) do not communicate. Through this analysis, it becomes possible to flesh out the Hologram of Good and Evil so that we may more clearly understand what effect this had on people at the time. For instance, this representation of the Tree of Life tells us (based on their numbers) that the gods of the left brain were seen as dominating. In contrast to the nature gods of the opposite side, they were also responsible for bringing civilization to humanity (which indeed the left brain does). They were also very masculine and deposed significant female deities who may have held the positions the male deities co-opted. Certainly, Marduk killing Tiamat was an important myth that symbolized the shift to male dominance that happened through the Sixth Wave.

It has been suggested that the Assyrians viewed their supreme god, Ashur, as the totality of the nine great gods, and the image in figure 5.2a helps us understand how polarized the ancient Assyrians experienced this god. Or more correctly said: this is how polarized the Divine was perceived after the Assyrians had projected the Hologram of Good and Evil onto it. The Divine was seen as dominated by the masculine powers that held the highest numbers, and the role of the only feminine power, Ishtar, was to keep everyone connected. Again, the nine great gods in the tree in figure 5.2a were most likely aspects or qualities of Ashur, who is hovering above the tree in figure 5.1. In this interpretation the Assyrians saw Ashur as the supreme deity who killed the female goddesses of the past (except for Ishtar). Maybe it is then not surprising that the Assyrians are reputed to have been the cruelest people in antiquity. Julian Jaynes speculates[10] that they became this way when they lost direct contact with their personal gods, which people commonly had in earlier times, and so became desperate. This loss would have coincided with their transition to believing in a single god, and the god they turned to, Ashur, who was often shown as a war god with a bow and an arrow, would naturally have been much feared.

THE CHALDEAN-JEWISH-CHRISTIAN TRADITION

From the perspective of world history, the Assyrian version of the Tree of Life is interesting for a few different reasons. One is that the Assyrians may have been the last significant power emanating from Mesopotamia (not counting the short revival of the Babylonian Empire). Their trajectory toward monotheism may then be looked upon as the completion of this ancient civilization, whose history goes back to the very beginning of the Sixth Wave. Another reason to pay attention to Assyria, is that in the history of religions, Mesopotamia is sometimes viewed as a starting point of the Chaldean-Jewish-Christian tradition. Israel and Judea had in fact belonged to Assyria in the late seventh century BCE, before the Babylonian captivity, in which the Jews remained until the mid–sixth century. Even if Chaldea, where according to legend Abraham came from, is not the same as Assyria and Babylonia, all three cultures were part of Mesopotamia and so shared a number of beliefs about the world and the gods. In fact, in the ancient world, these cultures had a prestige rivaled only by the Egyptians, and it seems obvious that the Jews, who lived under Mesopotamian empires for such a long time, would have borrowed significant religious ideas from them. It is no secret that some of the stories in the Book of Genesis, such as that of Noah and his ark, find their origin in Mesopotamian beliefs. This is a somewhat hidden connection to the past, and the Assyrian Tree of Life may through this have influenced not only Judaism but also Christianity and Islam.

This is not to say that the Jews simply copied the views that were prevalent in Mesopotamia. Most likely they were, however, given knowledge in captivity, which if they resonated with it would have modified it and from this created a variation around their own god, Yahweh. To believe that they just made it up or copied it without having any experiences of it of their own would be to completely miss the point. It is a central theme of this book that the phenomenon of the Tree of Life is real and that the duality it created could be directly experienced early in the Sixth Wave. Yet, there were cultural variations in how this experience was expressed, such as the Assyrian version and the Jewish one. Most likely, the Mesopotamian view of the Tree of Life, whether mediated by the Assyrians or the Babylonians, then strongly influenced how Yahweh, the Jewish god, was perceived and re-created by his people.

There is also little doubt that the Assyrian Tree of Life (fig. 5.2) is the original version, from which the Jews later developed the Kabbalistic Tree of Life. The original Jewish view of the Divine may then have been similar to that of the Assyrian Tree of Life (fig. 5.2a) and the male dominance this expresses. This would mean that Yahweh was also a projection of the Hologram of Good and Evil and so would express the very same imbalance. Although this admittedly is a reconstruction, it is reasonable and holds a strong explanatory power for the continued history of the Abrahamic religions.

THE GARDEN OF EDEN STORY IN GENESIS

This leads us to the Book of Genesis and the view the biblical story conveys about the Tree of Life. According to biblical chronology, Genesis may have been written as early as 1500–1000 BCE, but modern scholars[11] believe that it was finally put together much later, around 500 BCE. Because this happened after the Jews returned from their Babylonian captivity, we must seriously consider that Mesopotamian laws and ideas about the Tree of Life had a bearing on it. Genesis, in

Figure 5.3. Lucas Cranach the Elder's *Adam and Eve* (1526). Typically Adam and Eve are shown in such paintings on opposite sides of the Tree of Life (compare fig. 5.1), which creates duality. (*Courtesy of the Courtauld Institute, London*)

the Torah or the Pentateuch of the Christian Bible, however, contains many different parts. The first[12] is a description of how God created the world, which is similar to many such accounts from other traditions and is by itself not controversial. It also conveys the key knowledge that creation takes place in seven DAYS and six NIGHTS (if we count the resting DAY). This is indeed the rhythm of creation that was verified in chapter 3 (provided that we look upon the waves as leading up to the current time). The second part of Genesis is about Adam and Eve in the Garden of Eden and their expulsion from it, which has many questionable elements that we will look into here. The later sections of Genesis are about the continued history of the Jewish people and will not be discussed (see, however, *The Global Mind and the Rise of Civilization*, which deals with the Flood and Noah's ark).

In short, the story about the Garden of Eden begins with Adam and Eve living in paradise in peace with all the animals and with Yahweh. In the Garden two special trees are mentioned, the Tree of Life and the Tree of Knowledge of Good and Evil. Yahweh tells the couple that they can eat the fruit from all the trees except for the Tree of Knowledge of Good and Evil. A serpent appears and entices Eve to eat from this tree, and she then leads Adam to do the same. After having eaten from this fruit, their perception of themselves is changed, and they discover that they are naked. Yahweh appears and curses them for having eaten of this fruit, and as a punishment they are expelled from the Garden of Eden. Notably, the serpent is also cursed. Adam is told that he will be toiling for the rest of his life, and Eve will give birth in pain, as all women after her, as a punishment. Yahweh closes the Garden with a flaming sword, with a vague hint that it may at some point again be opened.

Needless to say, this is not about any actual physical garden. The Garden of Eden is a metaphor for a state of unity consciousness, which was reflected in the unity with the animals and nature as well as between the genders. Adam and Eve only experienced themselves as separate after eating of the fruit and seeing "that they were naked." They

THE ULTIMATE TRANSCENDENCE OF DUALITY 131

also experienced a unity with God before they ate the fruit; they could naturally talk to Yahweh. Based on what we have here learned about the Tree of Life and the serpents emanating from it, I interpret the story as a metaphor for the transition from one hologram to another. The serpent symbolizes the Sixth Wave carrying the Hologram of Good and Evil, which introduces dualities and marks an end to the experience of unity of the Fifth Wave. The transition from the hologram of the Fifth Wave to that of the Sixth meant that humans came to experience themselves as separate from both the Divine and nature.

Regarding the two trees in this metaphor, there has been a debate whether they are one and the same or two separate trees.[13] The solution that I am proposing to this quandary is that there indeed is *only one Cosmic Tree of Life,* from which waves in both the biological and the mental range in the spectrum (fig. 2.3, p. 35) emanate. The biblical Tree of Knowledge of Good and Evil is then only a special expression for one of the holograms carried by these waves, the hologram of the Sixth Wave. The Tree of Knowledge thus shares the axis of the Tree of Life, but its hologram is of another frequency, and hence the former is described as an altogether different tree. The serpent as a symbol of the Sixth Wave seeks to manifest itself through Adam and Eve eating from the fruit of the Tree of Knowledge, which is none other than the Hologram of Good and Evil. Eating its fruit simply means downloading the hologram of the Sixth Wave, with all of its consequences, including many aspects of knowledge as well as duality.

The notion of "the Fall," as this event has sometimes been called, really reflects the shift in consciousness that was precipitated by the downloading of the Sixth Wave hologram. This was indeed a fall in the sense of a departure from the earlier state of unity, but it was also an elevation to a higher frequency, which allowed humans to create civilization. Later Judeo-Christian interpretations have been eager to blame humans, and especially women, for this "Fall," and so have failed to recognize that one aspect of downloading the Sixth Wave is the creation of civilization, which in itself was a positive step.

Figure 5.4. Hunahpu uses his blowgun to shoot down Seven Macaw (a symbol of the hologram of the Fifth Wave) from the Tree of Life. Note the serpent hanging in the tree to the left, symbolizing the Sixth Wave. Similar to the Garden of Eden story, this story represents the transition from one wave to another, where the hero twins Hunahpu and Xbalanque introduced duality. (Courtesy of Linda Schele)

The story of a transition from a world of unity to one of duality, such as that in Genesis, is one with which several other ancient peoples would also resonate. The Chinese legend about Fuxi and Nuwa (fig. 3.11, p. 85)—the serpentlike couple that brought civilization—is one[14] and the Mayan story about the hero twins shooting down the vainglorious Seven Macaw[15] from the tree is another describing the end to unity. Seven Macaw, in this story in the Popol Vuh, was a symbol of the seventh DAY of the Fifth Wave and its unity. While he was sitting in the Tree of Life, he was shot down by Hunahpu (Hun Ahau = One Light) using a blowgun with the help of his dark twin Xbalanque (X = feminine aspect, Balam = Jaguar, a night animal): the two symbolize the duality of the Sixth Wave, which would take over after the unity of the Fifth Wave. In the Popol Vuh stories, the transition from one hologram to another was described as a matter of fact, as the Maya saw the shift as part of a cosmic plan, and these shifts were not condemned. Among the Maya and many Native American peoples, the serpent, for instance Quetzalcoatl, was, instead, honored for bringing civilization.

When we consider transition myths from cultures other than the

Jewish, where humans were not condemned, we may wonder what is wrong with seeking knowledge or knowledge about good and evil and why it would have been considered a "sin." Is it not obvious that if humanity is to evolve we will have to seek knowledge, including about ethics? The transitions between different waves and frequencies of evolution are the very mechanisms that cause life on Earth (as well as everywhere in the universe) to evolve. If Yahweh is the creator of the universe, why would he punish those who seek to perfect themselves by transiting to higher states of mind? Through Yahweh's vilification of Eve and Adam for eating the fruit, they were brought into a situation of "cursed if you do, cursed if you don't." And if the Tree of Life is the manifestation of the Creator, then who is Yahweh? It seems that what is unique in the Garden of Eden story among the creation stories of the world is the guilt, punishment, and concept of sin that was inflicted on humans and especially, through the "sin" of Eve, on women. Ironically, however, this is the creation story that, through its adoption by other religions, has become the most widespread.

I suspect that the origin of the condemnations in this story is that the Assyrian view of "god," which favored male dominance, is lurking behind the actions of Yahweh. Yahweh of the Garden of Eden story is similar to Ashur of the Assyrian Tree of Life. Yet, regardless of what influence Ashur might have had, Yahweh himself was a projection of the Hologram of Good and Evil by the Jewish priesthood. The author(s) of the Garden of Eden story most likely had a patriarchal and conservative agenda as they themselves were dominated by this hologram. We also must understand that women had been subjugated by this hologram for a long time when the Book of Genesis was written. The Garden of Eden story essentially served to legitimize the already existing plight of women.

The consequences of this primordial myth about the origins of humankind have been far-reaching and largely negative. If we assume that it was formulated before the midpoint of the Sixth Wave by a group of Jewish patriarchs, we may understand its purpose as political or, in other words, one of asserting power. It was to keep people, and especially women, down and to blame them for gaining knowledge, enjoying sexuality, and engaging in many other things that come with the curiosity of life and the eating of the fruits of creation. The doctrine of Original Sin—although invented much later by the church father Augustine[16] (ca. 430 CE)—is directly based on the cursing of Eve in the Book of Genesis. The concept of Original Sin, no matter how absurd, has for centuries been used by Christian churches, and especially the Catholic Church, to denigrate women.

YAHWEH

Because the Hebrew scriptures were incorporated into the Old Testament of the Christian Bible, Yahweh—even if he was a feared ancient war god at least partially modeled upon Ashur and Marduk—has much more widely come to be a model for what "God" is supposed to be like. This view has prevailed well into modern times as Yahweh has had a great influence not only in Judaism but also in the Christian church and Islam. More than half of humanity today belongs to the Abrahamic religions, which have all in significant ways inherited traits of Yahweh in their concepts of God. In reality, these traits were projections of a particular Hologram of Good and Evil, which has served to cement the power structures of these religions. Whether Moses, the presumed Egyptian prince who led the people of Israel from slavery back to their country and received the law from God on the way, is a historical person has also been questioned.[17] No Egyptian source seems to corroborate the story, and it may have simply served to cover up the Mesopotamian origin of Yahweh, whose male gods he seems to have more in common with than with the Egyptian pantheon.

In the Bible, Yahweh defines himself as jealous,* and his cursing

---

*"For you shall worship no other god: for the LORD, whose name is Jealous, is a jealous God." (Source: Exodus 34:14, King James Bible 2000)

of the serpent may be an expression of this jealousy. As we have seen, the serpent was the first symbol of humanity's experience of a power in the otherworldly realm. Yahweh may then have seen the serpent as a rival, much as Marduk had seen Tiamat—more than modern people have probably understood—and Yahweh's long curse of the serpent supports this explanation. In Genesis the serpent is referred to as the "craftiest of the animals." The serpent, as we now know, is notably a symbol of an evolutionary wave and the directed progress that humanity is supposed to go through. Cursing the serpent (for encouraging Adam and Eve to seek knowledge) then really means cursing evolution and progress, much in line with the desires of a conservative patriarchy, whether Mesopotamian or Jewish. By cursing the serpent, Yahweh attempts to keep humans, and women in particular, in a state of guilt for having embraced the continued evolution of creation. Yahweh (quite in contrast to the Popol Vuh, see fig. 5.4) curses what was meant to happen according to the divine plan, namely the transition from one level of evolution to another. Indeed, eating of the fruit of the Tree of Knowledge of Good and Evil was the right thing for the humans to do. Rather than facilitating the transition from the world of one hologram to that of another, Yahweh seems to have made it more difficult.

At the time the Garden of Eden story was written, its author(s) were probably convinced that Yahweh was the Divine All That Is. Because the Hologram of Good and Evil indeed emanated from the Source and was experienced as such, there was probably only a vague perception that the holograms would later come to shift. Although the Christians, through the New Testament, redefined humanity's relationship to God, compared to in the Old Testament, the Christian God was still looked upon as if it was the same entity as Yahweh. In the first centuries CE, there were discussions among the early church fathers as to whether the Old Testament with Yahweh should be included in the Christian Bible. Yet, the power of the Hologram of Good and Evil was such that it would defeat the critical voices, and the church as an institution accepted this veiled Ashur as "God." Although it may not be relevant today to reveal the origin of Ashur in the Hologram of Good and Evil (since he has no direct followers in the modern world), Yahweh remains an expression of this hologram that still profoundly impacts our world.

Before discussing this, I think it is important to recognize that in the ancient world there were many tribal and national gods that were war gods. Yahweh of the Jews was by no means the only one with such characteristics. Yet, he is the only one that has survived to the present time. He has become the model for all three of the Abrahamic religions for what "God" is, and this indeed seems to be a limited and very politically motivated view. As a consequence, when atheists today argue against the existence of God, they usually argue against some concept of God derived from that of Yahweh. Moreover, much of the current religious strife in the Middle East goes back to the view of God as jealous and of someone who condemns those who do not follow him. This is a perception that likely will never generate peace no matter what the protagonists of the Abrahamic religions say. On the contrary, the concept of a god to be feared and whose laws you have to obey is likely to block the road to lasting peace. For this very reason, this very powerful perception from the Sixth Wave is still influencing the world.

THE RISE OF RELIGIONS

Why then, if Yahweh was not the Divine All That Is but a dualist perception of the Divine, has he become so influential? The answer is that the Hologram of Good and Evil, because of its dualist nature has favored that some people have power over others. We saw this already from the emergence of slavery and warfare in the previous chapter. Subjugation was a universal consequence of the resonance with the Sixth Wave and was as such by no means created by the Assyrians or the Jews. Nonetheless, given this characteristic of the era, its duality, as we have already seen, profoundly influenced the kinds of deities people came to recognize and relate to.

Especially after the midpoint of the Sixth Wave in 551 BCE, people began to develop religions and thought systems around these deities. When, at this point in time, a prewave to the Seventh Wave was activated, one of the most significant paradigm shifts ever resulted. All over the world, human individuality (including the ego aspect) emerged. Historians refer to this era as the Axial Age.[18] The hologram that most people downloaded shifted in such a way that direct immersion in the spirit world (essentially the Fifth Wave experience) largely disappeared. In its place came religions, organized theological and ethical collective thought systems. Naturally, to the extent that people were then disconnected from their own direct experience of the world of spirit, they would become more inclined to subordinate themselves to a religion based on the experiences of a prophet or a founder of a religion.

The direct contact that people previously had with a whole range of spiritual entities, such as city gods, tribal gods, personal gods, demigods, legendary heroes, animal spirits, and so on, underwent a dramatic

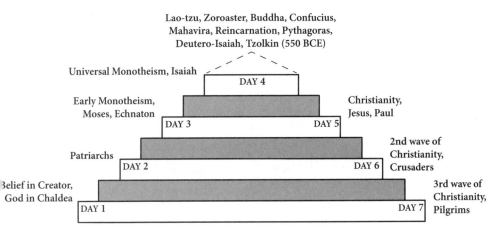

Figure 5.5. Pyramidal representation of the Sixth Wave with the explosion of religions at its midpoint. (*Diagram by the author, design courtesy of Bengt Sundin*)

change around 550 BCE as religions with doctrines, or at least elaborate thought systems, started to emerge (fig. 5.5). We can see the effects of this shift on all continents as the entire spiritual and psychological makeup of the human beings underwent this dramatic change, within a very narrow time frame. Different cultures altered their relationships to the Divine and developed new religions to account for their new experience of this. Hence, in Mesoamerica this is the time that the *tzolkin* first appears (ca. 550 BCE). In China, the wisdom teachers Confucius (551–479 BCE) and Lao-tzu (sixth century BCE) started to teach. In India, Buddha (born 563 or 552) and Mahavira (599–527), the founder of Jainism, appear, both proposing paths to enlightenment. The great epics of Mahabharata and Bhagavad-Gita were also compiled, and the belief in reincarnation established at this time. Another important religion to emerge was the dualist Zoroastrianism (550–523 BCE) in Persia, which at the time was the world's largest power. Pythagoras (570–495 BCE) began to teach about the harmonies of the spheres.

All of these religious thought systems emerged within fifty years from the actual midpoint of the Sixth Wave, a shift that had manifestations on a massive scale. Because of the global nature of this transformation, it is fairly obvious that all of these new religions and philosophies were reflections of a shift on the level of the global mind almost as profound as at the very beginning of the Sixth Wave (fig. 3.8, p. 78).

At this midpoint both Mesopotamia and Egypt, the ancient cradles of civilization, were conquered by the Persian Empire (550–330 BCE). The fact that these ancient civilizations were no longer able to uphold their old traditional beliefs is a confirmation that this shift generated something fundamentally new in the human relationship to spirit. The direct experience of spirit, which seems to have prevailed especially in Egypt, was replaced by more abstract religions. The oldest civilizations of our planet, instituted at the beginning of the Sixth Wave by "the gods," consequently came to an end. There is thus somewhat of a conflict between spirituality based on personal experiences and religiosity. The new mind field created at the midpoint of the Sixth Wave was no longer conducive to the ancient semishamanic ways of Mesopotamia and Egypt. After the conquest of these cultures by Persia, they were conquered by Alexander the Great, as the leading edge of the Mediterranean culture decisively shifted west to Greece and Rome, cultures with markedly individualistic traits.

Seemingly paradoxically, the emergence of religions on a worldwide scale coincided with the birth of the self-conscious individual, notably in Greece. This represents the end point of Julian Jaynes's *The Origin of Consciousness in the Breakdown of the Bicameral Mind;* it is really only after this shift point around 550 BCE that we know of individuals, such as Plato, Aristotle or Solon, whom we could imagine shaking hands with and having an interesting discussion with. Thales of Miletus (ca. 624–546 BCE), sometimes called the first mathematician and sometimes the first Westerner, is also from this time.

I will not here go further into the big topic of human individuality as it is outside the main focus of this chapter. Yet, I feel it is good to be aware that the first human beings who were self-conscious, self-reliant individuals, who could make choices without relying on the gods to make the decisions for them, emerged at this time. Individualism almost certainly had the same origin as the religious systems, as people at this time lost the direct contact they had previously had with the spirit world, and so what we have come to call the Western mind began.

THE MONOTHEISM OF THE JEWS

It is as part of this global shift in consciousness, leading toward the creation of organized religions, that the Jews developed their monotheism. The Jewish priesthood who had returned from captivity in Babylon around 550 BCE developed a theology that could serve as a basis for a theocratic state. The intention was for Yahweh to be the supreme leader of Israel and for its people to be subordinate to his rulings. Very importantly, at the time of this shift, Deutero-Isaiah (second Isaiah), who wrote the latter part of the Book of Isaiah, also expounded the view that Yahweh was the One God of the entire world (and not only of the Jews). This by itself provided a significant step toward a monotheism that could become a global religion. It is important to realize that the various steps in the development of religions do not simply appear out of the blue but are caused by shifts in the waves of creation that underlie our experience of reality and the Divine.

In Israel in this era, it was not the king but Yahweh who supposedly had given the law of the Ten Commandments to Moses. In the theocracy that developed, the priesthood made the important decisions, and the king became fully dependent on the prophets sent by Yahweh. The citizenry were obedient to the laws of Yahweh, because if an individual or the people deviated from this law, the revenge of Yahweh was expected to be gruesome. As the Jewish nation stuck with these laws, it remained a select, closed group; outsiders could only become Jewish with difficulty, and marriages outside the community were discouraged. This to some extent set the Jews apart from the mainstream of humanity and may explain the often hostile attitude that has been expressed toward them. They did in fact look upon themselves as a divinely chosen people and followed a law of their own. It is easy to see the parallels of this theocracy to the papacy in medieval Europe or the Sharia laws of Islam.

But then again, was Yahweh, who later significantly influenced the view of who "God" is in Christianity and Islam, truly the Divine All That Is? The Garden of Eden story indeed indicates that Yahweh was a projection of the Hologram of Good and Evil and by inference so does the Assyrian Tree of Life. We may also note that the Law of Moses was very much about creating separations—the pure from the impure, the Jews from the gentiles, and kosher from nonkosher. Mosaic law with its 613 commandments,[19] out of which 10 are famous, seems many times to maintain exactly such separations that you would expect from the projection of a dualist hologram.

Some of these commandments may be said to serve the orderly functioning of society, but others are not. The fourth commandment, "You shall not make any graven images," is, for instance, one that is not necessary for the peaceful functioning of a society. Although it is not observed by many Christian denominations, it still is in Judaism and Islam. Why have such a rule? It could be argued that a human could not make an accurate image of the Divine. True, but, on the other hand, no spoken or textual descriptions, which are not forbidden in the Torah, could give correct descriptions either. So why was a law instituted particularly against images? Part of the reason may be that jealousy was projected onto the Divine, but an even more significant projection is likely to have been the left-right duality of the Hologram of Good and Evil. For this argument, we shall remember that, overall, human language abilities, whether spoken or written, are mediated by the left brain (which is why someone who has damaged the left side of his brain may become unable to speak).[20] Images, on the other hand, are mediated through the right brain. Thus, the rule against graven images is really a law against communicating with the Divine through the right brain. Moreover, to allow only textual information about God will notably exclude those who cannot read or write, which will also allow a male priesthood, not relying on the intuition of the right brain, to control the connection of others to the Divine. Thus, the fourth commandment limits the direct connection to the Divine through the right brain so that the view of "God" will be one shaped by the left brain. All of this seems consistent with the suggestion that Yahweh is a perception of the Divine through the Hologram of Good and Evil.

Because people everywhere at the time were dominated by this same hologram, there is nothing surprising about this, and I should point out here that this is not meant to be an argument specifically against Jewish beliefs. Many of the new religions and philosophies that emerged around the midpoint of the Sixth Wave, such as Zoroastrianism and Confucianism, were markedly dualist as well. Yet, because the Jewish view of the Divine later profoundly colored both Christianity and Islam (the name Moses is mentioned 502 times in the Qur'an,[21] more than any other person), the effects of the ancient Jewish monotheism are of paramount importance also in the modern world. Rather than encouraging every person to develop his or her own relationship to the Divine, the Abrahamic religions have thus been limiting. Ultimately, these limits come from the boundaries inherent in the Hologram of Good and Evil, which has made people project the left-right duality onto the world, and this is what we today need to become aware of.

It is in this context of emerging religious systems and the birth of human individualism that took place in the Axial Age around 550 BCE that I believe we can understand the success of Yahweh in being seen as "God" on a wider scale. Ultimately, the shift that took place at the midpoint of the Sixth Wave goes back to the new interference pattern between waves, which created a hologram with even less divine light than the Hologram of Good and Evil. It is interesting to note that organized religions did not emerge because of an increased contact with the Divine. It seems to have been the other way around. They emerged because a new wave, a prewave for the Seventh Wave, emanating from the Cosmic Axis, hit Earth, and this began to eclipse the more direct spiritual contacts people had previously experienced.

MONOTHEISM IN THE
DAYS AND NIGHTS
OF THE SIXTH WAVE

The reader may now ask: What does the history of religions have to do with the fractal-holographic universe? Everything, it seems. The history of religions is very much a product of the movement of the Sixth Wave and includes the entire Chaldean-Jewish-Christian tradition. The hologram that rules in the DAYS of the Sixth Wave tends to favor steps toward left-brain-dominated monotheism as we can see in

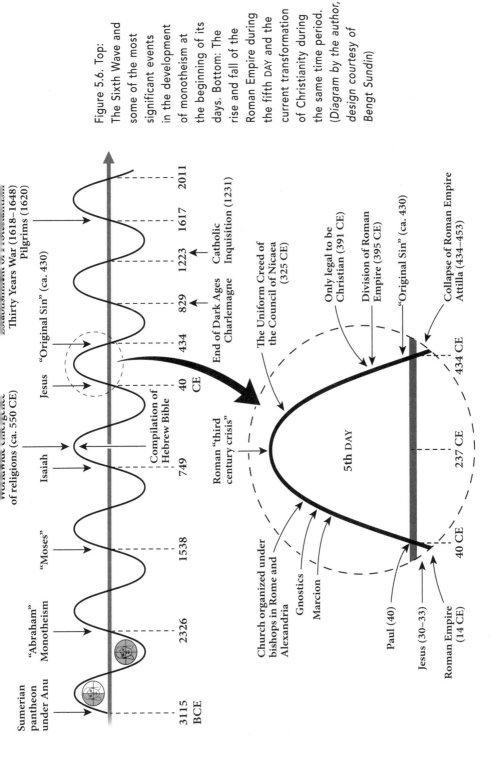

Figure 5.6. Top: The Sixth Wave and some of the most significant events in the development of monotheism at the beginning of its days. Bottom: The rise and fall of the Roman Empire during the fifth DAY and the current transformation of Christianity during the same time period. (Diagram by the author, design courtesy of Bengt Sundin)

the upper row of figure 5.6. In the time periods that are DAYS, a holo-gram with a light-dark polarity dominates, while during the NIGHTS the filter is complete. The periods that are DAYS are also, as we may see in *The Global Mind and the Rise of Civilization,* the time peri-ods that favor the rise of new civilizations. Thus, the same hologram has given rise to both the religions and the civilizations. The peri-ods that are NIGHTS often lead to the downfall of civilizations, and this incidentally is the reason why so many ancient civilizations have disappeared.

These shifts between DAYS and NIGHTS in the Sixth Wave account for much of the evolution of the theologies of the Chaldean-Jewish-Christian tradition. Steps in the direction of a more marked monotheism, and also the further expansion of this in the world, are taken in the time periods that are DAYS, because this is when new light enters to inspire its protagonists. *Because the light is limited to one brain half, it is, however, a limited, compartmentalized perception of the Divine that has emerged from this development.*

It should be noted, however, that especially in the first half of the Sixth Wave it is difficult to know what is historical fact and not, and while the dates of Abraham and Moses in the biblical chronology (fig. 5.6, upper row) may fit with the DAYS, their historicity is ques-tionable. Moreover, it is not always easy to identify which religious changes took place in the beginning of NIGHTS in the first half of the Sixth Wave. Yet, it is noteworthy that the two final NIGHTS—when we do have accurate datings—begin with the introduction of the dogma of an Original Sin (ca. 430 CE) and the Inquisition (1231 CE), respectively. Hence, it seems the theologies developed in the NIGHTS may have a quite different character from those of the DAYS. Islam, on its part, took its beginning at the midpoint of the fifth NIGHT (in 632 CE), and so its most expansive periods have been in the NIGHTS of the Sixth Wave, which it consequently is more in resonance with.

FROM JESUS TO THE
ROMAN CATHOLIC CHURCH

The continued road from Jewish monotheism to the message of Jesus to the establishment of the Catholic Church and later to the Protestant reformation is complex even if it is directly conditioned by the upturns and downturns of the waves of creation. The appearance of Jesus in Israel at the beginning of the current era, preaching about a God of love and compassion, obviously presented a great challenge to the priesthood of Jehovah or Yahweh, which, at least partially, was based on dominance and fear. In significant regard, the teachings of Jesus were different from all beliefs (not only Jewish) of earlier times, emphasizing forgiveness rather than revenge. The world would arguably never be the same after this message, and a hope of a more loving relationship to the Divine emerged.

After Jesus's crucifixion in 31 or 32 CE, his message began to spread outside Israel. Several different groups looked upon themselves as the inheritors of Jesus's legacy, and the world at the time seemed to be moving on a broader scale in the direction of monotheism. One movement emerged around Jesus's brother James, leader of the church in Jerusalem;[22] another movement, possibly a church, developed around Jesus's wife, Mary Magdalene, later forming the Gnostic tendency,[23] and yet another movement, especially of gentiles, formed around Paul.[24] With the Council of Jerusalem in 50 CE, the latter group broke with the Law of Moses,[25] stating that male members of the Christian community were not required to be circumcised (meaning, members did not need to be ethnically Jewish), and so the religion opened itself more broadly to the Roman world.

I think it is important to understand the emergence of these currents against the background of the fifth DAY of the Sixth Wave in 40 CE (see the lower part of fig. 5.6). The rise and fall of the Roman Empire, a very significant civilization in human history, has in this figure been blown up to be visible in detail as a function of the ascending and descending phases of this DAY. In the ascending phase of the fifth DAY, 40–237 CE, the Pax Romana, the empire is essentially expansive and yet stable. In this first half of the fifth DAY, Roman authorities still worshipped the traditional Roman pantheon of gods, including the emperor himself, and often persecuted Christians. At the midpoint of the fifth DAY, things started to change. The Roman Empire showed the first signs of disintegration with the third century crisis.[26] From this midpoint (237 CE) and onward, it would become increasingly difficult to defend the borders and maintain the unity of this vast empire, which then sometimes was ruled simultaneously by several competing emperors.

The descending phase saw increasing attacks of marauding Germanic tribes, eventually leading up to the collapse of the West Roman Empire at the beginning of the fifth NIGHT. At the latter time, the Roman economy was in shambles, and what followed upon the onslaught of the Huns has been called the Dark Ages of Europe. Centralized national structures hardly existed, and very few cultural expressions can be found from this era. This fifth NIGHT set an end to the world of antiquity, and the Dark Ages lasted until the beginning of the sixth DAY, in the early ninth century. At that time, the empire of Charlemagne was transformed into the embryos of new nation-states such as France and Germany,[27] which would soon be followed by others, eventually leading to an upturn of European civilization.

Because the holograms keep shifting between DAYS and NIGHTS (fig. 5.6, upper row), the human perception of the Divine is not static or immutable. In general, in parallel with the changing political conditions, as civilizations rise and fall in phase with the DAYs and NIGHTS, religions follow a parallel path. Sometimes, as in the case of the fifth DAY discussed above, we can follow in detail the changing theology from the ascending phase of 40–237 CE with a hopeful Christianity seeing the Kingdom of God as imminent. The light that then came in was such that it created expectations of a New Kingdom,

Figure 5.7. The apostle John (left) and Marcion of Sinope (right). (*Source: J. Pierpoint Morgan Library MS 748, folio 150 verso*)

especially among the already monotheistic Jews. Without this energetic background, no enthusiasm for a Kingdom of God is likely to have been generated, and hence there would have been little interest in the message of Jesus anywhere. As he was active shortly before the fifth DAY, Jesus, however, sensed and expressed this ascending energy. Thus, several groups based on Jesus's teachings survived, and a religion was created, even though it would become clear at the midpoint of the fifth DAY that the Kingdom of God would not manifest in that era.

After this initial phase, the church created by Paul would gradually become more firmly organized, with a hierarchy of bishops led by the church fathers in Rome and Alexandria. The church fathers formulated different doctrines and began to decide what books should be canonized as parts of the Christian Bible. Marcion[28] (fig. 5.7) argued that the Old Testament god Yahweh was inconsistent with the loving God of Jesus and should therefore not be included in the Christian

Bible. The Gnostics on their part rejected Yahweh altogether[29] and looked upon him as the demiurge in contrast to the pure Divine that they worshipped. This tells us that even if a particular hologram dominates an era, there will still be variations in the experiences of the Divine and in the theologies that are developed. In the end, however, the church fathers who advocated for the incorporation of the Old Testament in the new Bible got the upper hand, and this was canonized (meaning that its content was approved by the church authorities and consecrated) in the beginning of the third century CE. This obviously created the idea that Yahweh and the God of Jesus were the same.

It is noteworthy that the two tendencies, the disintegration of the Roman Empire and the emergence of the church hierarchy, developed in parallel in the descending phase of the fifth DAY. The Christian church then evolved into a worldly power through its church fathers and bishops to become the spiritual arm of the Roman Empire. When Emperor Constantine converted to Christianity and decriminalized the religion in 313, the tendencies converged. Constantine's conversion was presumably a desperate attempt to maintain the unity of the empire, whose capital was then moved to Constantinople, as the city of Rome was already in decline. At the First Council of Nicaea in 325 CE, a unified creed was agreed upon,[30] and the Christian church became a monolith in which Paul's theology dominated.

Books that did not fit into this theology were relegated to the flames. Emperor Constantine is known to have said about Arius, a leader of a theology that diverged from his own: "If any book written by Arius be found, it is to be consigned to the fire, so that not only his corrupt teachings may vanish, but no memory of him at all may remain."[31] We can be certain that this decree was not unique. During the reign of Emperor Theodosius, the Library of Alexandria was burned down in 391 CE, presumably with a similar motive.[32] Thus, we can understand that some of the books reflecting the views of the original followers of Jesus, such as the Gnostics, have disappeared, and the only reason some of them have survived to our own time is that they were hidden.

At the time that the Sixth Wave shifted into a NIGHT in 434 CE, Augustine introduced the doctrine of Original Sin (notably based on the Garden of Eden Story), as the Catholic Church became the main political power to succeed the Roman Empire. Around this point in time, the image of the suffering Christ* on the cross became predominant. Although in the beginning of the fifth DAY the power of the devil was downplayed by the church fathers, who believed in the imminent victory of God, he would become a powerful figure in the fifth NIGHT, as the Christian religion adapted to its new energy.

Yet, it should be said that during the Dark Ages that followed, the Catholic Church assured the continuation of certain aspects of Roman civilization. What then manifested, at least in Europe, was a variation of the theocratic power that had originally been envisioned by the Jewish priesthood for Israel. The pope became the center of what was a de facto theocratic superstate to which all of Christendom belonged. Hence, in medieval times, all European royal dynasties would receive their crowns from the pope and so became dependent on him for recognition. Without this recognition, a dynasty would not be seen as legitimate as the Vatican was then regarded as a higher power than the worldly. Emperors, such as Charlemagne and Otto the Great, the founder of the Holy Roman Empire, were crowned personally by the pope. The emerging power structure was very much a projection of the Hologram of Good and Evil, and the monotheism that came from the Jewish tradition fit right into this.

The winners of the political struggle in the Christian church proclaimed a theology that was, however, very different from most of the early followers of Jesus, who, in the words of Simcha Jacobovici and Barrie Wilson in *The Lost Gospel,* "advanced a theology of liberation

---

*The oldest representation of Jesus on the cross is believed to be in the Santa Sabina Basilica in Rome built in 432 CE, right as the fifth NIGHT began. (Source: "The Basilica of Saint Sabina," *Wikipedia*)

markedly different from the one we have inherited from Paul and his followers. It is a theology based on Jesus' marriage, not his death; on his moments of joy, not the passion of his suffering."[33] For generations after the victory of Paul's theology, in contrast women have been denigrated by the Catholic Church and to this day are barred from holding office in it. Because Eve was considered responsible for the Original Sin, all women were equally condemned (based on guilt by association), and the Roman Catholic Church over the centuries has held women in contempt. This seems to have been in direct contrast with the message of Jesus and really would be counter to any authentic spirituality.

The victorious theology was very much based on the idea that human beings are born as sinners, based on the Garden of Eden story, and that Jesus "died for our sins." Jesus was said to have been sacrificed by God to heal the rift that had emerged between him and humans as a result of the latter eating from the fruit of the Tree of Knowledge of Good and Evil. Needless to say, this idea did not originate with Jesus but with the later Christian church. We can see the background to this theology in a punishing god inherited from the Old Testament and ultimately from Mesopotamia. With this logic, the Catholic Church came to focus on the suffering of Christ rather than on a life-affirming theology.

TOWARD A MULTILEVEL THEOLOGY

Naturally, the theologies shifting in parallel with the DAYS and NIGHTS of the Sixth Wave raise certain questions as to what we humans may know about the Divine and the purpose of this creation. How solid can any theology be if over the ages the theologies that the humans developed have been profoundly influenced by the hologram that has ruled over them? What I have argued here is that the biblical God, and more broadly the God of the Abrahamic religions, is basically a projection of the Hologram of Good and Evil onto the Divine, which implies that it has become part of the ruling power structure. But we may then also ask if the theologies could have been any different from what they were. Was there an alternative? Regardless of what our answers may be to such questions, if we are now to continue the climb of the nine-story pyramid to fulfill the destiny of humanity, it is necessary to understand on a deeper level what happened in order to relieve ourselves of views from the past that may hamper this climb.

From the perspective of the nine levels of creation, it is not only the shifting DAYS and NIGHTS of the Sixth Wave that have created the theological uncertainty and the various schisms these shifts have given rise to. A fully encompassing theology would need to take into account what is created by all the nine waves and recognize the corresponding relationships to the Divine for what they are. Hence, when we consider that there are five different waves, each giving a fundamentally different hologram to our minds (fig. 5.8), things become more complicated, because each of these generates a particular relationship to the Source. From figure 5.8 we can also understand that *each hologram creates the framework for the types of theologies that are developed in a certain era.* The waves and their corresponding holograms have been activated sequentially, and through the interference patterns they have created with each other, the waves have contributed to the remarkable variation of religious traditions and viewpoints that have existed on our planet over the past five thousand years. But if humans have developed their views of the Divine based on different holograms, how can we possibly see only one of them as true?

Before attempting to answer this question, I would like to briefly go over the different holograms in figure 5.5 and their consequences for the human perception of the Divine. In the Fifth Wave, going back one hundred thousand years, the relationship of humans to the Divine is based on immediate resonance with unity. Presumably, there was under the influence of the Fifth Wave no experience of conflict between the world of spirit and human beings as people were in a permanent state of

9th Wave		March 9, 2011	Individual Connection to the Divine
8th Wave		Jan 5, 1999	New Age, Neo-Shamanism
7th Wave		1755 CE	Atheism
6th Wave		3115 BCE	Religions
5th Wave		100,500 BCE	Shamanistic State of Unity

Figure 5.8. The Destiny Chart of Humanity, continued: Different relationships to the Divine under the influence of different mental holograms. Note that "Shamanistic State of Unity" does not mean that what we today call shamanism was actually practiced at the time. Yet, a state of unity with the spirit world may be the closest we can come in terms of an experience of a modern person. (Diagram by the author, design courtesy of Bengt Sundin)

consciousness akin to what we today would call a shamanic state. The Fifth Wave created a unity consciousness, albeit at a very low material level of life, and we can liken the experience of the world to a Garden of Eden with no separation.

The Sixth Wave hologram, and the rational mind that it gave rise to, changed this, and humans gradually became more separate from nature, other humans, and the Divine from 3115 BCE onward. All the major religions existing today are products of the Sixth Wave and are based on its dualist hologram. Most of them incorporate traits of a judgmental God, or gods, and a conflict between this God and the human beings. Such a conflict was experienced not only in the Abrahamic religions but also, for instance, in the beliefs of the Maya and Aztecs, who sacrificed humans to appease the gods.

Also in the East the effects of the duality of the Sixth Wave holograms were evident. In the ancient yin-yang philosophy of China, the duality was not only about good and evil; it also influenced many other aspects of human life, such as gender relations. The duality of the yin-yang symbol (fig. 4.4c) can be approached in different ways. One would be to look upon yin and yang as two forces that can be harmonized; the other is to look upon them as forever separated by the duality inherent in our existence. Such different viewpoints are at the core of the two most significant religious-philosophical teachings of China: Confucianism and Taoism. While Taoism essentially advocates that we should go inside and avoid dualist thinking, Confucianism advocates that we should learn how to become "good" members of society. Regardless, both teachings saw the duality of the human mind, what we here have called the Hologram of Good and Evil, as a fact of life that humans had to learn to deal with.

The Seventh Wave, as we will see in the next chapter, essentially created atheism. This, paradoxically, is really a specific relationship to the Divine based on a perception of darkness, even if it is not always recognized as such. This hologram was activated in 1755 CE, when the industrial age opened to a new form of creativity and the focus of many shifted away from religions. No major religion has emerged since this hologram was activated. The Eighth Wave, which was activated in 1999, elicited, on the other hand, a return to a relationship with spirit, based on a duality with an opposite polarity to that which had dominated the Sixth Wave. The shift over to the light at the right brain has created a spirituality that is more holistic and feminine. Typically, the New Age and the eclectic philosophies that emerged under the influence of this wave were often expressions of spirituality without the recognition of the Divine. The Ninth Wave, with its unity consciousness, finally brings a return to a direct relationship to the Divine All That Is with no limits in perception.

When it comes to how we can create a unified theology based on all of these different holograms, I think we should first notice that these have not been randomly generated. Instead, the different holograms do form part of a unified structure, which allows them to be activated at precise points in time according to a preset logic, as we saw in chapter 3. A multilevel theology, where the consequences of holograms of different levels are explored, should then be based on the realization that these holograms are integrated into a whole. It is also important to realize that the different theologies are steps on a climb to levels of higher frequencies.

What in the past has generally been called theology has almost exclusively been limited to the Sixth Wave and focused on religions created by projections of its left-brain dualist hologram. From the perspective that is developed here, this will by necessity lead to a very limited view of the Divine, basically experiencing the Divine only through one of the hemispheres of the mind. Even today, especially in the areas of today's world where the Hologram of Good and Evil was first downloaded—the region from Egypt to present-day Pakistan—dualist theologies are very much ingrained, and as long as they are upheld, it will be difficult to have peace there. In this regard the subjugation of women may be the most important expression of this duality to overcome. If this does not happen, it may be very difficult to climb to the Eighth Wave, which has an opposite polarity and in principle favors women. The Eighth Wave is also a necessary step for climbing to the Ninth Wave, which is the one that finally leads to the manifestation of the destiny of humanity.

THE ONE THAT HAS NOTHING ABOVE IT

A multilevel theology must also be a unified theology based on the realization that there is a unified intelligence behind all the different human perspectives of the Divine. Even if it is possible to take the position that the Tree of Life and the waves that it emits are just like natural laws that for some inexplicable reason have led the world to what it is today, to me, at least, it seems more logical to conclude that there exists One Divine All That Is, and in chapter 1 I discussed how we may understand this. This Divine then exists beyond all the viewpoints humans have created through the influence of the holograms of the nine waves. That we have now started to resonate with the Ninth Wave would imply that finally we are able to develop and practice a theology of unity.

The idea that there is such a Divine with no limits and nothing above it is not new. Earlier, the Gnostics, which was a sizable group within Christianity in the second century CE and presumably had emerged from an early movement around Mary Magdalene, held the view that there was the One, which was above the Old Testament God. We know a fair amount about the views of this early group of Christians from the Nag Hammadi Library, a collection of thirteen Gnostic texts found in Egypt in 1945.[34] The Gnostics maintained that there exists the One True Divine, who in all respects was perfect, the head of all worlds in goodness. In one of these texts, The Secret Book of John,[35] a creation story is provided that is said to have come from Jesus himself. Interestingly, this is very different from the story in Genesis; in it Jesus actually claims to be the one who induced Adam and Eve to eat from the Tree of Knowledge. Moreover, in the same book, Yahweh and his father, Yaldabaoth, are not regarded as the One but as limited local gods. Yahweh's statement in the Old Testament that he is a jealous god and that there is no other god beside him is in this creation account countered by Jesus with the following words: "But by announcing this, he suggested to the angels with him that there is another god. For if there were no other god, of whom would he be jealous?"[36]

I am not saying that this early Christian text argues, like I have, that Yahweh, as well as Ashur and Marduk, are human projections of a particular hologram from the true Divine. Yet, the text does tell us that already two thousand years ago some Christians thought that the true Divine was something greater than the gods of monotheism embraced by the Abrahamic religions. According to Jesus (at least as it is written in the Secret Book of John) the one true God created a series of eons, each with a male-female reflection of this one true God. This expanded theology seems close to the holographic model that is developed here. In other words, when Jesus talks about the One, it may very well be the Creator, which manifested itself as the Tree of Life, as discussed in chapter 1, which is different from "God" in the sense of a projection of the human ego.

A more clarifying theology than what we live with now would have been based on the insight that each hologram in the Destiny Chart generates a particular projection, a male-female duality if you will, onto the Divine. All religions have in other words been created based on the waves that human beings have been in resonance with at a particular point in time. Upon this, a theology or a belief in a certain nature of God has been developed in practice and in theory. In this view, the nature of the Divine All That Is is indeed something much larger and much more encompassing than a God created exclusively based on the Sixth Wave polarity. In fact, a theology about this Divine All That Is may be beyond what may be described in any scripture, or mentally conceptualized otherwise. It may be that we can only know it through direct experience.

The One is the Source of all the different holograms and corresponding theologies, and from this we may understand that there is no reason to fanatically get stuck in any one of them and reject all the others. Because of the simplemindedness this has created, many people today do not want to use the word *God* for their experience of the Divine. The reason is probably not only that this word has been used to support a multitude of political and patriarchal agendas and still today is used to judge, condemn, and stigmatize people by means of an ancient theology. The reason may more profoundly be that the concept of "God" inherently reflects a limited view, which does not reflect who the One is. The One That Has Nothing Above It, as the Gnostics would say, is not the same concept as the "God" of the Abrahamic religions.

It is important to recognize that the holograms coloring our perception of the One Divine are parts of a unified whole and also that they all represent steps in a climb. There is a partial recognition in the Abrahamic religions that we are faced with such a climb. In the Jewish tradition, for instance, it is currently believed that, depending on humanity's actions, we will return to the Garden of Eden, also believed to be a Messianic age, sometime within the next 225 years.[37] But how could this happen and why would it be prophesied if there is not a process that could lead to such a return? A mechanism for such a return is provided here in the form of a climb to the Ninth Wave hologram (fig. 5.8). Yet, when this will happen indeed depends on the actions of humanity. For humanity to be able to return to the Garden of Eden, which is its destiny, it seems that a much more inclusive theology needs to be developed than those currently ruling the world. One of the last verses of the Book of Revelation in the Christian Bible also points in a similar direction: "Blessed are those that do His [God's] commandments, that they may have the right to the Tree of Life and may enter through the gates into the city" (Rev 22:14, translation from the King James Bible 2000). "The right to the Tree of Life" then presumably means having part in the Divine and being able to return to the state of unity.

6
The Seventh Wave

THE HUMAN PREDICAMENT

All of history, as we now are beginning to see, is a product of wave movements of very low frequencies. Given the nature of these waves, it is not surprising that people have at times experienced themselves as being controlled by some higher power or feel that they are not in control of their lives. And as we are now beginning to see, there is a lot of truth to such viewpoints. Through the centuries, people have experienced the holograms as expressions of the will of God. As a consequence, if they have seen the events created by these waves as positive, they have felt blessed by God, and if they have seen them as negative, they have felt punished.

Regardless of our own individual feelings about the course of events, they seem to be part of a process that has meaning on a higher level. What is meant to happen on a larger scale is indeed determined by the holograms that humanity is endowed with by the waves of creation. What we can now see through the quantum-holographic model is that the events in our lives are part of a much larger scheme, the Destiny Chart of Humanity. What happens in our individual lives, what roles we are playing in this climb, is then to a large extent primarily a function of which waves we are in resonance with. Maybe, if we accepted this fact rather than lived under the illusion that life is fully under our own control, we would be able to deal in a more realistic way with some of the world's large-scale problems.

The desire for power, for instance—so typical of the Sixth Wave—

may originate in an underlying frustration with this reality of not being in control of one's own life. For this to disappear, we must come to grips with how powerless humanity really is when it comes to designing its destiny. In the worldview emerging from the quantum-holographic model, it is the One that has already created the large-scale direction of the evolution in the universe. This is effected through the waves it makes available to living beings across the universe, including on our own planet. Maybe our own powerlessness has led us to create deities like the Abrahamic "God," which at least seem to have some power with which we might associate ourselves. And yet, this power has been illusory in the sense that it has been limited to merely one level of creation. The adherence to such a belief system is now becoming a major problem for humanity as it blocks the manifestation of its destiny, which is beyond exercising power over others.

The Hologram of Good and Evil has played the crucial role for giving human beings civilization and also an awareness of an individual self. However, in the previous two chapters we also saw that this hologram is the origin of slavery, warfare, and the subjugation of women in addition to having given us a view of God as someone who exercises power over others and creates fear. This may have led humanity to look in the wrong places for addressing many issues that have been plaguing it. If these issues actually find their origin in holograms emanating from the Cosmic Tree of Life, then in order to have lasting peace and justice on our planet, we will have to relate to the holograms. We need to address the root cause, which is the frequency we resonate with, rather than the effects of this, which are merely symptoms of a planet that in many ways appears to have become diseased. As long as we as a human collective, through religions or otherwise, are cultivating the power of the Hologram of Good and Evil, we will only distance ourselves from the true destiny of humanity.

I believe that the first step for us when addressing this is to recognize how the evolution of the universe is designed on a large scale. If we fail to understand how this is driven by different waves and created by the holograms these endow us with, we will not be able to discuss how to successfully deal with the problems of the world. Before going into this, I think it is necessary to look more deeply at the versatile role the creation waves, and the interference between them, has played in shaping the course of human life.

THE CONTEXT OF THE SEVENTH WAVE

The power a wave has in shaping human existence is especially evident after an entirely new hologram becomes accessible from a newly activated wave of higher frequency. This wave then starts to form interference patterns with the waves that have been activated previously, which results in a burst of novelty. This activity was very much evident around the time that the Seventh Wave was activated on July 24, 1755 CE. Even though I am here giving a precise date for when this wave started to affect life on our planet, this is not to imply that the world saw a dramatic change on this particular day. Rather, you might say that, over the following twenty years, the world that we call modern began to emerge. The Seventh Wave has a period (a full DAY-NIGHT cycle) of 39.4 years, and so shifts between DAYS and NIGHTS, and vice versa, take place every 19.7 years. Thus, this wave has a twentyfold higher frequency than the Sixth Wave.

As with all the waves, the Seventh Wave had a prewave, and these two waves created interference patterns with the underlying Sixth Wave (fig. 6.1). The seventh DAY of the Sixth Wave, which began in 1617 and ended in 2011, especially created interference with the prewave of the Seventh Wave (beginning in 1498) and the Seventh Wave proper (beginning in 1755). In terms of European history (and why Europe has a special role is explained in *The Global Mind and the Rise of Civilization*), the years 1498, 1617, and 1755 CE correspond, as exactly as can be, to the starting points of the Renaissance, the Scientific Revolution, and the Enlightenment, respectively. Needless to say, these three time points all meant paradigm shifts of paramount importance.

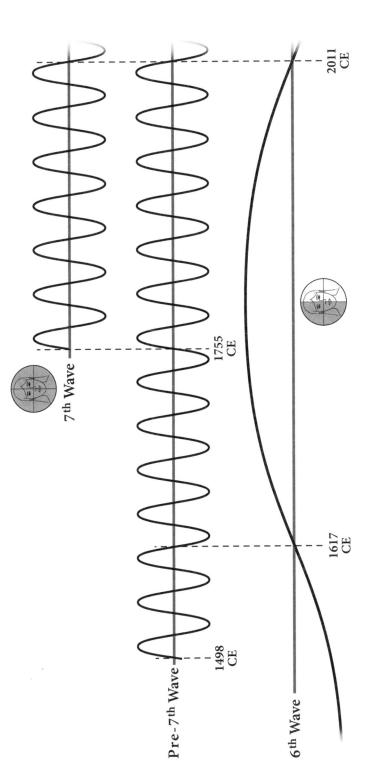

Figure 6.1. The interference of the Seventh Wave and its prewave with the seventh DAY of the Sixth Wave. (Diagram by the author, design courtesy of Bengt Sundin)

People born before the activation of the Eighth Wave in 1999 CE or its prewave in 1986 were born into this Seventh Wave. In other words, for many people who live today, the Seventh Wave was the wave with the highest frequency at the time of their birth, and for those of us to whom this applies we have a more direct and personal relationship to this wave than to the Sixth or lower waves. This in turn means, especially for those who lived in the industrialized part of the world during their formative years, that the frequency and hologram of the Seventh Wave created their basic approach to life and understanding of what life is about. Even though the Fifth and Sixth Wave holograms were a significant background against which the Seventh Wave emerged, the latter wave is likely to have provided the frame of consciousness driving people born during this period and giving them their main motivation for how to live their lives.

From the perspective of studying the manifestations of the different waves in human life, the Seventh Wave presents certain advantages. The most important one is that the dating of various events is much more accurate. This is in contrast to the Fifth Wave, where archaeological evidence is scarce throughout, and also to the first half of the Sixth Wave, where datings are notoriously uncertain. Early in the Sixth Wave, it is not always clear if events were mythological, and even if they were not, we do not always know exactly when they took place. The time frame of the Seventh Wave starting in 1755 CE is not significantly afflicted with such difficulties, and we usually know what happened, where it happened, and, very importantly from the perspective developed here, when it happened. This increased accuracy in the datings will allow us to see how multifaceted the effects of a creation wave actually are.

We have already learned about a few general facets of the Seventh Wave, for instance that it created trends toward equality (fig. 4.2, p. 96) and atheism (fig. 5.8, p. 152) and that these shifts were caused by the new hologram that became accessible with it. When a new hologram is activated, it gradually begins to dominate the already existing holograms, and based on the interference pattern of the waves, an individual hologram is created, which sets the frame for the human mind. The interference pattern will, however, be influenced by the shifting phases of DAYS and NIGHTS of the waves and is hence always in a state of flux, especially when waves of a relatively high frequency are involved. The new wave, in this case the Seventh Wave, always comes with a higher frequency and represents novelty and so attracts anyone who wants to be part of creating the new times, and many do because they sense that the novelty emanates from the Source. This is true also when the hologram is "endarkened" and actually blocks the human experience of the One. Regardless, the existence of interference patterns created by several waves means that no two people think alike or look at the world in the same way. We all have individual resonances with the various waves emanating from the Cosmic Tree of Life.

Hence, as mentioned, even as a new and higher wave has been activated, the lower waves always remain as a background against which the higher wave is expressed. What this means, for instance in the case of the religions that have been extensively discussed here, is that even if the driving mentality in the Seventh Wave has focused on the material world, such as the production and consumption of goods, the religiosity originating in the Sixth Wave has still survived. With the endarkened hologram on top, the enthusiastic following of religions has, however, in general, faded in the nineteenth and twentieth centuries, meaning fewer people may have had personal experiences of an otherworldly nature. Yet, it is not as if the new hologram has eradicated and replaced what had been created by the older one. Instead, the emerging world is created on top of the existing world, which is transformed as a result of the interference patterns that the two waves create with each other.

AN ERA OF NOVELTY: GLOBALIZATION

The types of novelties of the Seventh Wave, which, as in all waves, were very clearly noticeable in the wave's beginning, can be said generally to fall under the main headings of globalization, atheism, materialism, industrialism, and equality. One by one we will look at how in the past 260 years these effects of the new hologram have changed the world to what it is today.

I will begin with globalization. In previous books I have referred to the Seventh Wave as the Planetary Underworld, because under the influence of this wave the context of life shifted significantly from the national to the global. Up until this point, life very much belonged to the framework of the nations. The most important events marking this shift toward global awareness may already have taken place in the era of geographical discoveries that was initiated through the activation of the pre–Seventh Wave in 1498. Columbus sailed with his crew to America in 1492, and Vasco da Gama found the sea route from Europe to India in 1498. Most importantly, Ferdinand Magellan and Juan Sebastian del Cano circumnavigated Earth in 1519–1522, providing the final evidence that the world was spherical.

Around the time that the Seventh Wave proper began in 1755 CE, the mapping of almost all of the world's coastlines was completed by Captain Cook.[1] As a result, a trading network including the whole planet came to be established. In parallel with this geographical expansion, a mental shift took place toward globality. The identification of an individual to a nation, as well as to a religion, is primarily a product of the hologram of the Sixth Wave. One way of looking at the shift that took place at the beginning of the Seventh Wave is that people to some extent were disconnected not only from their religions but also from their nations by the new hologram. In the mid-1700s this manifested in the emergence of so-called cosmopolitans, individuals who sometimes were more wedded to their ideals than to a particular nation. An example is the French general Lafayette, who was led by his ideals to fight for the American Revolution. Others were prominent figures of the Enlightenment, such as Voltaire and Rousseau, who often had to flee their native countries because of their radical ideas.

The idea of a common good for all of mankind that would not be limited by national constraints also emerged in this era. An example of how this manifested was the world's first collaborative scientific project, which had as its goal to determine Earth's distance to the sun at the occasion of the Venus transits in 1761 and 1769. This collaborative project included 151 observers at seventy-seven different posts (including Captain Cook in Tahiti) in many countries,[2] including England and France, who in those days otherwise were mostly competing and at war with each other. Scientifically, the project may not have been successful, but the idea for the nations of the world to sometimes collaborate was established. This was a product of the new hologram, which downplayed the supremacy of national belonging.

We can here see that the nation-state, a creation of the Sixth Wave mind, did not simply disappear as the Seventh Wave was activated. It was not as if everyone on the planet suddenly became citizens of the globe, but the boundaries among the different nations and colonies lost some of their power in certain arenas such as science, commerce, and the exchange of ideas. Gradually over time, even if the nations at least until 2011 remained as a significant factor in shaping identities, all humans in the Seventh Wave became part of a global framework where what happens in one part of the globe has significant consequences everywhere else as well.

The point to realize is that these changes did not "just happen." They happened at a time when a new hologram, which was not dualist in nature, could be downloaded (fig. 6.2b, p. 166), and this provided humans with a dark filter through which they came to experience the world. Because this filter did not create sharp boundaries in the way that the Hologram of Good and Evil had, when humans projected this hologram onto their external reality, they did not impose as distinct limits between nations as they previously had. As we will see, it is for this reason that the current world, despite its materialistic nature, is a step forward compared to the state of the world prior to the activation of this new wave.

AN ERA OF NOVELTY:
ATHEISM AND ENLIGHTENMENT

This step forward happened because the hologram of the Seventh Wave eclipsed the divine light of the Sixth Wave, and so there was less awareness of what was going on spiritually. Unlike the beginning of the Sixth Wave, which produced a number of symbols all over the world, few symbols are extant reflecting the shift in hologram to that of the Seventh Wave. There is, however, one noteworthy Mayan representation of the shift in hologram from the Books of Chilam Balam[3] that refers to one of the prewaves of the Seventh Wave and shows the lords of the thirteen katuns. In the accompanying text it tells of how these lords, which are holograms for the various katuns, are "blindfolded"—meaning that they, and the humans downloading these holograms, will be unable to see the divine light.

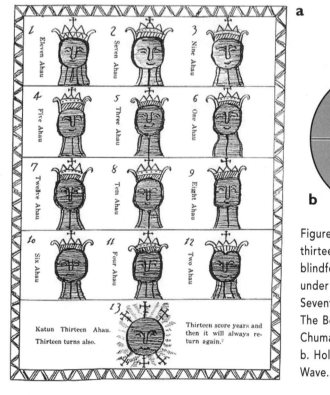

a

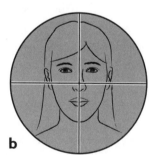

b

Figure 6.2. a. The lords of the thirteen katuns, showing the blindfolding to divine light under the holograms of the Seventh Wave katuns (*Roys, The Book of Chilam Balam at Chumayel, fig. 29*).
b. Hologram of the Seventh Wave.

In the previous chapter it was pointed out that a prewave of the Seventh Wave was already activated in 551 BCE and the ensuing disconnect from the One resulted not only in the rise of religions but also in human individuality. When the hologram in figure 6.2b became downloadable in the prewave beginning in 1498 CE, it similarly resulted in the enhanced individualism of the Renaissance. As part of this, Luther's Reformation beginning in 1517 CE developed a very different Christian creed. After the activation of the Seventh Wave proper in 1755 CE, individualism became even more emphasized. Typical of the individualism of the times is the example of the American Declaration of Independence, which markedly distanced itself from the earlier philosophy and emphasized the rights of the individual with these words: "We hold these truths to be self-evident, that all men are created equal, that they are endowed by their Creator by certain unalienable Rights, that among these are Life, Liberty and the Pursuit of Happiness." These words would have been unthinkable before 1755, and even more so in 1498, when for the most part the only rights that existed were those of the rulers.

In parallel with this trend toward individuality, for the first time in maybe fifteen hundred years people appeared, especially in the French Enlightenment milieu, who were outspoken atheists or at least non-Christians, including notably Voltaire, Diderot, and La Mettrie. La Mettrie's immensely popular book *L'Homme Machine* (Machine Man)[4] went as far as claiming that humans did not have souls but were machines. In the context of a still very dominant church, this idea was presumably liberating, and in this era for the first time we begin to see smiling faces in portraits (fig. 6.3, p. 168). Consequences of the new hologram were also the ideas that church and state should be separate and that people should have an individual freedom of religion. The separation of church and state became a reality through the American and French Revolutions, and a wave of anticlericalism swept through Europe. Later, throughout the Seventh Wave interest in religions would diminish markedly, at least in Europe, but more recently also in the United States. Under the influence of this hologram of darkness, no major religion

Figure 6.3. (left) Voltaire (*painting after Maurice Quentin de la Tour*); (right) La Mettrie.

emerged, and even among those that have professed to be religious, the focus of life has largely shifted over to the material values of life.

So was the Enlightenment really an endarkenment? This all depends on what values are important to you. Clearly, it has been an endarkenment in terms of direct spiritual experiences of the Divine (as we shall see later, this is now starting to change in the Eighth and Ninth Waves). In my personal view, many significant steps forward were, however, taken in the era shortly after 1755 CE that would qualify this as Enlightenment. Considering that the shift of the dominant hologram was part of a pattern of waves emanating from the Tree of Life and thus was part of a divine plan (see fig. 4.2 on p. 96), we may also wonder if the One truly would be adversely disposed against nonbelievers or would want to punish them, as is sometimes claimed by adherents to the Abrahamic religions. Such ideas do not seem to make sense at all, because if humans are going to climb the ladder and return to the unity with the Divine in the Ninth Wave, they also need to go through a level that disconnects them from the Divine. Paradoxically, maybe, sometimes someone who is an atheist may serve

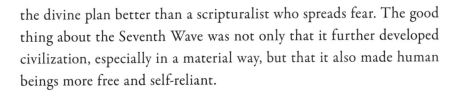

the divine plan better than a scripturalist who spreads fear. The good thing about the Seventh Wave was not only that it further developed civilization, especially in a material way, but that it also made human beings more free and self-reliant.

AN ERA OF NOVELTY: SCIENCE

What is done by what is called myself is, I feel, done by something greater than myself in me.

JAMES CLERK MAXWELL*

The scientific revolution was initiated through the works of Kepler and Galilei around the beginning of the seventh DAY of the Sixth Wave in 1617 (fig. 6.1), together with a burst of new mathematical theories (see fig. 3.10 on p. 81). At this point in time, before the activation of the dark filter of the Seventh Wave, no scientist looked upon his work as something in conflict with religion, and these pioneers were mostly interested in how God had created the universe. What was novel was that they used observations and experiments as well as mathematical tools to discover the underlying patterns of nature: Kepler's laws about the planetary orbits (published in 1619) are the first mathematical laws of nature. Most of us today looking at a planet in the night sky would not come up with the idea that its movement could be captured by a mathematical formula, and yet this is what he found. This may make us realize how remarkable this paradigm shift actually was. The idea of using mathematics to describe movements in nature was later generalized by Newton in his *Principia* in 1684, in which the law of gravitation was presented. If this connection between physical phenomena and mathematics had not been made, the modern world of science, technology, and industry would not have come about.

*Comment made by Maxwell to the Reverend Professor F. J. E. Hort in 1879 when terminally ill.

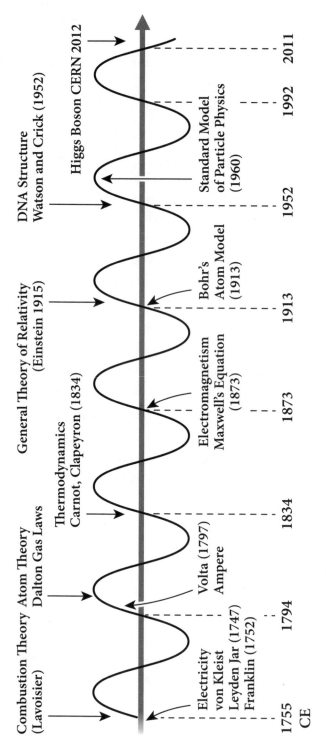

Figure 6.4. Major discoveries, especially theoretical ones, in science created by the Seventh Wave. In the lower row are noted especially the breakthroughs pertaining to electromagnetism.

(Diagram by the author, design courtesy of Bengt Sundin)

What came with the beginning of the Seventh Wave in 1755 CE with its endarkened hologram was a new relationship to the world, and for this the atheism mentioned in the previous section also played a significant role. Those who saw the light coming in through the Sixth Wave hologram might still regard Earth and nature as something holy not to be touched. Only as the endarkened hologram of the Seventh Wave entered and transformed human perception of the world would nature be looked upon as something that would be acceptable to transform with scientific and industrial methods.

The latter point is especially clearly illustrated in figure 6.4 (lower row) with the evolution of the study of electromagnetism. Electricity had hardly received any attention at all by researchers until the downloading of the Seventh Wave hologram. It was only in the years shortly before this that methods to generate electricity were developed in the form of Leyden jars, and in 1752, Benjamin Franklin provided proof that lightning was an electric phenomenon.[5] So before the Seventh Wave began, humans were not able to experiment with or even clearly distinguish electricity as a natural phenomenon. Maybe it was because lightning and other sporadic expressions of electrical or magnetic phenomena were considered as more otherworldly (such as, for instance, the Nordic god Thor or other lightning gods creating it). Regardless, only as the filter of the Seventh Wave was downloaded would researchers start to look upon it as a phenomenon that humans could experiment with, harness, and understand. Almost invariably the breakthroughs in the field of electromagnetism have taken place in the time periods that are DAYS in this wave and sometimes, such as in the case of Maxwell's equations, exactly at the beginning of these.

Sometimes a theory will not have a breakthrough until its validity and usefulness in science are demonstrated in practice. The important experiments setting the stage for quantum physics were made by Planck and Einstein in 1900 and 1905, respectively, and Einstein's special theory of relativity was published in the latter year as well. However, it was only with Bohr's atom model in 1913 and the actual verification of the general theory of relativity in 1919 that these theories gained widespread acceptance. In the fifth DAY, which followed upon Bohr's proposition, quantum physics was born out of a cascade of discoveries leading up to the Schrödinger equation in 1929. The reader may here note an interesting parallel to what we found when we studied monotheism in the previous chapter, namely that after a stepwise preparation of a phenomenon in the preceding DAYS, the real breakthrough takes place in the fifth DAY.

It should be obvious from figure 6.4 that paradigm shifts in science do not occur at random points in time. Instead, they are fundamentally conditioned by the shifts in the human mind that take place at the beginning of DAYS in the Seventh Wave. Naturally, it can be argued that the figure could include a number of other scientific discoveries and theoretical breakthroughs and that maybe some findings would have been made also in the periods that are NIGHTS. Overall, I am, however, convinced that these would be considered as less important than what has happened in the DAYS. Most, if not all, historians of science would agree that Maxwell's theory of electromagnetism as well as the theories of general relativity and quantum physics have been the most impactful within the time frame that is studied here.

Because the new endarkened hologram of the Seventh Wave indeed originated from the Source, we shall not be surprised that certain groups of people, especially in the milieus of scientists and skeptics, sometimes look upon science with the same zealousness as the adherents of theist religions. Sometimes this takes the form of denying the existence of anything that cannot be directly observed or measured. Certainly science has been the driving mode of thinking throughout the Seventh Wave, and yet many scientists who have made significant discoveries have reported that they have been guided to their findings by a power greater than themselves, as alluded to in the quote on page 169 from James Clerk Maxwell.

AN ERA OF NOVELTY:
MATERIALISM AND INDUSTRIALISM

The most dramatic change in human life that the Seventh Wave brought may, however, have been the introduction of technology on a massive scale—the Industrial Revolution. As mentioned above, this revolution would, in the era beginning in 1755 CE, to a large extent happen through a constant interaction with science. Sometimes some breakthrough in science, such as the understanding of electricity, led to a host of inventions and an enormous change in the everyday life of people. But very often practical problems, such as how to communicate over long distances or provide transportation, has prompted science to go in new directions and find new solutions. Ultimately, a new relationship of humans to nature, which in this wave was looked upon as a resource rather than a mysterious and spiritual phenomenon, was activated by the new hologram.

One significant step that was taken at the beginning of the Seventh Wave was the introduction of fossil fuels, which had never been used before. The actual beginning of the Industrial Age is usually set to the invention of the steam engine in 1769, which meant that an energy source was at hand that allowed machines to be run on a massive scale in factories. Because the locations of factories were no longer constrained by access to water streams, whole industrial towns were now built. The Industrial Age could also be said to have begun in England and Scotland in the first DAY of the Seventh Wave when the spinning Jenny, the automatic spinning machine, was invented in 1764. Later, it and other machines employed in the textile industry began to be run by steam engines in large factories.

A critical factor for industrialization was that persons, raw materials, and goods could be transported to and from mines and factories. In figure 6.5 (p. 174), we can see that, immediately after James Watts's steam engine was invented, the Frenchman Cugnot invented a steam car, which, however, was not very useful for mass transportation. Yet,

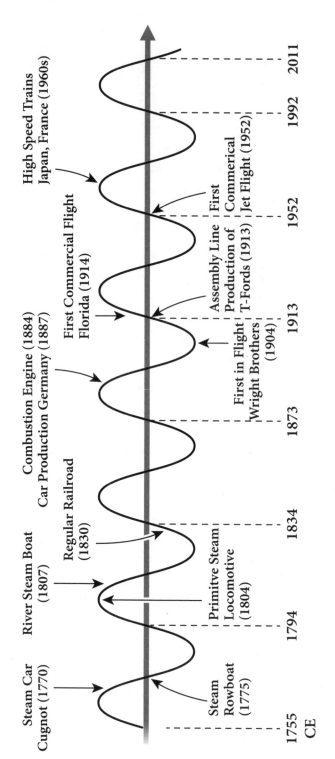

Figure 6.5. The evolution of transportation in the Seventh Wave. (*Diagram by the author, design courtesy of Bengt Sundin*)

step-by-step in the following DAYS the steam engine is made use of for transports on both land and sea. At the midpoint of the fourth DAY, the car was invented by Daimler and Benz in Germany, which, for the first time, allowed for an effective private means of transportation based on fossil fuels. In 1913, as the fifth DAY began, assembly-line production of cars is introduced at Henry Ford's factories in Dearborn, Michigan. A notable exception to the rule that all major inventions are made in periods that are DAYS was the invention of flight by the Wright brothers in 1904, which is close to the midpoint of a NIGHT. (I would call this an exception that proves the rule.)

In parallel with this development of the means of transportation is the use of different energy sources. In the United States, coal has been the primary source for generating electricity, followed by natural gas, with nuclear power and hydropower as other sources—all innovations based on the new hologram. There is no question that it is in the DAYS that significant inventions are made. For example, in the fourth DAY, the electric motor/generator (1873), the lightbulb (1875), and the phonograph (1876) were all invented as electric networks for public use became available. In the fifth DAY a range of household machines such as vacuum cleaners, refrigerators, and kitchen appliances were invented, and the stage was set for the mass consumption of these in the sixth DAY.

A field of technology whose evolution fits almost perfectly the movement of the Seventh Wave is telecommunications (fig. 6.6, p. 176); almost invariably breakthroughs to new techniques have taken place at the beginning of its DAYS. Step-by-step, more advanced and versatile techniques, going from the idea of creating a telegraph to the introduction of websites on the Internet (at CERN in August of 1991),[6] are prompted by new DAYS in the wave. Presumably this has occurred because telecommunications are very much related to the power of electricity—a technology that is directly a function of the Seventh Wave.

We should also consider the phenomenon of simultaneous and

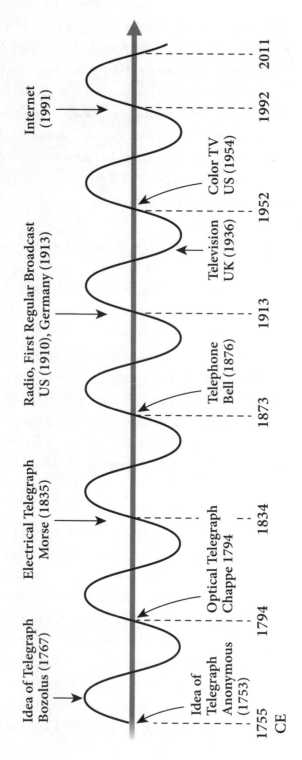

Figure 6.6. The evolution of telecommunications in the Seventh Wave. (*Diagram by the author, design courtesy of Bengt Sundin*)

independent discoveries in this context: for instance, Alexander Graham Bell submitted his patent application for the telephone only hours before his main competitor, Elisha Gray.[7] Such synchronicities can hardly be dismissed as random accidents. Rather, it is the unfolding of the wave that determines the "right time" for a new invention to be made. However, as different individuals are in resonance with the same wave, they may come up with the same invention at the same "right time." This synchronizing power of the waves is a very important factor of which to be aware. It does not necessarily mean that exactly the same thing is invented at exactly the same time. It may also mean that a whole range of phenomena that can be attributed to the same hologram emerge within a limited time frame. Take for instance how the beginning of radio broadcasts (1910–1913), jazz music (1914), the first abstract painting (Kandinsky, 1913), and the assembly-line production of cars (1913) together ushered in the era of modernity as the fifth DAY of the Seventh Wave began. These various emerging phenomena were then all related through their common origin in a specific hologram. In the fractal-holographic universe, everything develops according to a schedule determined by the waves.

AN ERA OF NOVELTY: EQUALITY

As was hinted at already in figure 4.2 (p. 96), the Seventh Wave hologram, because it lacks the basic polarity between yin and yang, will also bring equality to humanity, at least in certain respects. This was also a message of Jean-Jacques Rousseau's *Discourse sur l'Inegalité* (Treatment on the Inequality) published in 1755. If it is true that slavery, warfare, and subjugation of women in the Sixth Wave are products of its duality, then we would expect those phenomena to at least become less prominent in the Seventh Wave. The same would be true for the monarchic systems of governance, and we have already seen that the ecclesiastical control of people at large began to diminish.

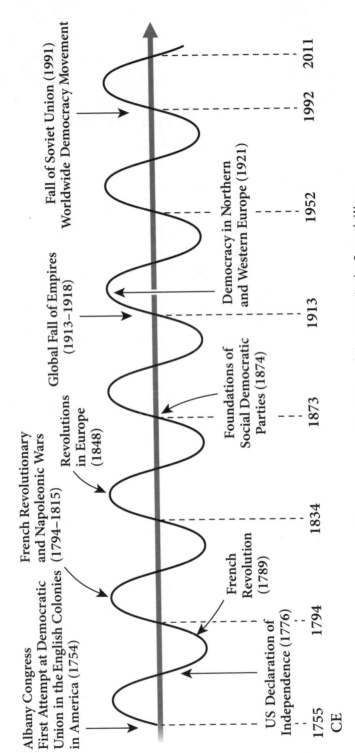

Figure 6.7. The emergence and evolution of democracy in the Seventh Wave. (*Diagram by the author, design courtesy of Bengt Sundin*)

Such deepgoing processes naturally cannot manifest overnight and will not necessarily develop with the same speed everywhere. Yet, up until 2011 there has been an overall trend toward democracy across the world, as we can see in figure 6.7.

Hence, one of the most obvious shifts that took place was in the way that nations were governed. Ever since the beginning of the Sixth Wave in 3115 BCE, nations were formed around monarchs who were more or less absolute rulers. Initially, such as in pharaonic Egypt, rulers were regarded as gods themselves, then later representatives of the gods, and eventually ruling by the grace of God. Until the beginning of the Seventh Wave in 1755, Switzerland, England, and the Netherlands were the only European countries that had some experience of republican rule, and only England and Sweden had different political parties in their parliaments.[8] However, only small proportions of the populations were eligible to vote, and, under the influence of the dualist Sixth Wave, monarchy seemed to be the only natural form of rule.

With the beginning of the Seventh Wave and its new hologram, this system of governance was challenged, initially in the American Revolution, where the colonists repudiated the rule of the British king and instituted a republican and democratic system. Even if slaves and women were excluded from equal rights in the United States at its outset, this new system of governance nonetheless meant a significant break with the past. Soon afterward, the French Revolution in 1789 led to the downfall of the monarchy in Europe's largest nation, and, over time, all the world's monarchies have been replaced by republics (today only a few, mostly politically powerless, monarchs remain).

It would take a book of its own to discuss how the Seventh Wave brought republics and democracy to large parts of the world. As in the case of the other processes that we have studied in this chapter, it was the fifth DAY that brought the largest change in this direction. At the beginning of this shift, the Chinese, Ottoman, Russian, German, and Austrian Empires, which had all been very autocratic, collapsed. In some of the new countries, democracies would emerge as well as more broadly in Northern and Western Europe, which in the 1920s also included the rights of women to vote. The process of democratization later culminated with the sweeping turn to such systems of rule around the beginning of the seventh DAY. The Soviet Union then collapsed, and simultaneously large parts of Eastern Europe, Latin America, and South Africa all gained new freedoms together with a shift in governance.

The idea of a filter to spiritual light may at first sound like a negative factor for human life. Yet, as it turns out, at least in my personal view, things are much more complex. With the introduction of this filter in 1755 came not only democratic ideals but also ideals that are generally referred to as humanistic. Groups that previously had been oppressed and treated with very little respect, such as prisoners, slaves, the mentally ill, women, and children, were now beginning to be treated humanely. Until the 1750s hardly any voices were raised against the slave trade,[9] but in 1807 Britain banned it and went on to ban slavery all over the British Empire in 1833. Eventually, the United States followed suit in 1865. Sometimes, it would take a war to go through progressive change, as in the case of the American Civil War, which led to the liberation of slaves. Similarly, the change to democracy in Europe largely depended on World War I to bring about the collapse of the autocratic empires.

All of these changes may in fact be looked upon as going in the direction of more egalitarian relationships in society, and the dark filter of the Seventh Wave does not necessarily mean evil. In fact, much of life was humanized, and most likely the reason was that the dualism of the previous filter was transcended. (Filters do not really disappear. As a new filter is introduced, it merges with the already existing one and morphs it into a new synthesis.) Under the dualist filter of the Sixth Wave, people tended to think that there is a good force and an evil force in the universe, and so they would by necessity seek to find some people who would appear as good—through the light aspect of the filter—and others that would be seen as evil or bad. If someone, like a heretic or slave, was seen through the dark side of the filter, he or she would come to be interpreted as an expression of the evil force of the universe. Naturally, if someone is seen as inherently evil, there will be no reason or possibility to be compassionate or humane in your relations with this person. This is why there was so much abject cruelty in the Sixth Wave and also why, as its filter was gradually replaced by the Seventh Wave filter, people tended to see the world differently and be open to equality.

It is not my intention here to present it as if all the problems were solved by the Seventh Wave, but only to point out that its new hologram created processes that in my view went in the right direction. Yet, even those processes have for the most part not been completed. It is also notable that the equality generated was more of an existential equality so that people, regardless of race, gender, or religion, would come to have equal rights. At least this came to be the professed ideal, which by itself was a step forward. This change toward existential equality has not, however, necessarily spilled over into the economic realm. We will return to this when addressing the Eighth Wave but should now take a look at the economic consequences of the Seventh Wave.

THE GLOBAL ECONOMIC CYCLES OF THE SEVENTH WAVE

To begin with, the globalization created by the Seventh Wave led to a significantly expanded world market of trade of all kinds of goods and services. At the beginning of this wave, we can hardly talk about a global economy in the sense that it exists today, in which each country is dependent on every other country for its economic well-being. The global nature of the technological innovations in the Seventh Wave, however, also created a global economy. Moreover, if the evolution of technology in the Seventh Wave follows the upturns and downturns of its DAYS and NIGHTS, this would likely mean that the world economy

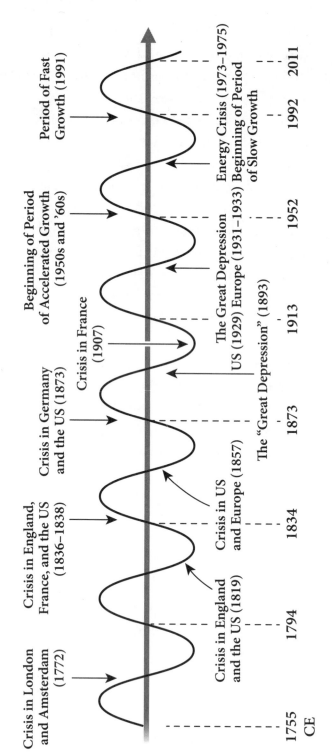

Figure 6.8. The world's economy with some significant crises in the Seventh Wave. (Diagram by the author, design courtesy of Bengt Sundin)

is very much influenced by this wave. Hence, if a DAY is a time period of technological innovation and cross-fertilization, then whenever a new DAY begins, you would expect an upturn in the economy as new products become available to people at large. As a consequence, GDPs and trade volumes would also be expected to rise. Conversely, if the time periods that are NIGHTS are characterized by a decreased rate of innovation, we would expect such time periods to be marked by economic depressions or recessions.

Economic crises may, of course, have many different causes, and, especially in the first half of the wave, the world's economy was so limited that only individual cities were affected. A crisis would then not necessarily spread across the world. In the second half of the wave, the world's economy behaves very much as would be expected based on the innovativeness in the DAYS. Hence, the fifth DAY brings the Roaring Twenties, the sixth DAY the long sustained period of growth of the 1950s and 1960s, and the seventh DAY a period of very rapid growth, notably based on the telecom industry in the 1990s. In contrast, the beginning of the fourth NIGHT saw the Panic of 1893, a serious economic depression. This was nothing, however, compared to the Great Depression, which started with the stock exchange crash in New York in 1929 and whose worst year in the world's economy was 1933, the beginning of the fifth NIGHT. The beginning of the sixth NIGHT did not produce mass unemployment on a similar scale; nonetheless, the energy crisis, which began in 1973, became a starting point for a long period of slower growth, especially compared to the sixth DAY. To conclude, in the latter part of the wave, a DAY clearly means an upturn and a NIGHT very clearly a downturn in the world's economy.

THE SPEEDUP OF TIME AND THE CRAVING FOR NOVELTY

We have now gone through a number of phenomena caused by how human beings perceive the world and studied how these may be related

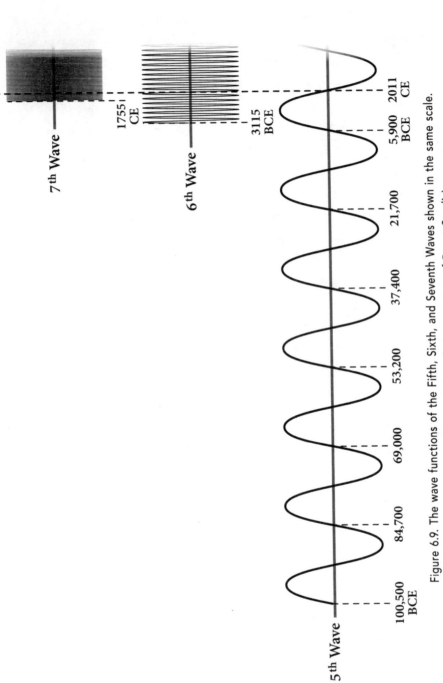

7th Wave

1755 CE

6th Wave

3115 BCE

5th Wave

100,500 BCE   84,700   69,000   53,200   37,400   21,700   5,900 BCE   2011 CE

Figure 6.9. The wave functions of the Fifth, Sixth, and Seventh Waves shown in the same scale. (Diagram by the author, design courtesy of Bengt Sundin)

to the Seventh Wave of creation. We can then see that certain phenomena have an almost perfect fit with their wave movements, in addition to the fact that it is possible to logically connect these phenomena to the proposed shift in hologram from the Sixth Wave to the Seventh Wave. These different evolutionary movements from the mid-1700s have so far been attributed to the change in hologram. There are, however, also certain aspects of the Seventh Wave best explained by the *twentyfold increase in frequency* compared to the Sixth Wave. I will end this chapter with a discussion of these, as the speedup of time may be relevant to our understanding of the shifts to waves with even higher frequencies, such as the Eighth and Ninth Waves.

The human experience of time and the rate of change in our lives very directly depend on the frequencies of the waves we are in resonance with. The Fifth, Sixth, and Seventh Waves are shown in the same scale in figure 6.9, which allows us to understand the frequency differences and how these have influenced the human experience of time and life in different eras.

As far as we can tell, the Ice Age people, living under the influence of the Fifth Wave where DAYS and NIGHTS shifted only every eight thousand years, did not experience an ongoing change in their lives or of their fellow tribe members. The way they clothed or adorned themselves did not change markedly over thousands of years, when you could wear a cave bear fur your whole life without it going out of fashion. Even though there might be daily dramas of survival, the nature of these dramas would not change much over time.

With the Sixth Wave came a marked frequency increase as the DAYS and NIGHTS would now shift every 394.4 years. Life would start to undergo change at a higher pace, and in retrospect we can observe that civilizations and religions would rise and fall with a certain regularity. Those who were living in the Sixth Wave were noticeably changing their habits over time, and it is, for instance, known that clothing fashions in medieval Europe would change approximately every ten years or so. With the Seventh Wave, the frequency speeded up further, and as mass consumption developed in the 1950s and 1960s in certain parts of the world (with the economic upturn of the sixth DAY), the phenomenon of "keeping up with the Joneses" became widespread, and fashion collections were presented twice a year. Fashions were thus changed roughly twenty times more often than in the Sixth Wave, which is consistent with the fact that the frequency of the Seventh Wave was twenty times higher.

As the Eighth and Ninth Waves were activated later in 1999 and 2011, respectively, with wave periods much shorter than a human lifetime—720 and 36 days—the fashion industry was no longer able to increase their number of collections proportionately. Instead, what emerged with the Eighth Wave was the phenomenon of burnout, where the rate of change from many different sources and the inability to keep up with this has sometimes led to physical and psychological symptoms.[10] Because of this frequency increase, there was up until 2011 a common experience among people that time was speeding up.

The frequency of a wave also influences the worldview of people. For instance, the frequency of the Sixth Wave was too low for people to become aware that they were part of evolutionary processes. During that time people did not think the world had evolved to what it was through a long-term evolution and believed, instead, in the Christian world at least, that God had created the world some six thousand years ago. With the Seventh Wave, a marked speedup of change, however, took place. Already at its beginning in 1755, Immanuel Kant in *Universal Natural History and Theory of Heaven* expressed the idea that the world might be hundreds of millions of years old,[11] quite in contrast to the biblical account. By the midpoint of the Seventh Wave, two important evolutionary theories were proposed, one about biology by Charles Darwin and another regarding socioeconomics by Karl Marx (who, even if they communicated, never met). As befits the Seventh Wave, both theories were based on a materialist worldview where the agents causing the evolutionary change were believed to be of a material nature. Even as we may now realize that both theories were wrong when it comes to identifying the factors that caused evolutionary change, they indeed were both right in that they looked upon evolution as a fact. Karl Marx's theories came to have an enormous influence on twentieth-century politics. The point here is that a worldview embracing evolution could emerge only with the increased frequency of the Seventh Wave, which made people directly experience that they were part of an evolutionary process. After all, the 39.4-year wave period of the Seventh Wave was, for the first time, within the range of a human lifetime.

The changing forms of popular dance music provide more direct evidence of how the frequency increase in the Seventh Wave on its different DAYS, as shown in figure 6.10 on page 188, has affected people. We can see that in the first half of the wave, the waltz with its relatively slow three-step rhythm was by far the most popular form of dance. With the beginning of the fifth DAY, the African American milieu of the United States created jazz music, which is based on syncopes. This amounted to a speedup in the rhythm of dance music, and in the Roaring Twenties, the Charleston sped up the rhythms even more. In 1952, right at the beginning of the sixth DAY, the term *rock 'n' roll* was coined, and the DAY continued with music of a high rhythm into the era of pop and rock in the 1960s. A final change in the rhythm of dance music came in 1991, as techno music was introduced in the beginning of the seventh DAY. The basic increases in the rhythm of popular dance music almost perfectly fit the beginning of DAYS in the Seventh Wave. What this tells us is that the waves of creation not only influence our minds and what they may be creating but also our bodies. The frequency increase of the Seventh Wave, which, even if it has been experienced only on a subconscious level, manifests in dance forms with increasingly faster rhythms. Again, things are not always what they seem, and remarkably, these trends all emerge from underlying waves of creation.

The Seventh Wave may be the best testing ground for correlating historic events with the shifts in the waves, because this wave does not

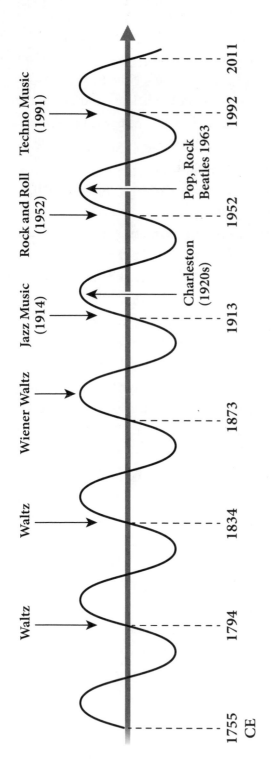

Figure 6.10. The evolution of popular forms of dance music in the Seventh Wave. (Diagram by the author, design courtesy of Bengt Sundin)

go back so far in time that datings become unreliable. In addition, its frequency is not so high that it becomes difficult to connect events with the shift in the waves, as is the case with the Eighth and Ninth Waves. Thus, overall it can be said that, at least in the second half of the Seventh Wave, novelties are almost invariably correlated with the beginning of DAYS.

7

Approaching
Our Present Time

THE EIGHTH WAVE AND THE
DIGITAL REVOLUTION

Something that is worthy of note is that different waves have initiated significant revolutions in human history. The Sixth Wave initiated the civilizational or, if you like, the pyramidal revolution, the Seventh Wave the Industrial Revolution, and the Eighth Wave, which we will look into next, the digital revolution. With the latter wave, and its corresponding revolution, we are now approaching our own time and are climbing one more step on the Destiny Chart of Humanity (fig. 4.2, p. 96). Much of what has been written so far is to prepare the reader for a new perspective on our own time. What is argued here is that underlying what we call reality are interference patterns of waves that we essentially are unconscious of and that yet play decisive roles for all evolution. Hence, if we are to understand where humanity is at the present moment and where the Destiny Chart of Humanity is leading us, it is necessary to be able to see how this underlying field has played out in the past.

The Eighth Wave was activated in 1999 (fig. 7.1), and its prewave was activated in 1986. Anyone reading this book has directly experienced the effects of this wave, and those born after 1999 were actually delivered into it. Yet, even if it coincides with our own time, in certain ways the Eighth Wave is more difficult to track than lower waves. Its frequency is so high (a DAY or NIGHT is only 360 common days and

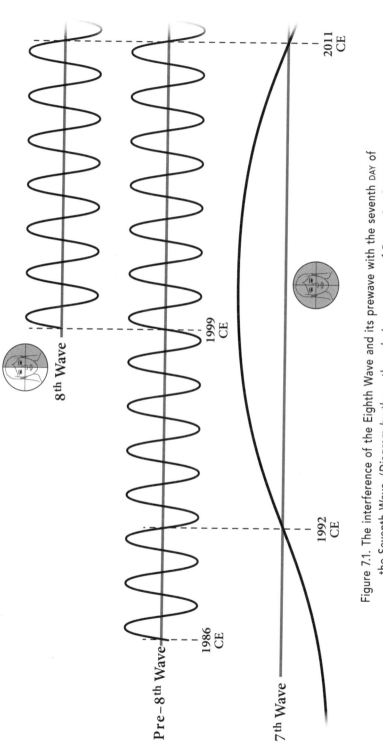

Figure 7.1. The interference of the Eighth Wave and its prewave with the seventh DAY of the Seventh Wave. (*Diagram by the author, design courtesy of Bengt Sundin*)

a full wave period 720 days) that it is difficult to follow the changes it gives rise to DAY by DAY or NIGHT by NIGHT, as can be done for lower frequency waves. This higher frequency gives the Eighth Wave a period that is considerably shorter than a human lifetime, which is why so many people in the twenty-first century have experienced a speedup of time. In reality there is, of course, no speedup of time, but there is a frequency increase of consecutive waves of creation, which, however, humans experience as a time speedup. Only the timekeeping system of the nine waves can explain why this experience of a speedup of time has become so prevalent.

The Eighth Wave brought a new dualist hologram (fig. 7.1) with a polarity opposite to that of the Sixth Wave. In the Eighth Wave it is not the left brain but the right brain that gains the light, and this has many consequences for the era that the wave informs. This new duality has, among other things, given rise to information technology and especially the Internet, which has flourished everywhere in the twenty-first century. The Internet has expanded to such an extent that it now seems as if our lives are taking place inside our computers: if you do not exist in the cyberworld, you really do not exist. Other areas that have been markedly affected by the new hologram are the relationships between the genders and among the hemispheres of the planet and the emergence of an eclectic spirituality.

We shall start by exploring the digital revolution and how this is connected to the new hologram of the Eighth Wave. In one sense, the Internet is the completing phenomenon in the long series of advances in telecommunications that was brought by the Seventh Wave (fig. 6.6, p. 176). None of the preceding phenomena of the DAYS had, however, been markedly affected by information technology or by the digital revolution. It is only as the Eighth Wave and its prewave created an interference pattern with the Seventh Wave that the Internet emerged. The most relevant starting point for the Internet is probably the first posting of a website by CERN in Geneva in August 1991.[1] This was conceived as a new means of exchange of information among scientific institutions, but soon people and businesses more broadly became interested.

However, the Internet became truly interactive only after the inception of the Eighth Wave in 1999. Entrepreneurs then began to see a commercial potential. Some people came to see the digital revolution as a parallel to the Industrial Revolution and rightly so, as there is a deeper meaning to this analogy in the parallels of two waves of creation. After some time, the interactive nature of the Internet in the Eighth Wave became evident in the form of blogging and forums for discussion. Most importantly, social media,[2] especially Facebook, which as of November 2015 has more than fifteen hundred million active users, came into existence. In 1999, the application of smart technologies for houses and cars was also beginning to be contemplated, and this is more recently developing into the Internet of Things. Hence, the digital revolution is by no means limited to the Internet; a whole range of techniques for robotization and automation have emerged as a result of it. Many experience the world of information technology as magic, as if it did not come from ourselves but was generated on some higher level of creation.

How then are these massive changes in our lifestyle, affecting billions of people, related to the new hologram of the Eighth Wave? To answer this we must first understand the origin of digitalization. We should then first notice that the hologram that came with the Eighth Wave is dualist in nature. In this duality we have a parallel to the Sixth Wave, which, as we saw in figures 3.8 (p. 78) and 3.10 (p. 81), gave rise to the first numerals and mathematics. This is not an accident. Because counting begins with duality, people could not count, at least not to any length, before they had downloaded a dualist mind. It was only when human beings some five thousand years ago projected the Sixth Wave hologram onto the world that they became able to count. If we consider a dualist hologram with a yin-yang polarity, we may note it is binary in nature: the light side is associated with one and the dark with zero much like in the binary system used in computer calculations. In reality, the world first became digitalized some five thousand years ago through the Sixth Wave hologram. Again, the principle of as inside, so outside seems to apply to everything humans manifest in the external world. Similarly, when the dualist hologram of the Eighth Wave was activated in 1999, all phenomena that humans could study began to be digitalized. Maybe without us knowing, counting and mathematics have come to play an unprecedented role for human society because of the new dualist hologram of the Eighth Wave. This finds its origin in a basically simple polarity brought to humans from the Cosmic Tree of Life as the Eighth Wave reached Earth in 1999.

The reason that people did not develop smart phones and the like five thousand years ago is that all processes involving the human mind have to develop stepwise. Only much later, with the Seventh Wave, did people become capable of using electricity, which obviously is a prerequisite for the digital revolution in our own time. But because the hologram of the Seventh Wave was not dualist, the digital revolution in the modern sense would not manifest until after the Eighth Wave hologram became accessible. It is fascinating to realize how humanity develops stepwise in accordance with the climb of the nine-story pyramid and often with a logic that seems preconceived. Each step prepares for the next, and no level can be skipped. As I detailed in the previous chapter, things—whether forms of governance, technological developments, or dance styles—evolve on a schedule and emerge at the "right time." In this case, the Seventh Wave led up to the Internet in its seventh DAY, preparing the world for the next step with the Eighth Wave. The pre-wave had also prepared us for this step as it made personal computers available before the Internet came into existence.

THE EIGHTH WAVE HOLOGRAM AND ITS EFFECTS ON THE BRAIN

The fact that the duality of the Eighth Wave hologram favors the right brain has had some special consequences when it comes to the digital revolution. For one thing, the right brain, which is more intuitive and holistic and favors connectivity, now gains the light. Such properties have had a lot to do not only with the intuitive use of technical products of the digital revolution but also with the emergence of social networks on the Internet as the new hologram was activated. You do not need a sharp logical intellect to use a smart phone; you can operate it quite intuitively, as befits a product of the Eighth Wave.

Another consequence of this shift to the right brain is the transition from using text to using images. Earlier it was mentioned that in the Sixth Wave, which favored the left brain, writing was invented, and so scriptural texts were considered as holy and important. A large number of people are now communicating by making videos rather than by writing. With the interactive Internet and the widespread use of cameras in smart phones, products of the Eighth Wave, we are seeing a shift to information being widely provided in the form of images. We are to a large extent communicating through exchanges of images or films, whether on the Internet or through smart phones. Video clips are replacing texts, a consequence of the shift over to the right brain through the new hologram. What is more, these technologies are now used all over the world. A quarter of the total number of Internet users, for instance, live in China,[3] about twice the number of those in the United States.

There is a further consequence of this shift to the right brain in terms of how writing is being done. Up until recently writing, at least for right-handed people, was conducted with the right hand, which was a product of the Sixth Wave hologram connected to the left brain. This accounts for some of the power that the written word has had, especially in religious scriptures. Written texts have simply been perceived as having more power than spoken words. At the current time, handwriting has, however, all but disappeared, and people have replaced it with keyboards on which they write by means of both hands while watching a screen (which is a sort of image). This means that now, after the downloading of the Eighth Wave hologram, both brain halves are active in the process. This new balance between brain halves is ultimately a reflection of the balance that has been created by the holograms of the Sixth and Eighth Waves. Hence, a brain half shift has taken place as a result of the new hologram, from which, in turn, a new inner balance is created. What goes on in the external world, such as in this case the way we write, thus reflects the balance of holograms brought to us by creation waves emanating from the Cosmic Axis.

Such considerations help us understand that following the downloading of the Eighth Wave hologram, the digital revolution is a product of the dualist human mind created by these shifts. This statement, however, goes against what most neurologists would say, namely that the human mind, in contrast to computers, is of an analogous nature. This view is based on the misunderstanding that the mind has its origin in the human brain. As we have seen here, it instead has its origin in holograms emanating from the Cosmic Tree of Life, which create a digital mind. In fact, if the human mind did not have a digital character, the digital revolution would never have taken place. It is true that computers are carrying out the digital processes, but it is always the human mind that figures out how information of the most varied kinds is to be digitalized; it is only a digital human mind that can perform such tasks.

MOORE'S LAW AND INCREASING ECONOMIC INEQUALITY

The digital revolution has had many consequences, not only of a technological nature but also social and economic. An aspect of this is the great threat that the rising economic inequality poses, especially in the United States, but to some extent almost everywhere in the industrialized world. In the United States, 95 percent of the total income gain in the period between 2009 and 2012 was taken by the wealthiest 1 percent of the population.[4] Despite a significant rise in productivity in the corresponding time period, most people have not had any rise in real wages since the early 1970s. This inequality, as we shall see, is very much related to the digital revolution. Before going into how this is happening (except for the obvious political reasons), we should note that this inequality is an expression of the dualist hologram of the Eighth Wave (fig. 4.2, p. 96).

Although the Internet in principle has served to democratize the information flow by making it possible for anyone to present his or her ideas, digitalization is also behind processes that on a very large scale threaten the survival of a high number of jobs, something that in turn may generate more inequality. How does digitalization threaten jobs and create inequality? Martin Ford's excellent book *Rise of the Robots* explains how inequality finds its origin in the digital revolution. In his book, Ford makes several important points based on his deep knowledge of economics as well as of robotics and computer science. Ford writes that because of Moore's law[5] (which states that computing power roughly doubles every eighteen to twenty-four months), robots will take over more and more jobs or at least gain the potential of doing so. As a result, human labor will become increasingly dispensable and decrease in value, so that in turn wealth will be increasingly concentrated in the hands of those who have the capital to invest in robots.

As robots learn to perform increasingly more sophisticated tasks, they will replace not only repetitive jobs but also jobs that require advanced degrees or specialized skills or training. As an example, Ford mentions radiologists who, needing as much as thirteen years of training to learn to interpret medical images, now find themselves being replaced by computers that can make interpretations both faster and more reliably. A large part of the workforce, including qualified college-educated persons, is at risk of being replaced by robots. There are few business areas, including trading on Wall Street, that have not been affected by this development. Because an increasing number of tasks can now be performed at less expense and better by robots, the next economic downturn may lead to a mass unemployment from which there may never be any jobs to return to.

This potential scenario is counter to the conventional wisdom of academic economists who have based their theories on the kind of growth and recession cycles that were typical of the Seventh Wave (fig. 6.8, p. 182). The common wisdom has been that if machines replace humans then this will free up the affected laborers to take other and sometimes more advanced and stimulating, jobs. Luddites, the group in the early days of industrialization in England (Seventh Wave) who saw the automated machines in the textile industry as their enemies, are held up as an example of wrong thinking. What these economists fail to see, however, is that the Seventh Wave is no longer dominating the economy. The Eighth Wave with a dualist hologram has taken over as the driving factor, and the digital revolution is not creating jobs on a large scale.

Ford argues that there are several factors in the digital revolution that now make the situation different from any earlier point. I believe he is right. The whole argument about technology always developing to create new jobs may very well have been valid during the Seventh Wave, but there are strong reasons to believe that the Eighth Wave is now canceling these job-creating processes as robots become increasingly more effective and computing power continues to rise. I also think it is important to be aware that the Eighth Wave has not created any new inventions of substance, such as the car, the refrigerator, or the telephone, which, in their original forms, are all products of the Seventh Wave. Instead, information technology is being applied to existing inventions, which then in different ways are robotized and automated. When substantial inventions were made in the Seventh Wave, jobs were created, whereas the digital innovations introduced in the Eighth Wave are, by their very nature, causing jobs to disappear, replacing workers with robots.

If indeed a new economic crisis hits and the owners of large corporations decide to replace humans with robots on a massive scale, this would likely lead to an even more extreme inequality in wealth and income favoring the richest 1 percent. If such a crisis hits the world, or at least the technologically advanced part of it, governments would face a political dilemma: On the one hand, robots would make it possible to liberate people from the imperative of working, but this could only happen as a result of a massive redistribution of income. On the other hand, if robots are allowed to replace the human workforce on a large scale, there will be no one to pay for the products that the robots are making. Most likely an intense power struggle will then surge around these issues, which we can now only see on the horizon. While such a crisis may be somewhat ahead of us, it is important to be aware of its potential risks.

We can now begin to understand the origin of the rising inequality in the Eighth Wave, which ultimately goes back to its dualist hologram. This wave presumably also provides an explanation for the origin of Moore's law. It is usually claimed that this law, which describes how computer power increases over time, is not a law of nature in the usual sense. This would, however, make it difficult to understand why it seems to be so exact. What I suggest is that it is actually the Eighth Wave, with a wave period of twenty-four months (within the range of prediction of Moore's law), that is creating a staircase of S curves describing the increase in computer power. Every time there is a DAY in the Eighth Wave, or one in its prewaves, there has been an approximate doubling in computer power. If this is true, Moore's law may not be a law of nature in the common sense but rather a law of nature that goes back to the frequency of a wave emanating from the Cosmic Tree of Life.

THE COMMON EVOLUTIONARY PATTERN OF THE CREATION WAVES

Creation waves, including the Eighth Wave, all develop according to an inherent rhythm and pattern. In previous books, I have extensively described a common pattern of these waves up until October 28, 2011. In this pattern, the first seven DAYS and six NIGHTS in each wave had features or qualities in common with the corresponding time periods of other waves. Also, in this present book, I have several times pointed out, for instance, the special role that the fifth DAY has had in the evolutionary process of a wave. This special role was exemplified by the birth of Christianity in the Sixth Wave (chapter 5) and the birth of modernity in the Seventh Wave (chapter 6). The two phenomena may seem quite different, but the fifth DAY is the period of breakthrough regardless of what wave we are studying (see fig. 7.2). The fifth DAY is, however, invariably followed by the fifth NIGHT, which, as in the case of the Sixth Wave and the Dark Ages of Europe, turns in to a period of destruction. Some significant phenomena of the fifth DAY and the fifth NIGHT in the eight lowest waves are shown in figure 7.2 (where the high frequency of the Ninth Wave is the reason that it is not included). It should be noted that in this table, the time periods that a DAY or NIGHT will last varies considerably between the various waves (see fig. 2.8 on p. 50). In the First Wave, the time period in which the solar system emerged was 1.26 billion years, while the iPhone in the Eighth Wave emerged in a DAY that was only 360 common days long.

There is in other words a common, inherent breakthrough-destruction pattern in all of the waves; for all the waves, the fifth DAY and NIGHT play comparable roles in the evolutionary processes. In the column to the extreme left in figure 7.2, we can see that in Mesoamerica, where these waves formed the basis of a prophetic art, these two time periods were ruled by Quetzalcoatl and Tezcatlipoca, the lord of light and the lord of darkness, respectively. These gods described the qualities of their respective time periods. When considering the birth of Christianity, we can see that this religion emerged with the fifth DAY.

Wave	1st	2nd	3rd	4th	5th	6th	7th	8th
DAY 5 Quetzalcoatl	Solar system	Reptiles, Transition to land		Fire	Cave paintings	Christianity	Democracy	iPhone
NIGHT 5 Tezcatlipoca	Meteor bombardment	Perm-Triassic extinction		Wurm ice age	Neanderthal disappear	Dark Ages	Nazism, WW II	Recession of 2008

Figure 7.2. Significant events in the fifth DAY and NIGHT in the eight lower waves of creation. (*Diagram by the author from* The Global Mind and the Rise of Civilization)

In the Dark Ages that followed in the fifth NIGHT, the message of Jesus was, however, placed in an entirely different context than originally. Similarly, the breakthrough to modernity took place at the beginning of the fifth DAY, but in the fifth NIGHT, beginning in 1933, it was replaced by the modern dark ages of some twenty years, beginning with the rise to power of Hitler in Germany in 1933.

I am showing this diagram here (a much more extensive scheme is shown in *The Global Mind and the Rise of Civilization*) for two reasons. One is to further back up the claim that there is a common origin to all the nine waves of creation. Even if the phenomena they develop are different, their evolution still follows a common pattern, at least up until October 28, 2011. Another reason is that the frequency of the Eighth Wave is so high that it is very hard to stepwise detail the significant events in its evolution. Despite this uncertainty, I think that the most characteristic phenomena of the fifth DAY and fifth NIGHT of the Eighth Wave are quite clear: The invention of the iPhone in 2007 stands out as a peak in the digitalization brought by the Eighth Wave, and you may look upon it as the main breakthrough of this wave. While it may seem strange to compare the launching of the iPhone to the emergence of Christianity or democracy, there is a parallel. Each wave has its special purpose, and so it is only logical that the Eighth Wave, which brought about the digital revolution, manifested the iPhone in its fifth DAY. In contrast, the fifth NIGHT of the Eighth Wave took the world to the brink of economic disaster with the downfall of several Wall Street banks and the Great Recession. It may be argued that this recession did not have the same persistent quality of destruction as the dark ages of the Sixth or Seventh Wave. On the other hand, in the high-frequency development of the Eighth Wave, this would not have been expected anyway.

To further substantiate that the Great Recession was caused by the Fifth NIGHT of the Eighth Wave, I should point out that in *The Mayan Calendar and the Transformation of Consciousness,* published by Bear and Company in 2004, I very exactly predicted when this economic recession would come to occur based on a scheme like the one in figure 7.2.

I several times stated that an economic downturn would be expected to hit when the fifth NIGHT of this wave began on November 19, 2007. As it turns out, the Great Recession is now considered by economists to have begun in December 2007, two weeks after the time I had predicted. Not only was I one of the few people who predicted that a recession was to come, I was, to my knowledge, the only one who predicted exactly when it would begin and well in advance of when it actually happened. This prediction, which may be one of the most precisely dated economic predictions ever, can be verified by anyone who picks up that book. Notably, it was not based on a detailed analysis of the economic situation, which I would not have been competent to make, but merely on the supposition that the same pattern of evolution in all of the waves would be reproduced also in the Eighth Wave.

THE RISE OF THE RIGHT/EAST HEMISPHERE

There are a few other aspects of the Eighth Wave hologram that deserve to be discussed in this chapter. One is the rise in importance in the world's economy of certain Asian powers, especially China. Another is the rise of women in many parts of the world, and the third is a rise of a new spirituality. The diversity of changes in the Eighth Wave again illustrates how varied the effects of a specific wave actually are, similar to the Seventh Wave, whose hologram was the origin of atheism, economic cycles, electricity, transportation, democracy, environmental destruction, and many other things, some of which may even seem contradictory. Although many of us may be tempted to conclude that a particular wave is "good" or "bad," things are not that simple. All we can say is that the Destiny Chart seems to be a climb toward something "good."

One seemingly contradictory effect of the Eighth Wave is the connection between the rise of the Asian powers and the rise of women. However, as we could see in figure 4.3 on page 99, and as is extensively discussed and explained in *The Global Mind and the Rise of*

Civilization, there is a direct relationship between the effects of the holograms on the level of the planet and of the human being. Hence, the origin of the left-right polarity that is ruling the human mind is always the west-east polarity that is ruling on the level of the planet. If the Eastern Hemisphere of the planet is favored, then the right brain of the human being is also favored by the hologram of the Eighth Wave. A favoring of the Eastern Hemisphere has also been visible, at least on the economic level, as especially China has become a very significant motor for the world's manufacturing business ever since the Eighth Wave began in 1999. The enormous amount of foreign currencies that China has accumulated also gives it the power to potentially influence the economies of other nations. Russia, another Eastern power, has also regained some of the power that it lost when the Soviet Union collapsed.

Because the rise of the Asian powers is caused by the hologram of the Eighth Wave favoring the right brain, you would expect this to also cause women to gain power. The rise of women was not discussed in the context of the Seventh Wave, even though it was something that very much started with this wave and was an expression of its equality. Women, for instance, played significant roles at the outset of the American (Edenton Tea Party, 1774) and the French Revolutions. (What brought down the French monarchy was the Women's March on Versailles in 1789.) What is noticeable about these events is that they really were the first times in history that women played a political role in their capacity as women.

During the course of the Seventh Wave, women continued, step-by-step, to achieve equal rights, at least formally, in the Western world (New Zealand was the first country, in 1893, to give women the vote). Gradually, women entered the many social arenas that previously had been the exclusive domains of men. Overall, the hologram of the Seventh Wave has been the driving factor behind this development as by its very nature it is nondualist and came to suppress the hologram of male dominance of the Sixth Wave. As the Eighth Wave, with a duality favoring women, was activated, women's rights have progressed rapidly in certain parts of the world. In Sweden, women currently earn nearly two-thirds of all academic diplomas, and the country has a government that is explicitly feminist.[6] In the larger cities of the United States, women under thirty have been earning higher incomes than men of the same age since 2000, and there is little to indicate that these trends will be reversed.[7] These are changes that are bound to have long-term effects in many other parts of the world as well.

At the same time, violence against women inherited from the Sixth Wave remains a significant cause of imbalance, in addition to being unethical. Notably in the Middle East, where the Abrahamic religions are the most ingrained, the situation may even have become worse for women, as sometimes a new hologram causes reactions. Overall, however, the Eighth Wave hologram is favorable to women. Although the balancing may still take some time, there is nothing to stop it from having long-term effects in the same direction. I think it is correct to see various advances regarding the rights of lesbians and gays as functions of the same hologram shift. After all, the oppression of these groups finds its origin in the patriarchal family created by the Sixth Wave, and as the hologram of the Eighth Wave has an opposite duality, it has tended to cancel it out.

We may also notice that the activation of the Eighth Wave hologram has taken place within a somewhat different context than the activation of the Sixth Wave hologram. Its effects are more complex, because the Eighth Wave hologram creates its effects against the background of several lower waves, which have created complex interference patterns among them. When the Sixth Wave hologram was activated some five thousand years ago, the result was the emergence of many kinds of dominance and subjugation. At the current time, the Eighth Wave hologram partially has the effect of balancing exactly those forms of subjugation. Yet, paradoxically maybe, it will still, as we saw earlier, create a new economic inequality based on digitalization. If the effects of the Eighth Wave hologram sometimes seem contradictory, it is because they are.

THE RETURN OF SPIRITUALITY

Adding to these multifaceted effects of the Eighth Wave is the rise of spirituality. The light on the right brain in the Eighth Wave has caused a shift to holistic thinking and the honoring of the more feminine qualities of both genders. A noticeable change that has been created by the Eighth Wave, and already with its prewave, is the emergence of a new expression of spirituality based on these qualities. This spirituality has had an eclectic character and has appeared especially in Anglo-Saxon countries and in Europe. Women have played the most prominent role in this spiritual awakening, which is exactly what you would expect, as it is based on the Eighth Wave hologram. This awakening has had a markedly different character from the male-dominated religiosity of the Sixth Wave, which is primarily based on scriptures. Hence, this new movement is not so much based on words as on direct spiritual experiences.

This new spirituality very much has the character of a return, *a return of the Divine beyond the limitations of earlier concepts of God.* The corkscrewing of the shifting filters (fig. 4.3, p. 99) generated a level (the Seventh Wave) that blocked experience of a divine source. The continuity of a wide range of spiritual traditions was thus broken because of this. The result of this mentality has been that, as the light again became accessible through the Eighth Wave and its prewave, seekers have sought and found spiritual inspiration in Eastern and indigenous traditions, which are linked to the right brain. Because of the disconnect from the Divine in the Seventh Wave, spirituality and paranormal phenomena were dismissed as irrational not only by skeptics but also by large parts of the public. On the other hand, you may argue that the very same disconnect from the Source has generated a self-awareness that may be supportive of the spirituality of the future, as humanity is re-creating the unity with the Divine. Self-awareness is necessary for anyone who wants to climb to the top of the nine-story pyramid and create a direct contact with the Divine without "middlemen," such as priests or gurus, who sometimes block such a contact.

206 of APPROACHING OUR PRESENT TIME

An important starting point of the new spirituality was the Harmonic Convergence,* which happened in 1987 at the beginning of the prewave of the Eighth Wave. The scripturalist religions have since been rejected, because they are based on the left-brain hologram of the Sixth Wave and are inconsistent with the right-brain hologram of the Eighth Wave. It also rejected the limiting and dualist idea that there is only one right path and instead embraced an eclectic approach, seeking inspiration from a wide range of different spiritual traditions. Consequently, it has included shamanism and indigenous traditions that are close to the spirituality of the Fifth Wave.

As I mentioned, atheism started to spread widely under the influence of the Seventh Wave and its endarkened hologram, with the result that, at least in Europe, churches have gradually emptied. But because the United States, as a Western country, has been favored (fig. 4.2, p. 96) with light by the Hologram of Good and Evil, Christian churches there have remained strongly immersed in the Sixth Wave. We could, incidentally, also call this hologram the Hologram of Western Dominance. Only more recently, presumably because of the activation of the Eighth Wave hologram, has atheism started to grow in the United States. Interestingly, as the light has begun to fall on the Eastern Hemisphere in the Eighth Wave, adherence to Christian churches has dramatically risen in China,[8] to the point that the number of churchgoers there now exceeds that of all of Europe. Hence, the rise of Christianity in China and the rise of feminine spirituality in the West find their origins in the same hologram.

The many different kinds of effects that are generated by the Eighth Wave may seem bewildering—ranging from digitalization to the rise of feminine spirituality. The effects are versatile because they are products not only of this hologram's duality but also of its particular form of duality, along with the entering of the light aspect, the frequency

---

*Harmonic Convergence was an event based on the Mayan calendar, which became a rallying point for the new spiritual energies that came with the prewave of the Eighth Wave.

increase, and the interference with other waves. From this, many different developments can arise, which are not easily predictable. This versatility is also why our individual lives on the level of the Eighth Wave are quite varied. Despite this complexity and versatility, the ultimate origin of all of these changes is fairly simple: a shift in hologram.

UP TO THE NINTH WAVE

In addition to the changes brought by the Eighth Wave, the Ninth Wave has now also been activated (fig. 7.3, p. 208). This happened on March 9, 2011, prepared for by its prewave, which began on July 18, 2010 (which was the date of the Conscious Convergence). The hologram of this wave is without filters, which brings a perspective of oneness to the world. The Ninth Wave notably completes the Destiny Chart of Humanity and plays a central role in the last chapter of this book. The ninth is the highest of the waves, and the one with the highest frequency, as its wave period is only thirty-six days, with DAYS and NIGHTS that each are eighteen common days long.

Because the Ninth Wave has such a high frequency, I had in *The Mayan Calendar and the Transformation of Consciousness* predicted that it would generate a rate of change higher than anyone had previously experienced. It, in fact, also started with a bang, as two days after it was activated, on March 11, 2011, a 9.0 earthquake with an ensuing tsunami hit Fukushima, precipitating a nuclear crisis that took Japan to the brink of disaster. Was this related to the activation of the Ninth Wave? To answer this would mean entering a whole new inquiry. Yet, what we saw in figure 4.3 (p. 99) is that when the activation of a new hologram happens on a global scale, this can have geophysical consequences. A significant precedent to the Japanese earthquake was the earthquake that devastated Lisbon in 1755, which had the same magnitude and occurred a few months after the beginning of the Seventh Wave.

But the earthquake in Fukushima was not the only thing that happened as the Ninth Wave was activated. A massive protest movement

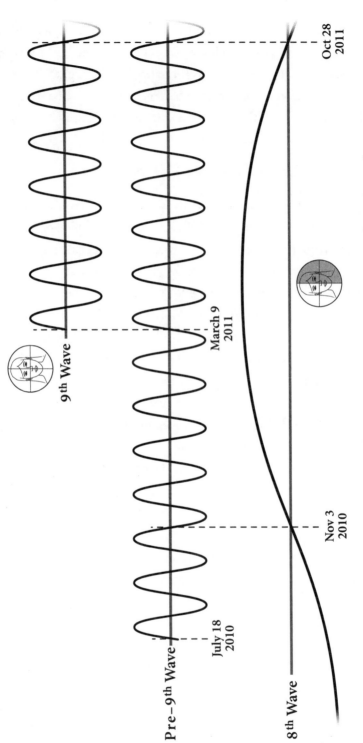

Figure 7.3. The interference of the Ninth Wave and its prewave with the seventh DAY of the Eighth Wave. (*Diagram by the author, design courtesy of Bengt Sundin*)

began against the ruling order all over the world (see fig. 7.4 on p. 210, marking the locations of the protests). The Arab Spring began, and for the rest of the year, protests erupted all over the world, including the Occupy Movement in the United States and many other countries. In Egypt and Tunisia, the revolutions prompted by the prewave were successful, and as the actual wave was activated, the wars in Syria and Libya began. Originally, these protests were secular and peaceful, and in the streets of Cairo and Damascus the main slogan was simply "one, one, one." This was in recognition of the fundamental oneness (or unity consciousness) of these movements in which religious and ethnic differences (for instance, between Copts and Muslims) were set aside. In Egypt, the women also played a significant role in the revolution that ousted Mubarak. The Ninth Wave started exactly as you would expect from a wave bringing unity consciousness into a world of duality.

The simultaneity of dramatic events as the Ninth Wave was activated was staggering. Two weeks after this time point, *Newsweek* magazine had "Apocalypse Now" as the headline on its cover.[9] The media simply found it difficult to cover so many different, consequential stories at the same time. I had written about this time in *The Mayan Calendar and the Transformation of Consciousness* (2004, p. 216) well in advance: "The enlightened consciousness developed in the Universal Underworld [that is the Ninth Wave] will be pulsed onto humankind in a wave movement of the Thirteen Heavens that covers a period of only 234 days. This reflects a frequency of change of the heavenly energies that by far surpasses anything anyone has ever experienced." It seemed as if at least *Newsweek* came to agree with this assessment.

The compounding of events as indeed took place was a result of a twentyfold increase of frequency as the Ninth Wave, the highest frequency wave, was activated. The protests against the established order, including revolutions in several countries, continued worldwide through most of 2011. They were also what you would have expected

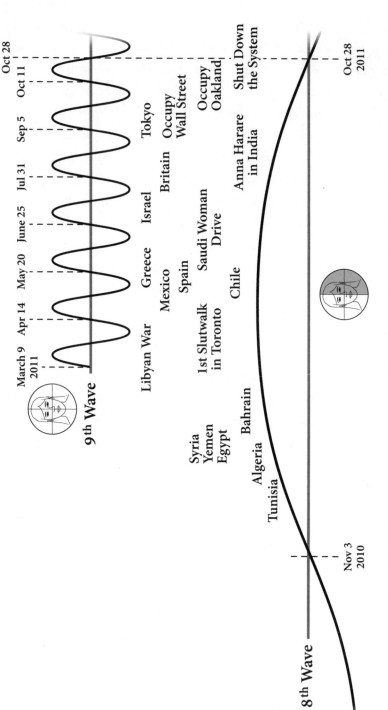

Figure 7.4. Different protest movements in 2011 and their relationship to the Ninth Wave. (*Diagram by the author, design courtesy of Bengt Sundin*)

as the veils were suddenly removed (fig. 7.4) or, in other words, as the Ninth Wave's hologram of unity was added to the dualist hologram of the Eighth Wave. The dominance of bankers and dictators, which the Eighth Wave dualist mind had still seen as natural, now with the unity mind of the Ninth Wave came to be seen for what it is— injustice and oppression.

At the end of 2011, shortly after the 234 days, *Time* magazine decided to make "The Protester" its "Person of the Year"[10] as reflective of the year's spirit. Not to name a particular individual for this was also indicative of the Ninth Wave, as many of these protests had as their aim the good of all rather than serving particular interest groups or new leaders. It seems quite clear that all of these activities surfaced because some people started to resonate with the unity consciousness of the Ninth Wave. What emerged was a novel approach to politics and economics such as that of the Occupy Movement. Rather than representing particular interest groups, this movement aimed to look for the highest good for all. This is also exactly what you would expect from a frame of mind that is not dualist and that allows you to see that everything is connected to everything else. At least temporarily, the thinking of the world order created by the dualist mind was transcended after the Ninth Wave had been activated. If it had been difficult to follow the Eighth Wave DAY by DAY because of its high frequency, this was even truer for the Ninth Wave, with its seven DAYS and six NIGHTS leading up to October 28, 2011, in only 234 common days. It is easy to now be cynical and say that nothing happened, because the enthusiasm, which reigned during those 234 days, would not last after October 28, 2011. Yet, it is a fact that a new political philosophy did emerge with the Ninth Wave, whether in Cairo or in New York. I think it is very important to realize that even if the movements created by the activation of the Ninth Wave waned, this does not invalidate their existence. From the time period of March 9 to October 28, 2011, we do have some significant information about the effects of the hologram that the Ninth Wave carries.

Figure 7.5. Protests in 2011. a. Tahrir Square, Cairo, February 8, 2011. (*Photograph by Mona*) b. Madrid, May 20, 2011. (*Photograph by Fotograccion.org*)

Figure 7.5 (cont'd). c. the Occupy Movement in New York, September 28, 2011. (*Photograph by David Shankbone*).

OCTOBER 28, 2011

October 28, 2011, was the date that this creation had been leading up to, at least in the sense that at this point in time the nine waves had all gone through seven DAYS and six NIGHTS. They would also all be synchronized, *as they would all be in their seventh DAY on that date.* This was the date when the cosmic dragon in Chinese mythology would have moved through its 9 × 13 (= 117) scales, and when the 9 × 12 (= 108) transformations of Shiva in Indian mythology had been completed. Most clearly maybe, in the Mayan understanding, it was the point in time when Bolon Yookte K'uh, the nine-level entity of creation, would "appear in his full regalia."

And yet, and this came as a surprise to me and many others, after this point of completion and synchronization, the protests started to slow down. The Arab Spring lost much of its original enthusiasm and became increasingly colored by Muslim infighting as well as signs of disintegration in some of the affected countries. The Occupy Movement faded away after pledging to "shut down the system" on October 28. The year 2012, which followed upon this, was an uneventful year with little drama. On December 21, 2012, the date claimed by archaeologists and many astrology-inspired researchers to be the end of the Mayan calendar, nothing at all happened. On my own part, even though I had predicted exactly the onset of the economic crisis in late 2007 and the frequency increase that occurred on March 9, 2011 (and hence had verified that the October 28, 2011, was the correct shift date), I had to admit that what followed the shift was not what I had expected. The change was in many ways confusing and disappointing.

So what had happened? The mistake I made, or at least my biggest shortcoming, when it comes to elucidating how this creation works, was not to have fully understood what would happen as the waves completed their seven DAYS and six NIGHTS. The mistake was not that I had fallen into the trap of the archaeologists' Mayan calendar end date of December 21, 2012, and then made up some reason why the Maya would have chosen that date. It was not that I had calibrated the calendar incorrectly or failed to recognize its nine-level nature. Yet, some of my writings predicting the end to systems based on duality had been overly optimistic, and I had been naive regarding the time frame in which deep, long-lasting human change could take place. In short, my main mistake was that I had tried to squeeze in the climb to the ninth level within the time frame leading up to October 28, 2011, and this, as it turned out, was not correct.[11]

A CHANGE IN THINKING
ABOUT THE SHIFT

Because I became aware of these limitations in my understanding of the post-shift era, it became necessary for me to reconsider the Mayan sources and what those actually had said regarding this shift in our own time. What I then found was that the views of different Mayan scholars interpreting the duration of the Long Count were contradictory. Michael Coe, professor at Yale, had claimed that the Long Count calendar of the ancient Maya (which here has gone by the name of the Sixth Wave) was limited to thirteen baktuns, and most Mayanists had come to share this view.* He believed that a new count of thirteen baktuns was to begin on December 21 (or 23), 2012, and this was the view that went out to the world (as well as his comment—based on nothing—that the Long Count would end "with a bang," which ultimately was what started the millenarianist view of the Mayan calendar). Yet, it had been known for a long time that in Palenque there existed Mayan Long Count dates 4,100 years into the future. Based on such and a survey of the ancient inscriptions, Mayanist Mark Van Stone has pointed out that there really was no Classical Mayan source saying that the Long Count would be limited to thirteen baktuns.[12] The Palenqueans instead saw it as continuing without interruption to at least twenty baktuns, and maybe more.

Hence, the year 2011 (or 2012, as the archaeologists claimed) would not be the end to the Long Count calendar, and like any wave, the Sixth Wave would just continue deep into the future after the shift point. Yet, even so it was indisputable that this shift date had

---

*In his book *The Maya,* Michael D. Coe wrote: "following the Thompson correlation, our present universe would have been created in 3113 BC, to be annihilated on December 24, 2011, when the Great Cycle of the Long Count reaches completion" (1966, p. 149). Remarkably, his book, which was widely read, initiated the apocalyptic interpretations of the Mayan calendar.

been regarded as so important to the ancient Maya that they made the inscription in Tortuguero some fourteen hundred years ago stating that Bolon Yookte K'uh, the nine-step entity, would then appear in "his full regalia," and this was not something that could readily be dismissed. This raised the question why they considered this date so important if it was not an end date. As I now see it, the answer is that the ancient Maya did not look upon this shift as important because it was an end date, but because it was a unique time when all the nine waves had been activated and were synchronized, something that had never happened before in the history of the universe. Indeed, the year 2011 was the first time when all the nine waves were accessible to resonate with, and for this reason it remained true that it was a very significant time point.

None of the waves then actually ended in 2011, and in terms of the language of the Mayan calendar, we are now in the fourteenth baktun (or seventh NIGHT), in a never-ending Long Count (Sixth Wave). The other eight waves will similarly continue without end. As a consequence, there were no discontinuities in the development of the waves, and there was no reason to believe that something very abrupt, like the end of the world or the sudden birth of a new world, would happen at the very date of the shift. The world changed on October 28, 2011, as it does with all the shifts in the Mayan calendar, and it was maybe a more significant stage-changing shift than ever before, but it was not a jump outside the established movements of the waves. Based on these insights, it has become possible to outline how the nine waves will develop in the future beyond 2011.

The time of the shift and synchronization on October 28, 2011, was thus indeed a very significant date in the history of the universe. It was not significant in the sense that I, and many others, had originally envisioned, but it did, as we will see next, set a completely new stage for our existence, and I think it is in the nature of a profound shift in consciousness that no one can completely foresee what it will result in. The human potential for creating resonance with the Ninth

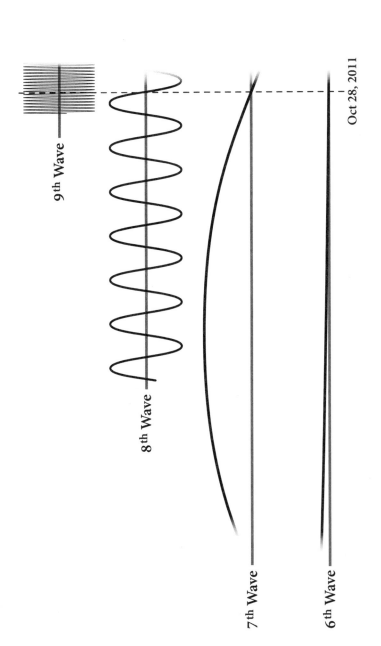

Figure 7.6. The four higher waves with shifts between peaks and valleys (DAYS and NIGHTS) leading up to the shift on October 28, 2011, and beyond. (Diagram by the author, design courtesy of Bengt Sundin)

Wave has not yet been fully realized, and the evolutionary process climbing to the top of the nine-story pyramid has not been completed by many and certainly not by humanity at large. Collectively speaking, the shift has not yet been fully assimilated and only a minority has developed resonance with the Ninth Wave. Yet, for the first time in human history, the nine waves are now all accessible; nothing is blocking the climb to the top of the pyramid, at least not on the underlying quantum level.

8

The Deactivation of the Hologram of Good and Evil

THE NEW STAGE FOR LIFE

Up until October 28, 2011, new waves and prewaves with higher frequencies and new holograms were thus sequentially activated, which allowed for the entry of more light (see fig. 7.6 on p. 217). In fact, at the very end of it, in the time period October 11–28, 2011, all the different waves were in their DAY modes. This, in reality, was a completion of an evolutionary process of 16.4 billion years, and it is no wonder that the many people who at the time participated in the global protest movement saw new possibilities. Possibly this would then also generate a new more democratic form of doing politics in which dictators, billionaires, and big corporations did not decide everything.

The experience, consciously or subconsciously, of this sequential activation of higher frequencies in more spiritually oriented people created expectations of some kind of "mystical boom" at the end of the Mayan calendar when everything, literally everything, would suddenly change from one day to another. An elevated consciousness would immediately take over and reshape the whole world for the better, or so at least many believed. This did not quite happen, and I think we can now say with some certainty that this was not how the cosmic plan was designed either. Hence, there was no discontinuity on October 29, 2011. As all waves do, *the nine waves of creation at this date just continued and turned into their valleys, or* NIGHT *phases.* In

219

other words, the laws of nature, such as these that have been created from the Cosmic Tree of Life, did not change. Yet, despite the absence of a discontinuity, the shift would set the stage for an entirely new energy field created by the nine waves. These had never previously all been activated, and especially the activation of the Ninth Wave was fundamentally new. It is this new stage on which we now live that we will look at in this chapter.

Yet, even if there was no "mystical boom," the time after the activation of the Ninth Wave on March 9, 2011, had given clear indications what direction this, the highest and final wave, promises to take humanity over time. The Ninth Wave is designed to take us away not only from the dominance of bankers and dictators but also from nationalism and religious fanaticism. If these tendencies became much less evident immediately after the shift on October 28, 2011, it was not because of the Ninth Wave but because the simultaneous shift in the lower waves came to influence the world, and this is what we will look at in the present chapter.

As a result of this, the world at the present time (2016) appears contradictory. On the one hand, when it comes to religions the Catholic Church after the shift for the first time in its history gained a pope, Pope Francis (elected in 2013),[1] who has left many of the earlier divisive and judgmental dogmas behind. Transforming the Catholic Church toward a source of unity is obviously not a change that could happen overnight but is nonetheless proceeding at a very high speed, and this speed would have been unthinkable without the Ninth Wave as a background. On the other hand, as we look to the Middle East, we see crimes committed in the name of religion on an almost unprecedented scale. The explanation for these contradictory tendencies is that all nine waves are now for the first time running in parallel, and how people experience reality and what actions they take fundamentally depend on which wave(s) they are in resonance with. Some people are in resonance with the Ninth Wave and may truly experience unity with the Divine All That Is, while others, who are primarily in resonance with the Sixth Wave, may be in a very dark place as this wave has now gone into a NIGHT. *The shift in 2011 thus did not generate a sweeping change affecting everyone in the same way.* Instead, creation evolves on several different levels in parallel—it is, if you like, multidimensional—and so how someone experiences the present reality depends on what waves he or she is in resonance with.

After the 2011 shift, the waves have created a new interference pattern unlike before the shift, when wave after wave were added on top of those that had already been activated (see figs. 6.9 on p. 184 and 7.6 on p. 217). Instead of the previous situation, which generated a feeling of escalation, the different waves after the shift just continued to oscillate in the way shown in figure 8.1 (p. 222). Hence, immediately on October 29, 2011, the waves all went into their NIGHT phases (which is actually only a logical consequence of the fact that right before the shift, on October 28, 2011, they had been in their DAY phases). Some of these waves will not return to their DAY modes for a very long time. This indeed has meant that a fundamentally new stage has been created upon which life is to be lived.

To understand what the new stage means, we should be aware that what happens in a NIGHT is very different from what happens in a DAY. Whereas a DAY is a time period of creativity and forward movement, a NIGHT is a period of rest, integration, and sometimes destruction. Given this, what is the interference pattern in figure 8.1 telling us about our future?

When answering this question, I think it is important to be aware of a significant qualification when it comes to using figure 8.1 to foretell our future. The interference pattern in it shows the *potentialities* for the current era, which is not the same thing as how things will actually be manifested. In the interference pattern in figure 8.1, a conscious human being may collapse the wave function and download the hologram from any of the waves, and depending on what hologram he or she downloads, different courses of evolution may manifest. To make

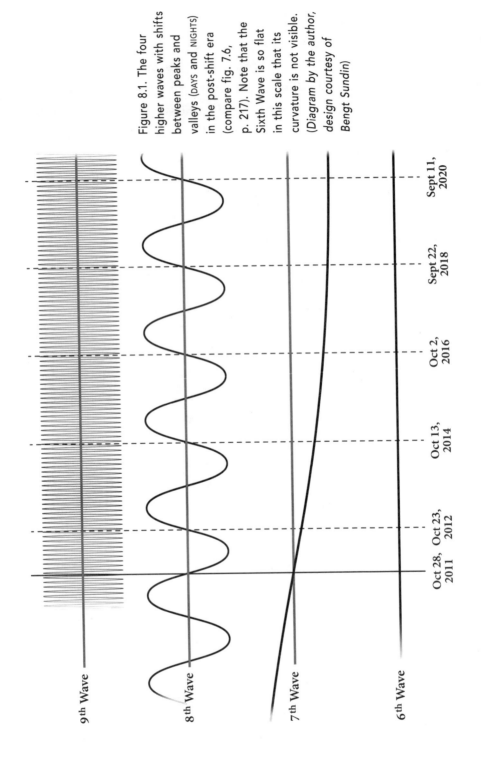

Figure 8.1. The four higher waves with shifts between peaks and valleys (DAYS and NIGHTS) in the post-shift era (compare fig. 7.6, p. 217). Note that the Sixth Wave is so flat in this scale that its curvature is not visible. (*Diagram by the author, design courtesy of Bengt Sundin*)

9th Wave

8th Wave

7th Wave

6th Wave

Oct 28, 2011 Oct 23, 2012 Oct 13, 2014 Oct 2, 2016 Sept 22, 2018 Sept 11, 2020 things even more complicated, as I will exemplify later, what is happening in the short-term is often a reaction to what the long-term tendency will generate and may even be directly opposite to this. Much of what happens at the current time may thus be reactions (manifested by people in resonance with lower waves) to the long-term changes that the Ninth Wave will bring.

MOVING INTO THE FUTURE

With this qualification in mind, we shall now take a more detailed look at the interference pattern that dominates our world and how we may interpret this new stage according to the holographic model. The first thing to note is the time points at which the various waves will return to their DAY modes. From figure 8.1 we can understand that this happens in accordance with an exact schedule, determined by the different lengths of the NIGHT periods of the different waves.

The Sixth Wave, as we can see in figure 8.1, is after the shift on October 28, 2011, on its way down into a long NIGHT and will only return to a DAY in the year 2406, while the Seventh Wave will return to a DAY in July of 2031. These points of return to DAYS of the Sixth and Seventh Waves cannot be seen in the scale used in figure 8.1 as they are too far into the future. Yet, the Eighth Wave, with its relatively short wave period of 720 days, returned to a DAY already on October 23, 2012, and has continued to oscillate between DAYS and NIGHTS ever since. The Ninth Wave, because of its high oscillation frequency, came back to its DAY mode on November 16, 2011. There thus seems to be a fundamental difference between the Sixth and Seventh Waves, which will not return as DAYS in the short term, and the Eighth and Ninth Waves, which because of their high frequencies at the time of writing (July 9, 2016), are in their ninth NIGHT and fifty-fifth DAY, respectively. In conclusion, even though in the short term the two highest waves are accessible in their DAY modes, the long-term shift into NIGHTS in the Seventh and especially the Sixth Waves means that the phenomena carried by those waves will not appear in a long time.

What will transpire as a result of this new interference pattern, with all the waves running in parallel, is a sort of competition between the different waves when it comes to which ones of them will have the greatest effects. The way I see it, the only way humanity will have a future is if people transcend the Sixth Wave and climb to a point where they can create resonance with the Ninth Wave. In this sense, a critical factor for our future is how conscious people are of which waves they are in resonance with. It is often said that the key to the future is in consciousness, but the real challenge is for us to be specific about this. Raising consciousness means becoming aware of the frequencies we should resonate with in order to download the holograms of unity.

Already from this brief analysis, it should be clear that the world is now operating under very different premises compared to before the shift. In the situation prior to the shift, higher and higher frequencies (such as in fig. 6.9 on p. 184) were automatically being activated and directly gave rise to a sense of purpose and direction. *The role of conscious choice among the holograms is now more important than ever, as there is not another wave to wait for.* Hence, we need to choose between waves that are already up and running. I have already pointed to the positive long-term potentialities of the Ninth Wave. Here I will, however, discuss the more negative short-term consequences of the shift in the Sixth Wave into a NIGHT. This is what we may refer to as the deactivation of the Hologram of Good and Evil.

The downturn of the Sixth Wave into a NIGHT may partially account for the nature of the shift on October 29, 2011, which meant that even as the Ninth Wave continued to oscillate at a high frequency after the shift, this was drowned by the massive effect of especially the Sixth but also the Seventh Waves turning into NIGHTS at the same time. Only a very small minority of the world's population had developed a resonance with the Ninth Wave at this time, and as the new stage emerged, it was not possible for this minority to counterbalance the effects of the NIGHTS in the other waves. The years 2012 and 2013, up until the midpoint of 2014, were thus generally quite uneventful in terms of world events. Only in 2015 did the high frequency of the Ninth Wave again become as strongly felt as it had been immediately after its activation in 2011, and only at the current time are significant events on the world stage again taking place at a high rate as the Ninth Wave influences them. Partly, the lull between the shift in 2011 and 2014 is explained by the very immensity of the stage change, meaning that even those that were not the slightest aware of what was happening on a deeper level had to adjust to a new and largely unanticipated underlying field of creation. We all take our actions against some sense of where things may be going, and a NIGHT will invite a quite different attitude toward life than a DAY. If all nine waves shift into NIGHTS, obviously some readjustments would have to be made by everyone. If we are totally uncertain about what the energies are, we will hesitate to take action, and this was essentially the situation in the world until 2014. Since then the interference pattern in figure 8.1 has increasingly become assimilated and come to provide a more meaningful basis for what is happening.

The pattern in figure 8.1 does allow us to partially grasp the situation in terms of what the potentialities are and what tendencies they may give rise to. It is, however, important to distinguish the long-term consequences of the higher waves, endlessly continuing to run, from the short-term effects generated by the downturns into NIGHTS of the Sixth and Seventh Waves. I believe that the sooner we realize that this evolutionary stage of humankind is profoundly different from previous ones and analyze and understand it, the better able we will be to develop a new script for how to approach the future and take action accordingly.

THE DECLINING POWER OF THE WEST

If it is the DAYS of the Sixth Wave that has led to Western dominance it is relevant to ask if the current turn of this wave into a NIGHT will set an end to this dominance. At first sight such an end to Western dominance (understood here essentially as U.S.–U.K. dominance) may seem far from at hand. The United States has a military power superior to any other nation, a larger GDP than any other nation, and, for instance, the whole range of hardware and software companies in the computer industry are American. But what I am thinking about here is the deepgoing processes driven by the creation waves and in particular the Sixth Wave, which has been the source of Western dominance.

If the Sixth Wave has now turned into a NIGHT it is relevant to ask what happened in the West the last time the Sixth Wave turned into a NIGHT, which was in 1223 CE. Of direct relevance for North America is then the almost simultaneous demise of the most significant Native American civilizations that had emerged during the previous DAY. Hence, in connection with this shift, the urban centers in Cahokia (ca. 1250 CE), Tula (1179 or 1224 CE),* Chichén Itzá (1224 or ca. 1250 CE), Chaco Canyon (ca. 1140 CE), and Mesa Verde (1285 CE) were all abandoned.[2] According to traditional native sources, the abandonment of the urban centers in Mexico was a direct result of the wave shift and happened close in time to this. How was this expressed? In the account about the demise of Chichén Itzá, the Plumed Serpent was said to have moved from this city to Mayapan, directly connecting it with the shift from DAY to NIGHT. Yet, it is an open question whether the centers farther north were immediately shaken by the shift or if, following this, there was a relatively slow decline over a few decades. These cities were at the time the largest urban centers in North America;

---

*Several sources claim that Tula was sacked in 1224 CE; see, for instance, Hardoy, *Pre-Columbian Cities*.

Cahokia in present-day Illinois, for instance, had a population of about forty thousand inhabitants before its decline set in. North America would not again have a city with such a population until Philadelphia reached that number in 1780.[3]

To exactly date the decline of all of these civilizations is quite difficult. Yet, to me at least, it seems clear that the ultimate reason that the main urban centers in North America were abandoned was the shift from a DAY to a NIGHT in the Sixth Wave (which was symbolized by the Plumed Serpent). It is noteworthy how different the explanations of the Mayan and Toltec sources (which in my view come much closer to the truth) are from those of modern archaeologists. While the former emphasize the power of Quetzalcoatl and the wave shifts this deity could bring, the latter attribute this demise to material factors. Modern archaeologists consider the Plumed Serpent a fantasy and have in my view been unaware of the true causes for the upturns and downturns of civilization. They have instead attributed the demise of these civilizational centers to warfare, famine, drought, religious change, or some other tangible factor. From a quantum-holographic perspective, we can now instead understand that the decline of all of these sites was caused by the shift to a NIGHT (and the deactivation of the dualist hologram favoring the West), and the physical factors were secondary phenomena.

As we know, the collapse of these cities was not the end of native culture, however. The Native Americans survived, and eventually new cultures arose, such as that of the Aztecs, but nonetheless a remarkable transformation seems to have taken place because of this shift into a NIGHT. Applying this outcome to our current situation, we can conclude that if we want to be part of the transition to the Eighth and Ninth Waves (which are the only waves that in the foreseeable future will provide light) and the kinds of cultures these create, we should plan accordingly. There is a real risk that politicians, who are completely unaware of the underlying reality, will precipitate a social, political, economic, and geographical collapse in the United States at a time when the Hologram of Good and Evil is no longer active. *What the current time after the shift in 2011 calls for is long-term thinking, which is not based on competition with other nations but is a transition to a civilization based on the feminine and unity consciousness of the Eighth and Ninth Waves, respectively.* We should be aware that in the Sixth Wave we are at the very beginning of a long-term shift into a NIGHT and that it is not uncommon that the immediate effects are opposite to its long-term effects.

To understand the long-term decline of Western power at the beginning of the current NIGHT, it is also meaningful to study the events that took place as a new DAY in the Sixth Wave began in 1617 CE. After all, it was this DAY that came to an end in 2011. The new DAY in 1617 marked the rise of rationality and the scientific revolution, which, in accordance with the logic I am applying here, would now at least partly be on their way out. It was also this time, at the beginning of the seventh DAY, that saw the beginning dominance of the West—a logical consequence of the activation of the global hologram favoring this (fig. 4.3, p. 99). Neither Western dominance nor the existence of the nation-state are, however, eternal phenomena and depend directly on the shifting phases of the wave. As a result of the current shift, political systems are now heading in directions other than what we have been used to during the past four hundred years.

Not everyone realizes it, but the four hundred years of dominance by the West coincide fairly precisely with a DAY in the Sixth Wave. Western dominance is thus a direct effect of the hologram dominating Earth during this time period (fig. 4.3). As an expression of this, at the beginning of the seventh DAY of the Sixth Wave in 1617, France, the Netherlands, and, most importantly in the long term, Great Britain became colonial powers. The Pilgrims arrived in Massachusetts to found its first lasting land-based colony in 1620, and during the nineteenth century Great Britain would become the center of an empire where "the sun would never set," and in which about a fifth of the world's population would live.[4] If we add the former colonies of Spain and Portugal, as well as those of France, the Netherlands, Germany, and Belgium, the proportion of people dominated by Western European nations would be even larger. After World War I, and even more so after World War II, the United States, a nation formed by former English colonies and located even farther West, would take over as the dominant world power. People living today have thus lived their whole lives within the context of a family of nations under the dominance of the West.

Before 1617 CE, it was not taken for granted that the West would lead or dominate the rest of the world. At the beginning of the preceding shift, 1223, the Mongol Empire emanating from the East had for instance instead come to dominate the world, an empire that may have been the largest the world has ever seen.[5] With the current deactivation of the hologram of the Sixth Wave, the West is thus not likely to maintain its superiority long term, although it is likely to come back in some form around the year 2406 CE. This will naturally have a profound effect on the United States, which has been the main expression of Western power in more recent times.

So we may ask, Are there are any tangible signs that the era of Western Dominance is now coming to an end? I would answer affirmatively on this. The Union of the Crowns,[6] when England, Scotland, and Ireland got the same king, was instituted in 1603 and may be regarded as the political foundation upon which the British Empire came to be based during the time period of 1617–2011. After the shift in 2011, this foundation has, however, started to weaken. There was one (failed) referendum for Scottish independence in 2014,[7] and the Brexit committing the U.K. to leave the European Union in 2016.[8] The latter seems to lay the foundation for a breakup of the Union of the Crowns in the time ahead, and at some point in time the disintegrative effects of this are likely to spread even farther West, to the United States.

In this perspective I think it is noteworthy that U.S. ground troops were removed from Iraq in December of 2011, just a month after the shift,[9] an event that may have been the most significant immediate result of the shift on October 28, 2011. While some may think of this merely as the end of yet another war that the United States has been involved in since World War II, I think it goes further than this. The departure from Iraq may be a military event on a par with decisive battles in human history such as Tours, Waterloo, or Stalingrad—in other words, a military outcome that will define the relationship of power for a long time to come. It goes without saying that the threshold for the United States for engaging in full-scale military operations overseas has now been raised considerably. This new situation is based on the new distribution of light on a global scale (fig. 4.3, p. 99) and goes much deeper than temporary political considerations. Very often, the agents of change do not even know why they are participating in bringing about a particular change. The decline of Western power reflects such a long-term tendency, which is now becoming clearly visible.

Although this shift in power may create a hope for a new balance in the world, the most immediate international reaction has been that certain Eastern powers, ISIL and Russia—each in its own way—and maybe further down the line China, are stepping in to fill the gap. The United States itself bears witness to reactions to the downward trend into a NIGHT in the form of supremacist rhetoric among presidential candidates and racist murders or mass shootings conducted by men wedded to supremacy. Most people in the United States and elsewhere are subject to energy changes they do not even know exist. The Maya and the Toltecs knew that the Plumed Serpent was about to leave for some time, but no corresponding awareness now exists. The underlying energy changes generated by the deactivation of the Sixth Wave hologram will manifest in one way or another no matter what we think about it. Personally, I am wary of this end to Western Dominance, but on the other hand I am aware that if the world is ever to come to balance and a true state of disarmament, then the dominance of the Hologram of Good and Evil must come to an end.

THE DECLINE OF THE NATION-STATE

Another consequence of the deactivation of the Sixth Wave hologram
is that the nation-state is showing signs of disintegration. Modern
people take the nation-state[10] for granted and look upon this as a self-
evident framework of governance. Yet, the nation-state, like Western
dominance, is only a product of the last DAY in the Sixth Wave and is
a result of the changes that took place in northwestern Europe when
this DAY began. Hence, up until 1617, European countries were ruled
by various dynasties headed by monarchs. Among them, the Holy
Roman Emperor, to whom the rest were supposedly subordinate, was
at the center. The monarchs looked upon the countries they ruled as
their God-given personal estates. Already with the prewave (activated
in 1498) to the Seventh Wave, this system had been shaken, especially
with Luther's reformation in 1517. Several dynasties then broke with
the Vatican, even though the emperor remained at the center defend-
ing the old order. In the seventh DAY of the Sixth Wave, or shortly
thereafter, the Dutch established a republic, which fought for independence from Spain, and England for a time came under parliamentary rule with Cromwell. Both these events showed that a country
did not have to be ruled by a royal dynasty. In Sweden, the monarchy remained, but the governing agencies, to use a modern term,
became autonomous and were not directly ruled by the king. These
changes all pointed forward toward the modern nation-state, in which
the king belongs to the nation rather than the nation belonging to
the king.

The Thirty Years' War (1618–1648), the most devastating conflict
in European history, resulted in the de facto end to the rule of the Holy
Roman Emperor above the various monarchs in the German lands. The
Westphalian Peace Treaty in 1648, which concluded this war, is usually looked upon as the birth of the modern nation-state.[11] This was the
world's first international conference, and the nations participating recognized each other in principle as equals. Each country would from now

on be sovereign to decide what Christian creed it would embrace. This immense change at the beginning of the seventh DAY of the Sixth Wave was what would give the modern nation-state its structure. The nation-state was a product of this DAY and is most likely not as strong in the NIGHT. When much later, in the second half of the twentieth century, the colonies of the European nations became independent, these new nations also adopted the nation-state model rather than the structure of rule (sometimes tribal) they may have had prior to becoming colonies.

Because of the origin of the nation-state in a DAY of the Sixth Wave we thus have reasons to believe that as we have now entered a NIGHT, its structure may weaken and even collapse. This change also holds both opportunities and risks. On the one hand, there is an opportunity for a world no longer separated into nation-states that often have been competing or even warring with each other; a world without boundaries as envisioned by astronaut Edgar Mitchell on his return to Earth from the moon. All kinds of global collaboration could be envisaged in a world without nation-states. On the other hand, the end to the nation-state can also, as we have seen in Somalia, Libya, and Syria, lead to anarchy, with countries disintegrating through warfare among different factions.

Recent European history has been profoundly influenced by the decline of the nation-state, which may be attributed to the shift from DAY to NIGHT in the Sixth Wave. In this area of the world where, as described above, the modern nation-state was born, the shift to a NIGHT has had significant consequences for its systems of governance. The majority of European countries now belong to the European Union and most of them also to the Eurozone. Already this has weakened the previous nation-states whose powers are not as obvious as they used to be. Even though each country still has its own system of taxation, member states in the EU are now so deeply integrated that it is difficult to notice, for instance, when you cross the border separating the Netherlands and Germany. This strong integration, with the nation-states yielding much of their individual powers, was intensified with the signing of the Maastricht Treaty in 1992[12] and the institution of the euro currency as the Eighth Wave began in January 1999. When we are talking about such a long-term wave as the Sixth, it is often meaningful to look at the changes it effects within a window of about twenty years around the shift, and within such a time frame a decline of the power of the nation-state in Europe is quite obvious.

This decline of the nation-state brought about by the NIGHT in the Sixth Wave seems at the current time (2016) to be creating a reaction in the form of increased nationalism in many European countries. The most immediate manifestation of this may be in the exit of the U.K. from the EU, but the push for independence in Scotland and Catalonia has the same origin. Similarly, in many other countries, such as for instance in Eastern Europe, nationalist parties have emerged that are either anti-immigration or in favor of independence of some province. In the United States, Donald Trump's idea of building a wall against Mexico reflects exactly the same sentiments. I am, however, convinced that the current rise in separatism and nationalism is a reaction caused by the decline of the nation-state, which does not represent the long-term direction of the world. As the Sixth Wave shifts into a NIGHT, the nation-state, which was created in a DAY, is increasingly getting weaker, but as a reaction to this, especially older people (as was very evident in the Brexit vote) react by becoming more nationalist in their ideology.

We can see that the shift of the Sixth Wave at the current time can have both negative and positive consequences. The potentialities that are actually manifested are not predetermined by the underlying interference pattern of waves but rather depend on the choices we as individuals and as humanity make. This in turn depends on how conscious we are of this underlying interference pattern. To take this into account implies a completely new approach to strategizing about the future compared to how this has been done in the past. With an understanding of the roles of interference patterns, we should realize that it does not really make sense to merely react to events in the world. *What needs to be done is to set long-term goals for unity based on the potentialities that we now know exist, and this includes those created by the Eighth and Ninth Waves.*

THE MOVEMENTS FROM THE EAST

Another consequence of the shift to the NIGHT is the massive immigration into Europe, which has taken place after the shift in 2011 and in particular in 2015.[13] In Europe there is a planetary midline that goes through Rome and Berlin along the twelfth longitude east and separates the Western and Eastern Hemispheres of our planet. The origin of this line, which has played such a significant role in European history, is extensively explained in *The Global Mind and the Rise of Civilization*. To substantiate this, I have in all of my previous books shown maps, such as the ones in figure 8.2, charting migratory movements to and from this midline.

These movements display a clear and precise wave movement of expansion and contraction in relation to the midline. When DAYS begin and global duality is established along the planetary midline, separation is created, thus resulting in movements away from this line. On the other hand, when NIGHTS begin and the duality along the midline collapses, movements toward the midline, and especially from the East, take place. As we can see in the maps in the column to the right, violent swarms of nomadic peoples have in the past hit Europe from the East when NIGHTS began. To complete the picture, a new map could then also be placed in the bottom of the column to the right in figure 8.2 showing the migrations in 2015 coming toward Europe from the East.

Even if the current wave of refugees does not have the same violent character as in past NIGHTS, it seems that it has the same origin, namely a change in the global field created by the Sixth Wave. The periodicity in figure 8.2 is very clear, and we may also note that the countries that have been the most favorable to receiving refugees, Germany and Sweden, are located directly at this planetary midline. Superficially,

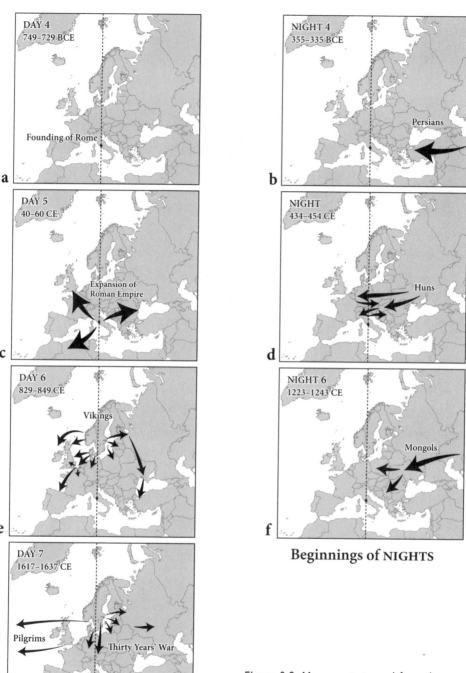

DAY 4 749–729 BCE Founding of Rome **a**	**NIGHT 4** 355–335 BCE Persians **b**
DAY 5 40–60 CE Expansion of Roman Empire **c**	**NIGHT** 434–454 CE Huns **d**
DAY 6 829–849 CE Vikings **e**	**NIGHT 6** 1223–1243 CE Mongols **f**
DAY 7 1617–1637 CE Pilgrims Thirty Years' War	**Beginnings of NIGHTS**

Beginnings of DAYS

Figure 8.2. Movements to and from the planetary midline at the beginning of DAYS and NIGHTS, respectively. (*Diagram by the author, design courtesy of Bengt Sundin*)

it may seem that the influx of migrants is caused by the situation in Syria, but because at least half of them are coming from other countries, including such faraway lands as Afghanistan and Bangladesh, I think we have every reason to interpret it as a result of the collapse of the duality of the Hologram of Western Dominance on a global scale. The fact that at least some European countries have been so open to this immigration also indicates that this immigration originates in the shift between DAY and NIGHT in the Sixth Wave. In a sense you may say that this migratory movement also serves to weaken the nation-state and Western dominance and has generated similar kinds of reactions as mentioned in the previous sections. *It is another example of how the actors in a drama are not aware of its origin in the holographic universe.*

The recent return of Russia as a global power player under Putin most likely finds its origin in exactly the same energetic movement from the East that is now manifesting. In an article from 2006, I predicted that Russia would return to the status of superpower based on such considerations,[14] and it seems at the current time that this has, at least partially, taken place. Russia, or as we mostly say, Putin, is attacking Ukraine, threatening countries in Eastern Europe, including the Baltic states, as well as carrying out bombing raids in Syria, and is generally aggressive toward the West. The latter example includes provocative flights toward countries like Sweden, Denmark, the United Kingdom, and even the United States. This is a recent phenomenon, which began at the start of 2014, but has only taken on such dimensions after the shift in 2011.

It seems to me, however, that this power play is another unconscious reflection of the westward energy resulting from the current collapse of the planetary midline. Putin does not have a clue about how the holographic universe works, but he senses the wind at his back and decides to play along to see if he can gain something. This assertiveness is not necessarily part of a conscious strategy on his part, with actual national goals for Russia. As I see it, the Soviet Union is not coming back, and the relatively weak economy of Russia may mean that this power play may seriously backfire. In the end, China represents the true power of the East. Regardless, Russia taking back Crimea and executing bombing campaigns in Syria would have been unthinkable before the shift in 2011, resulting in the U.S. retreat from Iraq and is a direct consequence of the new post-shift interference pattern.

ISIL AND THE VIOLENCE IN THE MIDDLE EAST

A large part of the world's Muslims live in the Middle East, a transcontinental region that stretches from Turkey to Pakistan, which is another expression of the Eastern Hemisphere. At the current time, much attention has been focused on the ISIL group, a terrorist group that with immense brutality has proclaimed an Islamic caliphate beginning in Iraq and Syria. It is linked to Islamic terror groups not only in the Middle East but also in Africa, Europe, and elsewhere.

I think it should be recognized that the main reason for the emergence of this organization was the U.S.–U.K. invasion of Iraq in 2003, spearheaded by George Bush and Tony Blair. In addition to this, there are, however, a number of factors pertaining to the Sixth Wave that have contributed to the emergence of ISIL. We should, for instance, notice that this organization has emerged in the very part of the world where civilization first emerged, in the region where current-day Syria, Turkey, and Iraq meet. This is where Göbekli Tepe, the world's oldest temple,[15] was built and where agriculture first began to be practiced some ten thousand years ago. *As a consequence, people have been influenced by the Hologram of Good and Evil for the longest time in this area and so have been very ingrained by duality.*

The rise of ISIL raises two questions about our own time. Why has it been relatively successful? And where does its brutality come from? The attacks on innocents in Paris in November 2015 are just one example of the brutality and lack of respect for life that this group has demonstrated time and again. When it comes to why terrorist Islamic groups have become very visible and to some extent successful exactly at this time there are a few factors emanating from the wave shift that I think deserve to be considered: (1) The global tendency toward disintegration of the nation-state, (2) the decline of the West, and (3) the beginning of a NIGHT and the significance of this for Islam. To begin with the two first factors, the Middle East has been profoundly affected by the disintegration of the nation-state and the fading role of the West as leader of the global family of nations. This part of the world was the last to become part of the global family of nations. Until 1922, this region was not organized as nation-states but by a Muslim sultanate, the Ottoman Empire. As a result of the demise of this empire in World War I, England and France then divided the region, drawing lines in the sand to create nations. As long as the Sixth Wave was in its DAY mode, which favors the structure of the nation-state, this worked fairly well, and a number of newly formed countries became part of the global family of nations under Western leadership.

Yet, as the Sixth Wave approached its NIGHT, these nation-states became increasingly vulnerable and this is part of the origin of the current chaos in the region. Because we are now (after 2011) in a NIGHT of the Sixth Wave, nation-states in the Muslim world created by European powers have a tendency toward disintegration, especially if they have been subject to military attack. In the cases of Syria, Libya, and Yemen the Ninth Wave inspired popular uprisings, but when the Sixth Wave turned into a NIGHT, some of these nations collapsed. In Somalia, Sudan, Afghanistan, Iraq, Syria, Libya, and Yemen, the nation-states have all partially disintegrated, and the same thing may very well happen also to other countries if they are disrupted. Once the national structure collapses, such as happened in Libya, it is very difficult, if not impossible, to re-create it.

A very important reason for the current rise of fundamentalist Islam, and the attempts to create a new caliphate, is that, in contrast to Judaism and Christianity, Islam was not born in a DAY but in the mid-point of a NIGHT, the fifth NIGHT in 632 CE. (Therefore, its symbols are the crescent moon and the evening star, symbols of the NIGHT.) As a result, Islam has historically been most expansive in periods that are NIGHTS in contrast to the West, which has been expansive in periods that are DAYS. For this reason, this region has not had an inherent tendency to create nation-states, which are products of DAYS, but rather has sought for caliphates or sultanates as religiously organized empires favored by the NIGHTS.

Hence, the reason ISIL turns up at the beginning of this new NIGHT, and seeks to create a state with laws from the seventh century CE, is that the NIGHT resonates with the NIGHT in which Islam was born and when it was expansive. Because we are now in a NIGHT, there is a desire for some Muslims to create a caliphate in which the word of one man, the caliph, is the law. However, the emergence of a caliphate requires that in principle all Muslims must be united into one system of rule. The animosity between Shia Islam in Iran and southern Iraq and the Sunnis in Saudi Arabia and ISIL is, however, very strong, rooted in a conflict over who was the legitimate successor of Muhammad as a caliph.[16] The conflict has created a kind of civil war within the Islamic world, making it difficult to realize the goal of a unified caliphate. Because we are in the beginning of a new NIGHT in the Sixth Wave, the idea of a caliphate is, however, again being activated, which is not merely a fantasy as you hear some commentators in the West say. In fact, it is the very reason that the old Sunni-Shia conflict at this very point in time has again been activated.

The emergence of ISIL is thus based on the shift to a NIGHT in the Sixth Wave, which leads to the disintegration of nation-states and creates a desire among some Muslims for a caliphate to replace them. Moreover, the shift to a NIGHT in the Sixth Wave weakens the West in the area, and ISIL and other terrorist groups can exploit the new energy field. The Islamic world has been in NIGHTS before, and even if Islam has not been peaceful, it was not necessarily worse than the Christians during the crusades. What now may make it more belligerent is that for a long time in the previous DAY in the Sixth Wave the West has had the upper hand and so in this NIGHT there might be a tendency to overreact and reverse this.

Even if it is naive to think that there would be a simple road to peace in the Middle East, I think it is important to understand the underlying tendencies in the wave field. What is happening there, as well as elsewhere, is *not accidental.* The main reasons for the intensified conflicts and the terror are that the Sixth Wave has gone into a NIGHT and that the duality of this wave and its hologram is so ingrained in the Middle East. The Middle East was never really industrialized (except for the oil industry), and so few people in the area have climbed to the Seventh Wave and onto the Eighth. For this, *it may be critical to support Middle Eastern women in meaningful ways,* because, after all, they are the ones that will find it the easiest to download the Eighth and Ninth Wave holograms and make peaceful use of them.

THE WORLD ECONOMY AFTER THE SHIFT

The speed with which different parts of the world are affected by the shift between a DAY and a NIGHT depends essentially on their distance from the previously mentioned planetary midline at the twelfth longitude east. As a consequence, the effects of this substantial shift in 2011 may appear later in the United States and China than in the United Kingdom, Europe, and the Middle East. Naturally, many other parts of the world, such as the BRIC countries, Latin America, Africa, South Asia, and Australia, will also go through their processes as a result of this shift, but I will leave these outside of the discussion.

Much of the future of the world will, of course, depend on how the global economy develops, and in this regard the key country to look at is probably the United States. We may then first note that after the shift, the political situation here has become marked by strong tendencies toward the disintegration of its entire political system, where the rules are increasingly being broken. This may possibly lead to a serious economic downturn, which could bring with it much of the rest of the world, including China. The economy of the United States may currently give the appearance of having a reasonably stable character, but it is in reality very vulnerable for a number of reasons. First, the governmental and foreign debts are very large and are not likely ever to be reversed. Second, the strength of the dollar still depends directly on the petrodollar system, which gives it an artificially high value, and third, there is an extreme income inequality (fig. 8.3) coupled with

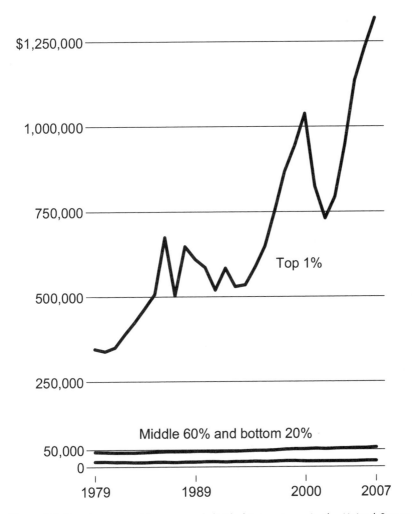

Figure 8.3. Development of incomes subdivided into groups in the United States, 1979–2007. (Created by Lane Kenworthy using data from the Congressional Budget Office; used with permission)

digitalization, which threatens to cause massive unemployment. In fact, if we simply go by what we would expect from the Seventh Wave, which plays the dominant role for the economic cycles (see figure 6.8 on p. 182), a serious economic downturn should be expected in its seventh NIGHT (2011–2031). No one can say with certainty whether this will happen, but it seems wise to consider this as a serious possibility, especially as there are many signs of a deepening of the crisis of the political system of the United States, including the two-party system, the Supreme Court, Congress, and possibly even the presidential institution. What the shift into a NIGHT of the Sixth Wave means among other things is a decline of rationality and structure, a process that is most likely going to continue to express itself in the political arenas of key Western countries, and if it does a serious economic decline is likely to follow suit. Politics is certainly not something separate from the economy.

As mentioned in the context of the digital revolution brought by the Eighth Wave, the increasing economic inequalities and the disappearance of the middle class adds to the risks of an economic crisis. In the United States and Western countries in general, a middle class with a relatively high living standard has enjoyed a relatively high standard of living for a few generations, but because of the digital revolution and the abovementioned vulnerabilities of the U.S. economy this social stratification is now being threatened.

As we can see from figure 8.3, for instance, it is only the 1 percent with the highest incomes who have had substantially increased incomes during the past forty years or so. The top 20 percent have also had a slow increase of income (although very slow), while the lower 80 percent have had virtually no rise in income at all. The graph shows the income distribution up until the Great Recession beginning in 2007. In the years after this, the income distribution has, however, become even more extreme, with the top 1 percent accruing 95 percent of the total income gain.[17]

BALANCING THE HEMISPHERES WITH
THE EIGHTH WAVE

It thus seems that the downturns of the Sixth and Seventh Waves could create fairly difficult times even in the rather unlikely best-case scenario with no worldwide economic crisis. The scenario that now unfolds also notably takes place against a background of a serious climate crisis and overpopulation. Yet, the notes I have made about the future above are not predictions in the sense that they are bound to happen. They are potentialities, and they are formulated exclusively on the basis of the Sixth and Seventh Waves. These potentialities are described based on what we know about the manifestations of these waves at earlier points of their development and against relevant parallels.

To the change in the relationships between the hemispheres of the planet should also be added that the Eighth Wave is in its DAY mode every other year (fig. 8.1). After a long time of Western dominance, this rapid oscillation may serve to create a balance between the global hemispheres (and hence by resonance also between the brain halves of human beings). *I believe that with every time period that is a DAY in the Eighth Wave (see fig. 8.1) there is an increased potential for more spiritual and feminine values to be manifested.* Still, we cannot know how the potential interference pattern created by the Eighth Wave will manifest as this is not predetermined.

It could, as we have seen in the beginning, after this shift mean that different Eastern powers seek to increase their role on the global scene. On the other hand, Indian spirituality could also spread more widely. People in the West could also download the new holograms to approach the Divine in a new inclusive and holistic way, which, especially through the Ninth Wave, would have positive effects for the whole.

Climbing to the level of the Eighth Wave is thus part of balancing the world and creating a holistic approach, which will not be equally easy everywhere. It is, however, almost certainly easier for women to do so. There are several reasons that the success of humanity in manifesting its destiny depends on the rise of the feminine on a global scale. In principle, the hologram of the Eighth Wave, which favors the right brain in both genders, will encourage the increasing strength of the feminine. As this happens, a more holistic and intuitive thinking may be mediated by our minds. Both genders become more androgynous and can enjoy the freedom to express themselves through either modality. *What I think we must realize here is that equal respect for both genders and the recognition of an equal connection to the Divine is something that is not only of interest to women.* This equality has the added dimension of helping all of humanity to manifest its destiny and develop a unity with the Divine, because it is nearly impossible for someone to make a frequency increase from the Seventh Wave to the Ninth Wave without passing through the Eighth Wave. Moreover, it seems impossible to conceive of someone climbing to the Eighth Wave without first balancing him- or herself with the other gender. Hence, the issue of the equality between the genders is a key part to fulfilling the destiny of humanity.

The climb to the Eighth Wave is most likely more difficult in the Middle East, where the Sixth Wave hologram is so ingrained and fewer have moved into the Seventh Wave. Different parts of the world are thus affected in very different ways by the waves that in principle are accessible all over the planet. This is mostly a function of how different locations are related to the planetary midline on the twelfth longitude east, but local habits may also play significant roles. In the United States, for instance, with its business dominance, the Eighth Wave hologram may be used more for information technology than for creating a holistic approach to life.

It seems clear that wherever a person is positioned, either geographically or in terms of the climb to the different levels of insight, understanding of the holographic universe is a critical factor for the outcome not only for the individual but also for humanity at large. Hence, it is imperative to know that humanity is engaged in a climb to the ninth level of the cosmic pyramid, because having this knowledge is the only way to remove the barriers on the climb. There are essentially two fundamental aspects of the new stage of life that people need to know about. One is that the Sixth Wave has now turned into a NIGHT, and the other is that the path to the return to the Garden of Eden is now accessible. Even if it is a climb, meaning effort may be necessary, there is now nothing preventing us from continuing the climb as resonance with the Ninth Wave is now possible.

9
Manifesting the Destiny of Humanity through the Ninth Wave

THE ERA OF FULFILLMENT

The current (2016) erosion of both the nation-state and Western dominance (to name only two of the trends discussed in chapter 8) may actually be preparation for an entirely new world that is being created by the Eighth and the Ninth Waves, if we are able to deliver the cosmic plan to a Golden Age. As the Sixth Wave and the Seventh Wave have turned into NIGHTS (until 2406 CE and 2031 CE, respectively), space will be created for the phenomena of the Eighth and Ninth Waves to manifest in this post-shift era. The new interference pattern upon which this will be built holds both risks and possibilities, but I believe that our understanding of, and intentions for, the climb will play a big role for how this new world will turn out. The next decade or two are likely to be very challenging for humanity as the shift is not likely to uphold the previous structure of the mind and its connected sociopolitical systems. Ultimately what the world seems to be going toward may best be described as *divinely guided anarchy* and so as part of this unfolding we must expect many reactions from people wanting to go back to the old paradigm. This is already becoming obvious as the world is becoming divided between those trying to stay with the old and others who are moving directly into the new interference pattern. *Whether humanity will make it through is likely to be deter-*

mined in this upcoming period, but again, this requires that the long-term direction created by the Ninth Wave is upheld and promoted.

Existentially speaking, the most significant aspect of the new stage of life, the new interference pattern, may be that the path toward unity with the Divine will increasingly become open. We can, in other words, now complete the climb to the ninth level of the staircase, and while there likely will be hurdles on this, there are no longer any insurmountable "blocks." Within the grand evolutionary plan for the universe we have thus now come to a new and very significant point in time where the underlying energy field looks very different from previously, and so creates entirely new challenges and opportunities, especially after the Ninth Wave was activated in 2011. We are now faced with the challenge of manifesting the Golden Age.

When considering this, I believe it is important to realize that when it comes to the actual course of events, there is both a short-term and a long-term perspective and that the two are different. The short-term perspective may be dominated by the fact that both the Sixth and Seventh Waves have gone into NIGHTS and that many people are reacting to this by trying to hold on to their DAYS, which are now gone. In the long-term perspective, however, both the Eighth and Ninth Waves are increasingly providing the predominant expressions of creation. Thus, even if the time until 2031 may be very challenging for humanity I believe that by 2041 the interference pattern in figure 8.1 (p. 222) will have stabilized enough and enough people will have created a resonance with the Ninth Wave that a world of peace will be generated from which violence will never again be re-created. The reason is that the unfolding of the nine waves is designed in such a way that the establishment of a Golden Age can never be reversed if the Ninth Wave eventually comes to rule on Earth. As we may understand from the previous discussions, this is not just wishful thinking but a logical consequence of the fact that the wave with the highest frequency, the Ninth Wave, has now been activated and in the time ahead is bound to increasingly shape the human perception of who we are.

The DAYS of the Eighth and Ninth Waves thus have time on their side. As we go more deeply into resonance with those two waves, people who have been fully born into them (after the years 1999 and 2011) will increasingly influence the global course of events. At the current time, these highest waves are, however, only beginning to manifest in public life, but we can be certain that these are the waves of the future and that eventually their expressions are going to take over life on Earth. *In the "struggle" between the Waves, it is the Eighth Wave and even more so the Ninth Wave that are constantly gaining.* This means that everyone who wants to leave behind a better world for their children and their children's children will have to take seriously the paradigm shift that is now happening in accordance with the new interference pattern and prepare themselves and their children for this Ninth Wave.

ANCIENT CONCEPTS ABOUT THE CURRENT SHIFT

As part of our understanding of the world, I believe it is important to see that several ancient traditions and religions saw their own era as leading up to the shift that we have now gone through. They saw time not as cyclical in the sense of being based on endlessly repeated identical cycles but as fundamentally directed in accordance with a Divine Plan. The universe had a purpose and was meant to fulfill this. We have here (fig. 4.2, p. 96) seen that humanity has gone from unity to separation and back to unity through a sequence of holograms with different polarities. It was because of their intuitive grasp of this that several ancient cultures pointed to the shift we have been through as the beginning of the Era of Fulfillment. This is not just the end of a cycle and the beginning of a new cycle. The shift was the inception of a new interference pattern creating an entirely new stage for life.

To find support for the idea that the ancients looked upon the recent shift as important we may begin with the Hindu view that the universe is created by 108 movements by the god Shiva, the god of creation and destruction.[1] His dance is a reflection of the twelve transformations between peaks and valleys (creation and destruction, if you like) in each of the nine different creation waves (equaling $9 \times 12 = 108$ transformations, which were completed on October 28, 2011). The number 108 incidentally also plays a crucial role in Buddhism and several other Eastern traditions. A very similar example is the Chinese scheme of $9 \times 13 = 117$ scales on the cosmic dragon,[2] which similarly we have reasons to associate with the shift on October 28, 2011.

The Hindu and Chinese schemes admittedly were not dated (and translated to chronological years), but according to the Mayan inscription at Tortuguero monument no. 6, the creation god Bolon Yookte K'uh (meaning the Nine-Step, or Nine-Support Entity)[3] would appear in his full regalia as the thirteenth baktun (seven DAYS and six NIGHTS) had been completed. The appearance in full regalia of this god, in other words, meant that all nine waves had been activated and considering that up until October 28, 2011, they each went through thirteen steps we can understand that the Plumed Serpent (like his Chinese counterpart) then had shifted between 117 scales on his back. A very important conclusion to draw from these examples is that in the views of these ancient traditions there were not more than Nine Waves. This in turn means that the Ninth Wave creates the highest state of consciousness that is available to us. This would mean that the state of the ninth level indeed is what we are to aim for.

All of these observations point to the momentous nature of the shift we as humanity have recently gone through. But as far as we know, the ancient Maya or the other ancient peoples did not have much to say regarding the future beyond this. When it comes to the Maya their prophetic use of numbers only went to thirteen, and we are now in the fourteenth baktun. Possibly this lack of knowledge on their part is because what is now about to happen on our planet is not cut in stone. The cosmos has created an opening for us to create unity consciousness, a product of the highest frequency Ninth Wave, but after this, the future is largely up to us, and our choices, both individually and as humanity, will be crucial for what emerges.

When considering the absence of information in ancient traditions (which are all generated by the Sixth Wave) regarding what our current time would mean, we should also consider that these were dominated by the Hologram of Good and Evil. Even if they, as we have seen, were clearly aware that creation was developed by Nine Waves, they had no knowledge of what kinds of mental states the Seventh, Eighth, and Ninth Waves would bring to humanity and what types of phenomena these would manifest in our time. What this means is that when they were trying to look into the future they would almost certainly be subordinated to a Sixth Wave duality in understanding their visions. This would generate a view of God as judgmental (as was extensively discussed in chapter 5). Hence, even if the Abrahamic religions also have hints at a scenario with the potentialities that have been presented here, their so-called apocalyptic scenarios often are markedly judgmental in nature and include ideas about separating "the good" from "the evil," the end of the world, and so on, which is what you would expect from people dominated by a hologram of duality. Personally, I believe that the concept of a Judgment Day is simply a projection of the dualist hologram of the Sixth Wave onto ourselves and that there has never been an intent on the part of the Creator to set an end to the world or punish anyone.

What supports such a statement is that according to the interference pattern in figure 8.1 on page 222, we do not seem to be approaching any significant discontinuity in the evolution of the waves that would justify the idea that the world would now be primed to come to an end. The waves generating our holograms may instead be expected to simply continue to flow endlessly without any foreseeable discontinuity. This, of course, does not preclude that humans create an end to the world or a destructive apocalyptic scenario, but I still feel it is important to see that there is no plan for the destruction of the world integrated into the nine waves of creation. *The apocalyptic scenarios are perpetuated by people with dualist minds.* Moreover, there is nothing to indicate that the wave pattern points to any disruption in the form of a Judgment Day, when everything would stop and people would be separated into "the good" and "the evil." Instead, the creation waves will from now on simply continue forward ad infinitum, and the future of ourselves and of humanity will be created in accordance with the waves with which we resonate.

Yet, despite their origin in the Sixth Wave, I think there are certain viewpoints from the world religions that indicate that some of their texts shared the perspective given here about an Era of Fulfillment that we now after the shift are entering. In Jewish eschatology, for instance, it is a prominent idea that humanity is to return to the "Garden of Eden." Such a return, I believe, should be interpreted to mean that there will come a point when the Ninth Wave dominates humanity. The reason for this connection to the "Garden of Eden" is that the Ninth Wave resembles the consciousness of the Fifth Wave, which was what created the Garden of Eden in the first place. Thus, it only makes sense if the Ninth Wave means a return to the same state of mind as in the Fifth.

According to Jewish tradition, depending on the actions of humanity, this return is believed to happen no later than six thousand years after the expulsion from the Garden of Adam and Eve. The date Jewish eschatology has placed for this expulsion is 3761 BCE, and as a consequence, this transition would be expected to take place sometime within the next 225 years.[4] Such a viewpoint is quite consistent with the one presented here, with the difference being that we now have an explanation as to why such a "return" to the "Garden of Eden" would indeed happen based on the resonance people develop with the underlying wave pattern of creation. Another similarity is that the actions of humanity will be critical for the manifestation of this era. It is not something that will happen automatically.

Moreover, in the Book of Revelation, the last book of the Christian Bible, there are descriptions of progressive developments in terms of seven trumpets, seven vials, and so on, indicating that the universe has been developed by processes in seven steps. This is exactly what we have seen in chapters 3 and 6, where up until 2011 several processes driven by the nine waves were developed stepwise through seven DAYS (see fig. 6.9 on p. 184). Also in these metaphors, we have thus been led to the place we are today according to a plan, and the same book goes on to describe a meeting with the Divine (Rev 20:11). In Christian eschatology it is also often prophesied about a coming Kingdom of God (which in my interpretation is what may be generated from people's resonance with the Ninth Wave), and one of the last verses in the Book of Revelation talks about the righteous having "rights" to the Tree of Life: "Blessed are those that wash their robes so that they have the right to the Tree of Life and may enter the city by the gates."* This seems appropriate for the Era of Fulfillment and points toward our own time, especially in that it is now that the Tree of Life has been rediscovered by modern science. It is only now that we can understand the entire evolution of creation from the birth of the universe to our own time as a result of waves broadcast by this very Tree of Life.

The Qur'an also has an interesting description of the Judgment Day, stating in the Cleaving Asunder Sura 82:17–19: "And what will make you realize what the day of Judgment is? Again, what will make you realize what the day of Judgment is? The day on which no soul shall control anything for another soul and the command on this day shall be entirely Allah's." The emphasis on equality between humans in this sura does provide guidance for how someone wanting to be part of the Kingdom of God should not seek control over others. This also points to the Ninth Wave, whose transcendence of duality is designed to set an end to such control.

MANIFESTING THE DESTINY OF HUMANITY OR FOLLOWING IDENTICALLY REPEATED CYCLES

The idea proposed throughout this book that humanity has a set destiny on which we should focus, may very well by itself be controversial.

---

*Rev 22:14: the "city" then presumably refers to the New Jerusalem, or in my interpretation, the New World.

Most modern Westerners would probably be highly skeptical against it, and many would rather believe that events in the world are essentially random and not subject to a time plan. This is because on the surface the world may very well seem to be driven by more or less random power struggles, conspiracies, and accidental technological innovations. Alternative explanations such as those provided here are not taken into consideration. It may then seem easy to go to the conclusion that this world is not going anywhere in particular and that it is not meant to go anywhere either.

What I hope is that the present book has shown this view of evolution as random and uncharted is not correct. If you have as a background the existence of nine waves of creation that have been sequentially activated to create the universe as it is now, it does seems clear that events are not random or meaningless but instead are subject to a fairly exact timing. There is always an underlying quantum field of waves that govern our existence, and most phenomena in our own time can be understood against the background this provides. Even if because of their very long wavelengths these waves are outside of what we can directly detect, they nonetheless exist and are the primary determinants for how the universe is being created.

To recognize that the totality of the nine waves has a direction, and hence the creation of the universe has a purpose, I believe is very important. This view of a direction to evolution is consistent with the abovementioned references to ancient spiritual and religious traditions. Creation has, in other words, been going somewhere ever since its inception, and as we can understand from the model presented here, its intended end result has been part of the nature of the universe ever since it was born. Because of this strong emphasis on manifesting the destiny of humanity, intrinsic to the design of the waves, I think it is important to here clarify that the underlying worldview is very different from that held by people who embrace a purely cyclical view of the universe, more common among alternative than mainstream researchers. At this time I also find it imperative that each one of us makes a clear choice as to whether we embrace a cosmology that has a purposeful direction or one that is fundamentally cyclical.

In recent decades a worldview where the universe does not have a direction has become widespread. Astrologers, who are studying endlessly repeated identical cycles, such as notably the so-called 26,000-year precessional cycle, or Great Year,[5] typically embrace such a view. Leaving aside that I am not aware of any evidence that this cycle has played a role for the evolution of the universe, it is important to be aware that such a worldview based on identically repeated astronomical cycles has important consequences for how you approach the future. If you look upon the universe as a product of endlessly repeated cycles that has no ultimate purpose or goal, you will obviously not be intent on co-creating a lasting Golden Age. If, on the other hand, you look upon your individual life in the context that I have provided here—as part of a process toward the Golden Age created by purposeful and directed waves—you will be thinking more in terms of providing lasting solutions for humanity.

I should add here that the nine waves of creation do not lack a cyclic component. Obviously they have such a component, as a DAY-NIGHT sine wave period (see fig. 2.8 on p. 50) can be called a cycle. The point is rather that in these creation waves the cycles are not identically repeated but are part of a progressive sequence of holograms that with every new step expresses itself more fully. The fifth or fifty-fifth DAY of a wave thus creates much more profound expressions of the wave than, for instance, its third DAY does. The waves are, in other words, going somewhere much like a serpent as the ancients would symbolize them. The "cycles" that are part of the creation waves are thus not identical but form part of progressions with deepening expressions. Because each of the waves has a forward movement and a direction we can say that they each carry a particular purpose as broadcast by the Cosmic Tree of Life. When we look upon the different purposes of these in the context of the sequential activation of the nine waves, we can understand that the sum total of these is indeed the Destiny Chart of Humanity. I cannot emphasize enough how important it is that the reader makes a choice whether to follow waves with the direction or purpose of creating a Golden Age or follow astronomical or biological cycles that are identically repeated such as the 26,000-year cycle. Such cycles, even if they may have some energetic effect, are not going to create a lasting alteration in the state of mind of humanity. It should also be noted here that among the thousands of calendrical inscriptions from the ancient Maya a 26,000-year-long cycle is never mentioned, and hence it played no role in their calendrical system.

To choose the Destiny Chart of Humanity in practice means not to embrace cosmologies or calendrical systems that are based on identically repeated cycles or beliefs that the events in the world are just randomly generated. If this book, based on its empirical evidence, has been able to convince you that the purpose of your individual life is to be part of opening the gateway to the Golden Age through acting in accordance with the hologram of the Ninth Wave and creating resonance with this, then this will have very significant consequences for your ability to make sense of and face the difficulties we may expect to encounter in the time ahead (briefly discussed in chapter 8). If you are developing resonance with the Ninth Wave, then these difficulties will not necessarily lead you to be discouraged but instead may be seen as hurdles created by the underlying waves of duality. If, on the other hand, you believe, as many do, that the universe simply goes through identical cycles, then any difficulty may be understood as a long-term downturn or simply that this universe is not a good place to be. *So the choice between a purposeful universe designed to create a Golden Age and one of repeated identical cycles that are not going anywhere is very crucial for who you are going to be in the times ahead—and how you are to approach these times.*

THE EGO AND ITS TRANSCENDENCE BY THE NINTH WAVE

The reason that a Golden Age is set to be created in the time ahead is that human beings may be expected to change as they deepen their resonance with the Ninth Wave. As this happens we will transcend our egos and our personalities and modes of operating will be altered. To see this, it may now be meaningful to discuss the ego and its relationship to your higher self. The ego emerges from the experience of separation from the Divine, which as we have seen is created by our experience of dark fields in our holograms. On the basis of this ego, a personality is created, which serves this very separation. Several spiritual teachings have over the centuries been developed with the intention of having people become aware of their egos, or even slaying the ego, as it is expressed in some Eastern teachings. These teachings recognize the ego's addiction to catering to the individual person and how this is different from living a spiritual life based on your higher Divine self. If we are constantly aiming to serve our own person and its perceived separation from others, rather than the divine plan, then we will indeed cement the power of the ego. The ego is, however, not an eternal psychological entity but is something that has a history and so is directly related to the evolution of the nine waves.

The ego did not exist in the Fifth Wave for the simple reason that there was then no dark field in the hologram creating an experience of the individual as being separate from the Source. As I touched upon in chapter 5, human individuality in any sense close to the modern did not emerge until the midpoint of the Sixth Wave (ca. 550 BCE), and it was only then that an ego emerged. Because the Ninth Wave shares the absence of a dark filter with the Fifth Wave, this would, however, mean that over time the ego would disappear. From this perspective, the ego may then not really be something that should be "slayed," but rather something that should be transcended as we climb to the top of the nine-story pyramid. As we find the tools to do so and open our beings fully to the Divine and subordinate ourselves to what it guides us to do, we will also transcend the ego and lessen the grip this has over us. *Incidentally, much of what is said here about transcending the ego would apply equally to transcending evil.*

The different place of the ego in different waves has consequences

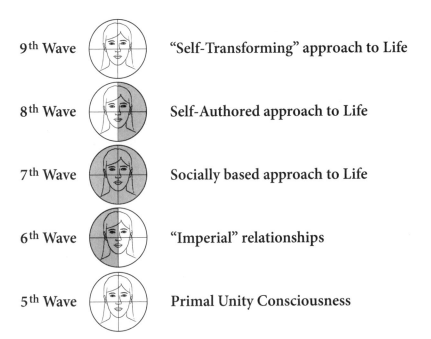

9th Wave	"Self-Transforming" approach to Life
8th Wave	Self-Authored approach to Life
7th Wave	Socially based approach to Life
6th Wave	"Imperial" relationships
5th Wave	Primal Unity Consciousness

Figure 9.1. The Destiny Chart of Humanity, continued: Climbing to the top of the nine-level pyramid implies going through different levels of relating. (*Diagram by the author, design courtesy of Bengt Sundin*)

for the kind of personalities and modes of operating we develop in these waves, as is hinted at in the Destiny Chart of Humanity in figure 9.1. Here, we will look at how we can make parallels between the different holograms and the developmental scheme of a human being developed by Robert Kegan.[6] The developmental phases that human beings go through during the course of their lives are thus reflections of their resonances with different holograms (fig. 9.1).

Hence, in a similar sense to how different holograms have been sequentially activated during the course of human history, the different holograms are sequentially activated over a human life. The individual's climb begins with the infant's state of unity with its mother before its ego has emerged. This may be likened to the state of unity with nature and the Divine that people experienced under the influence of the Fifth Wave. In the next phase, that of the duality of the Sixth Wave, we tend to develop "imperial" relationships, where we look upon others as if they were there mostly to serve our own needs, and this is when our egos are created. At the next level, which corresponds to the teenage years, we typically become very sensitive to what other people think and create our lives on this basis. This corresponds to the Seventh Wave, which because of its darkness does not provide much guidance from the Source and so leads us to become dependent on other humans. On the next level, we start to liberate ourselves from social constraints and allow the light of the Eighth Wave filter to inspire us. At this level of evolution individuals become self-authored: their life is not created by their imperial mentality or their concerns of fitting in socially.

On the ninth level finally, there is no dark filter separating us from the Divine, and for this reason it is not meaningful to say that our lives are self-authored. Instead, if we reach this level of development, which has only been fully possible after the Ninth Wave was activated in 2011, our will and how we create our lives is essentially a product of our unity with the Divine, and not of our ego. Life then, as shown in figure 9.1, becomes "self-transforming," or in other words, our selves are automatically being transformed by our unity with the Divine to the detriment of the ego. At this level the ego is not running a separate agenda, or maybe better said, an agenda of separation, and our actions become expressions of the All That Is Divine with which we are unified. This self-transforming level and its transcendence of the ego are only beginning to be available. I believe, for instance, that Patricia Albere's Mutual Awakening[7] is a reflection of the self-transforming nature of the Ninth Wave and is a product of the absence of filters from its hologram. There may be many other teachings with which I do not have experience that similarly may aid your transition to the ninth level's way of being.

At the ninth level we can hardly talk about a free will, because if the ego plays no separate role and your actions are determined in resonance with All That Is, we can hardly talk about will as free. At this highest level, when we are fully in resonance with the Ninth Wave, our lives will not be about running separate individual agendas but about fulfilling an aspect of the divine plan for humanity. There will no longer be a separate ego that acts only on the individual's behalf. Instead, as we in a unity state of consciousness surrender to our higher selves, we act on behalf of the Divine and its plan for humanity.

This disappearance of the ego in the Ninth Wave may be appreciated by some but not by others. But how could we possibly arrive at a Golden Age of peace unless we all surrender all agendas that are contrary to, or not aligned with, the divine plan? It is only if all our actions are informed by our contact with the Divine so that the largest possible view is taken into consideration that all of our individual lives can ever be harmonized. Joy will then never come from your agenda of being separate, but from the harmony that is created with All That Is.

BECOMING AN EMBODIMENT OF UNITY CONSCIOUSNESS

The reason that the Ninth Wave may be expected to generate a Golden Age in the time ahead is thus that its hologram does not include any darkness or duality, which in turn means that conflict-generating agendas of the ego will recede. With duality gone, separation and division between humans will disappear together with the superior/inferior dichotomy. For those that will be able to develop resonance with the frequency of the Ninth Wave, the perception of dark fields will no longer be projected onto Nature or the Divine, and this in turn will create a profoundly different foundation for human existence in the Golden Age. Developing resonance with the Ninth Wave is the same thing as moving in the direction of, and eventually attaining, a state of unity consciousness.

How then do we as a human collective attain such a state of unity consciousness to which the destiny chart points? There are many aspects of this, one of which is to learn to recognize the Ninth Wave and its consequences in yourself and humanity at large. Because this wave will from now on always be accessible to humanity, and will never be in its

NIGHT mode for more than eighteen common days, it is easy to follow and monitor the effects of the wave in ourselves. Thus, we may be able to more directly experience the personal consequences of this wave compared to waves with lower frequencies (and longer wave periods).

The current interference pattern is, however, complex and involves also the Sixth, Seventh, and Eighth Waves. This complexity gives us an even greater reason to monitor our individual processes by following the Ninth Wave to keep us on track. *A critical factor here is to decide for yourself what you are committed to—duality or unity—and to set your intentions for the future based on this.* If you do not know where you want to go on the stormy waters, it does not help much to have a compass.

I will, however, assume that the reader does want to go toward the unity consciousness of the Ninth Wave. After all, unity, and the disappearance of dark fields of consciousness, seems to be the goal of the divine plan, and we are now living in a time when this may be fulfilled. Personally, I think it is clear that unity consciousness is what this entire creation is striving toward and so also that it is the only guarantee for the survival of our species. Yet, there will be difficulties and it may sometimes require courage on our part to deliver this plan. With little doubt there will be strong pressures against its manifestation, not the least from those who have become comfortable with a life of duality or maybe are unable to see an alternative. It is at these times that the knowledge of, and resonance with, the Ninth Wave of creation may become the most valuable. It may seem to some that the Ninth Wave will automatically do its job like all the other waves have in the past and that accordingly we can ignore to be aware of, or follow the Ninth Wave, but I do not think so. I think our future depends on enough people setting the intention to resonate with the Ninth Wave and manifesting this through their actions.

I will then here submit a few ideas of what there is for us to do to attain unity consciousness, but again a critical step for this will always be the intention.

1. Understanding the Nature of this Creation

To understand the nature of how our universe works and evolves according to a preset time plan is critical for knowing where to go. A part of this knowledge, which is an important part of the Fulfillment Era, has been provided in this book. It is possible that some people may create resonance with the Ninth Wave without any intellectual understanding of the processes involved. On the other hand, such understanding may also play a significant positive role for our planet. I believe it does provide support for peoples' processes to know that the creation waves exist and are part of a divine plan for the evolution of the planet. I also believe that we now know where we come from and where we are meant to be going. For these reasons, help spread this knowledge and develop community around the Nine Waves!

2. Using a Calculator to Align Yourself with the Ninth Wave

As mentioned above, the Ninth Wave was activated on March 9, 2011, and has ever since been alternating between energies of DAYS and NIGHTS every eighteen days. As all creation waves, the wave periods of the Ninth Wave have four phases, an ascending DAY phase of nine days, a descending DAY phase of nine days, a descending NIGHT phase of nine days and finally an ascending NIGHT phase of nine days. As in the many other waves we have studied in this book, these different phases have different qualities and will in different ways influence how your life's projects develop. Because the hologram of the Ninth Wave has no dark fields, it tends to create unity consciousness in the DAYS, whereas in the NIGHTS this effect is not as evident. A person in resonance with this wave will find that in the DAYS all his or her projects that are consistent with and supportive of the emergence of unity consciousness will progress well.

The NIGHT phases of the Ninth Wave (as in all waves) have a different character from the DAYS. In the NIGHT phase, the Ninth Wave is essentially deactivated. But also NIGHTS have a purpose: rather than just moving forward you will have to deal with unresolved issues from your own or humanity's past, creations of the lower waves, that are inconsistent with the unity consciousness of the Ninth Wave. NIGHTS are also time periods when you need to process the actions of all of humanity, as the Ninth Wave breaks down the separation between individual and collective destiny.

We have previously seen that all human evolution proceeds in phase with the creation waves. The Ninth Wave is no different. If you seek to develop your life based on resonance with the hologram of unity consciousness, it then only makes sense if you follow the actual wave period of the Ninth Wave as a means of correcting your course. Over time, I also believe that the Ninth Wave will become a synchronizing factor for those among humanity who are committed to be part of this return to unity. To learn how to follow the Ninth Wave (which is the compass for the stormy waters) and develop your life and your life's projects in phase with its ups and downs you will, however, need to know how this wave develops over time (see the next section). As mentioned, becoming aware of its existence and understanding the Ninth Wave intellectually is meaningful, but this knowledge on the mental plane cannot replace direct personal experience. To follow this means having a tuning fork for the highest frequency level that the universe offers and raising your consciousness to this.

3. Healing Yourself

We have in previous chapters seen how the lower waves, and especially the Sixth Wave, in a multitude of ways have created separation—separation both within ourselves and from others. Sometimes this may take the form of judgmental attitudes toward yourself or others. The filters of the lower waves may also often have caused you to limit yourself to less than what you are. The Sixth Wave hologram may have subjugated, oppressed, or suppressed aspects of yourself, and some of the effects of this duality may have been passed down through generations creating wounds that need to be healed. You can only fully flourish in a state of unity consciousness that does not filter out any expressions of yourself.

In this case this means to rid yourself of all the negative effects of the dualities created by the lower holograms. A discussion about different forms of healing is not part of this book, and yet it is important to acknowledge that your own healing is an important part of your own transition to unity consciousness. Part of creating unity with All That Is and attaining a state of unity consciousness is to become whole and leave behind the painful separation from others and nature that has been created especially by the Sixth Wave hologram.

4. Political Action

The world does not change automatically just because we become spiritually awakened or are able to heal some aspects of ourselves. In the now emerging paradigm, where everything is seen as connected, it will not be possible to separate spirituality and politics. The Ninth Wave also on a larger scale holds the potential to heal the world by eliminating the various forms of separation that dominate it. The step to manifest unity consciousness on this larger social scale and make it part of our everyday lives may then be what requires the most courage. The Ninth Wave is about making unity consciousness a practical reality, and this includes political action against the many forms of oppression that the world has inherited from the Sixth Wave. This implies that the overriding political themes for anyone resonating with the Ninth Wave will be *equality and balance.* Exactly what course of action you should take will need to be based on your personal dialogue with the Divine. Each of our tasks is different, and yours should be based on your particular talents and specific purpose to the extent that you may use them to support the climb of humanity to unity consciousness.

5. Developing a Personal Relationship with the One

To develop a personal relationship with the Divine, and to base all your actions on the guidance you receive from this Source, may be greatly facilitated by the Ninth Wave. Be uncompromising when it comes to following this guidance; cut out all middlemen and develop a direct relationship with the One. It is in the very nature of the Ninth Wave that it alters our perception of the Divine and so alters our relationship to the One to become *a direct personal relationship* (see fig. 5.8 on p. 150). In our own time, the concept of Oneness is by some seen as something that only refers to relationships with other humans or with nature. *I, for one, do not think that the relationship with the One is something that can be ignored by anyone seeking to manifest the destiny of humanity.* After all, we have seen that the entire climb to unity consciousness emanates from a unified Source, the Cosmic Tree of Life. How then could we complete this climb without a direct contact with this Source? In order for us, as a species and also as individuals to fulfill human destiny, I therefore believe we need guidance directly from the Source for directing our lives. In my own experience, the Oneness University in India[8] provides the most effective support for those who want to develop a relationship that is personal and direct with the Divine. This university also offers a number of auxiliary means for spiritual awakening such as Deeksha, Oneness Meditations, and Sacred Chambers. It is one of the few movements or organizations in the world of today that envisions a Golden Age within a reasonable time frame, but others will hopefully also come to the same realization in the time ahead.

PRACTICAL TOOLS FOR DEVELOPING RESONANCE WITH THE NINTH WAVE

An individual can develop several projects as expressions of unity consciousness—and the term *project* is probably not the best word to use. One project could be to be a good mother or a friend, another to cure cancer or harmonize the income distribution of the world. I believe that anyone who already is in resonance with the Ninth Wave will have some desire to express his or her unity consciousness in actions in the external world through developing such projects. I also believe that whatever you are working with and whatever projects you are already engaged in, you can turn them into expressions of unity consciousness.

Regarding practical tools to monitor the resonance of your projects with the Ninth Wave, there are at the current time two websites that allow you to directly follow the DAYS and NIGHTS of the Ninth Wave. One of them is www.4-ahau.com,[9] which is essentially a Mayan calendar website, and in the charts posted on this website you can see how the Ninth Wave is connected to the traditional Mayan sacred calendar count. Another calculator, which very clearly shows the Ninth Wave and at what point in the wave you are on any given day, is also available (fig. 9.2).[10] This can be used to tune in to the Ninth Wave on a daily basis. A third possibility is to download a calculator[11] for the Ninth Wave (fig. 9.3, p. 265).

This calculator gives substantial information about several waves, and in a very clear way it also shows where you are in the Ninth Wave. Over time, more tools and websites are likely to be developed to follow this wave, but the currently available tools are quite adequate for

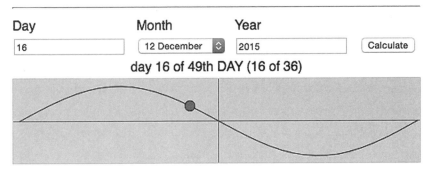

Figure 9.2. The Ninth Wave calculator, which can be used for following your path toward unity consciousness, can be found at www.xzone.com.au/9thwave.php.

Figure 9.3. The downloadable calculator that can be used for following several waves, including the Ninth Wave, can be found at www.2near.com/edge/carl.

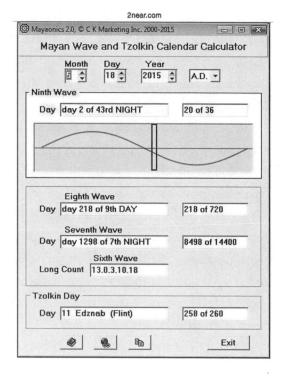

anyone who seriously wants to develop his or her resonance with the Ninth Wave.

If you follow the Ninth Wave for a reasonably long period of time, such as three or four wave periods, and do not experience its upturns and downturns or see them mirrored in your life's projects, then most likely you have not yet established resonance with the Ninth Wave. To the extent that your projects are aligned with the destiny of humanity, progress in them would be expected in the periods that are DAYS in the Ninth Wave. If this is not the case and you cannot experience the effects that the Ninth Wave has on your projects, I advise that you ask yourself if your projects are truly aligned with the destiny of humanity. There is no reason for you to judge yourself for this, but you should look upon it as an important observation.

There are other possible explanations for not experiencing resonance with the Ninth Wave. One is that the projects you are working on (and I mean project here in a very wide sense, including personal relationships) are not consistent with the unity consciousness of the Ninth Wave, or that you are not conducting your projects in a way that is consistent with unity consciousness. Possibly you are in fact working with something that is a dead end and does not serve the spiritual awakening or wholeness of yourself or others. If this is the case, you may want to consider whether you should continue with the project. This is really a question about your personal relationship to the Divine, and you will find your answers for how to deal with such issues from this relationship. The point is to use the Ninth Wave in such a way that you yourself become aware of how your life can become part of the destiny of humanity. To follow the Ninth Wave and become aware of its effects on you may serve as a self-correcting or troubleshooting tool for yourself. The more your life and your projects are expressions of the DAYS of the Ninth Wave, the more likely it is that you are on the path of the Destiny Chart of Humanity.

OPENING TO THE DIVINE

It is noteworthy that no technological revolution (at least as far as I am aware) was activated as the Ninth Wave began in 2011. This is in contrast to the Sixth, Seventh, and Eighth Waves, which all created distinct technological revolutions at the times of their inception that are still continuing. This tells us that the fields of darkness in the corresponding holograms of those waves is of fundamental importance for the development of human technologies and that the darkness is not there just to create an ego or evil. Moreover, the fact that the Ninth Wave hologram has no darkness, and that no technological revolution was initiated in 2011, indicates that the development of technology is not the main focus of this wave. The Ninth Wave is instead likely to make us use the technology developed in lower waves more wisely so that it serves the totality of our ecosystem rather than very limited interests of particular individuals.

The chief purpose of the Ninth Wave seems to be to make it possible for us to finally bring everything together in the Era of Fulfillment. The Ninth Wave provides us with a frequency that does not lead us to be separate but helps us see the unity of all things and how everything is connected. This in turn will mean that we will start to listen to and base our decisions on our heart rather than on the mind. The heart is not something amorphous, vague, or unfocused, but a coherent source of wisdom and love connected to the divine Source. It is something that emerges and is allowed to flourish as the power of the mind recedes in the opening to Oneness. This is what we need as a center of our being to fulfill the purpose of creation, which also requires developing unity with the Divine.

Thus, what we may expect from the Ninth Wave is a return to a direct contact with the Divine without any experience of separating dark filters, and this by itself will change us. The more we resonate with the Ninth Wave, the more self-transforming we become. Reaching the ninth level, however, does not mean that from now on we will only live in a state of consciousness generated by the Ninth Wave. We will still have parts of all the previous waves, even as we reach the top of the Ninth Wave, and we will perceive the world through holograms created by interference patterns among the different waves. However, to the extent that we create resonance with the Ninth Wave, everything will be subordinated to the unity with the Divine.

To develop unity with the Divine does not mean that you no longer have an individual personality. Rather, resonance with the Ninth Wave will help you craft your individual personality and destiny so that they are harmonized with the divine plan. Resonance with All That Is helps to make decisions that you as an individual would have a too limited perspective to make. No longer will your life's goals be run by a separate mind-ego agenda in conflict with this. To the extent that we surrender to the Divine, without which we cannot really speak about Oneness, our individual destinies will also become part of the overall collective destiny of humanity. Developing an experience of Oneness with others is always a product of a deepened state of Oneness with the Divine. When we have attained the point where we cease to be separate from the Divine, everything we do as individuals will actually be expressions of the Divine taking individual form. The Ninth Wave thus takes on a special meaning as a wave that can create unity with the Divine and make us aware of being Divine.

To some, the idea of being one with the Divine may invoke feelings of being all-powerful or possessing magical powers, but I believe such ideas are probably ego projections emanating from the Sixth Wave hologram. Being divine as a result of resonating with the Ninth Wave is rather about manifesting an aspect of the Divine that serves this creation, and it is the absence of filters in this wave that makes this possible.

Following the Ninth Wave is not about manifesting your destiny as a separate individual. It is about making your destiny a part of the divine plan and as you do so you will become more and more Divine yourself, and your ego's agenda will recede more into the background. This does not mean that every step on the way will be easy and pleasant, and yet this is the only true path to joy and happiness.

THE PURPOSE OF THE UNIVERSE

A theory has been developed here about how life in the universe is created and how it evolves. This does not immediately answer what the purpose of this creation is, although I think it narrows down the number of possible answers as to why we are here considerably. I can suggest a few possible answers as to what the purpose of the universe may be. One is that the universe, and we ourselves, have been created for the sole purpose of having a good, or at least interesting, journey through life. In this view, we have been created to have experiences and possibly the experience of happiness. Another possibility is that we have been created to climb the nine-story pyramid, so that at the top of this a paradisiacal state of unity with the Divine, a homecoming, can be attained and we can live in a state of pure joy, a Golden Age. A third possibility is that we have not merely been created for our own sake but also for the sake of the Divine. There is an Islamic Hadith, which speaks of this when the Prophet David asks God why he had created the universe. God responds: "I was a hidden treasure and I wanted to be known—so I created the world."[12]

I obviously cannot say with any certainty which one of these is the right answer and can only say what seems reasonable to me. I do think, however, that we can now be certain that the universe has an inherent direction and that we have now entered the Era of Fulfillment. The universe is not something that just came about, or had its particular characteristics, by accident. It has a purpose. My personal guess is that the reason it exists and continues to evolve is some combination of the second and third answers above. The universe was created for humans to attain a state of pure joy while at the same time giving full recognition of the role of the Divine, and this I believe is the direction in which we are now going. This would mean that the Divine wants to be known as the treasure that it is through our unity with it. As far as I can see, this can only happen if humanity creates a world based on the unity consciousness created by the Ninth Wave. Otherwise the Divine will not be experienced for what it is. If this is true, then we humans are confronted with a choice as to whether we want to participate in manifesting this state of consciousness. If we do, we will have to develop an ethic where the highest good is what serves the creation of such unity.

The world that would be created from such a unity would be very different from the world of dominance that we know today, even if it is now about to lose its grip. The actions of all human individuals will be shaped by this unity with the Divine, and in this way their harmony with universal law would be guaranteed. Creating resonance with the Ninth Wave is, in other words, the same thing as creating unity with the Divine. The Divine is about to be known in a way it has never been known before, because our filters and the fear these have created will be removed and our vision cleared. Everything is now available for us to go in this direction toward Oneness with the Divine and unity among ourselves. If we want to know the Divine for the treasure that it is, then this is where we need to go. This, as far as I can tell, is what the fulfillment of the Divine purpose of our lives means.

Notes

CHAPTER 1.
THE ORIGIN OF THE UNIVERSE

1. "Georges Lemaître," *Wikipedia.*
2. "Edwin Hubble," *Wikipedia.*
3. Kragh, *Cosmology and Controversy,* 55.
4. "Georges Lemaître," *Wikipedia.*
5. "Fred Hoyle," *Wikipedia.*
6. "Cosmic microwave background," *Wikipedia.*
7. "Steven Weinberg," *Wikiquote.*
8. "Dark energy," *Wikipedia.*
9. Frank and Gleiser, "A Crisis at the Edge of Physics," www.nytimes.com/2015/06/07/opinion/a-crisis-at-the-edge-of-physics.html?_r=0.
10. "Cosmological principle," *Wikipedia.*
11. "Cosmic background explorer," *Wikipedia.*
12. "Axis mundi," *Wikipedia.*
13. Bennett et al.,"First Year Wilkinson Microwave Anisotropy Probe (WMAP) Observations."
14. Tegmark, de Oliveira-Costa, and Hamilton, "High Resolution Foreground Cleaned CMB Map from WMAP"; de Oliveira-Costa, Tegmark, Zaldarriaga, and Hamilton, "The Significance of the Largest Scale CMB Fluctuations in WMAP."

15. Magueijo and Land, "Examination of Evidence for a Preferred Axis in the Cosmic Radiation Anisotropy," 071301; Land, "Exploring Anomalies in the Cosmic Microwave Background," thesis, University of London, 2006; Land and Magueijo, "The Axis of Evil."

16. Dominik Schwarz, Universitaet Bielefeld, personal communication.

17. Cho, "A Singular Conundrum: How Odd Is Our Universe?"

18. Ibid.

19. Hutsemékers, Cabanac, Lamy, and Sluse, "Mapping Extreme-Scale Alignments of Quasar Polarization Vectors."

20. Longo, "Does the Universe Have a Handedness?"

21. Ibid.

22. Carl Sagan Quotes, www.goodreads.com/quotes/371944-our-planet -is-a-lonely-speck-in-the-great-enveloping.

23. The Principle (official movie site), www.theprinciplemovie.com.

24. "The Principle," *Wikipedia*.

25. Aron, "Planck Shows Almost Perfect Cosmos—Plus Axis of Evil."

26. Ibid.

27. Fisher and Courtland, "Found: Hawking's Initials Written into the Universe."

28. Taylor and Jagannathan, "Alignments of Radio Galaxies in Deep Radio Imaging of ELAIS N1."

29. See www.theprinciplemovie.com/wp-content/uploads/2016/04/The -Axis-of-Evil-Just-Got-a-New-Brother.pdf by Robert Sungenis for an analysis.

30. Singal, "A Large Anisotropy in the Sky."

31. Tiwari et al., "Dipole Anisotropy in Sky Brightness."

32. Zhao, Wu, and Zhang, "Anisotropy of Cosmic Acceleration."

33. Vogelsberger et al., "Properties of Galaxies Reproduced by a Hydrodynamic Simulation."

34. Ghosh, "Universe Evolution Recreated in Lab."

35. This is a term originally used by Nassim Haramein, http://holofractal .net/the-holofractographic-universe.

CHAPTER 2.
THE NINE WAVES OF CREATION

1. "Black-body radiation," *Wikipedia.*
2. "Photoelectric effect," *Wikipedia.*
3. "History of quantum mechanics," *Wikipedia.*
4. YouTube: Search on "Wave Function Collapse."
5. "Albert Einstein," *Wikiquote,* https://en.wikiquote.org/wiki/Albert_Einstein.
6. "Holography," *Wikipedia.*
7. "David Bohm," *Wikipedia.*
8. "Karl H. Pribram," *Wikipedia.*
9. "Michael Talbot," *Wikipedia.*
10. YouTube: Search on "The Holographic Universe."
11. YouTube: Search on "Leonard Susskind on The World As Hologram."
12. "Gravitational wave," *Wikipedia.*
13. "Electromagnetic spectrum," *Wikipedia.*
14. Redd, "How Big Is the Universe?"
15. Longo, "Does the Universe Have a Handedness?"
16. "Antenna (radio)," *Wikipedia.*
17. Calleman, *The Purposeful Universe,* 47; Van Stone, *2012: Science & Prophecy of the Ancient Maya,* 41–45.
18. Longo, "Does the Universe Have a Handedness?"
19. Ward and Brownlee, *Rare Earth,* 97.
20. "9 (number)," *Wikipedia.*
21. Ibid.
22. "Chinese dragon," *Wikipedia.*
23. "9 (number)," *Wikipedia.*
24. Singal, "A Large Anisotropy in the Sky."
25. Schneider, *A Beginner's Guide to Constructing the Universe.*
26. "Ennead," *Wikipedia.*
27. "Realms of the World Tree," Mythology Wiki, Wikia, http://mythology.wikia.com/wiki/Realms_of_the_World_Tree.
28. O'Dubhaim, "The Elements of the Dúile from Ogham Divination."
29. Quipoloa, "The Aztec Universe."
30. "Hopi mythology," *Wikipedia.*

31. "Hanukkah," *Wikipedia.*

32. Van Stone, *2012: Science & Prophecy of the Ancient Maya,* 80–102.

33. Calleman, *The Mayan Calendar and the Transformation of Consciousness,* 236–44.

34. Freidel, Schele, and Parker, *Maya Cosmos,* 71–75.

35. Kimball, *Quetzalcoatl: The Ancient Legend.*

36. Van Stone, *2012: Science & Prophecy of the Ancient Maya,* 58–61.

37. Ibid.

38. "Solar System," *Wikipedia.*

39. "Synchronicity," *Wikipedia.*

CHAPTER 3.
WAVES AND SERPENTS

1. "The Four Creations," www.gly.uga.edu/railsback/CS/CSFourCreations .html.

2. Singal, "A Large Anisotropy in the Sky."

3. Tegmark et al., "Cosmological Parameters from SDSS and WMAP."

4. Calleman, *The Purposeful Universe,* 187–95.

5. See YouTube: Cymatics, Science vs Music by Nigel Stanford, or http:// cymaticsource.com; Cymatics, Insights into the invisible realms of sound.

6. Bianki and Fillipova, *Sex Differences in Lateralization in the Animal Brain.*

7. Binney and Tremaine, *Galactic Dynamics.*

8. "Galactic year," *Wikipedia.*

9. Longo, "Does the Universe Have a Handedness?"

10. Poirier, *Understanding Human Evolution.*

11. "Lucy (*Australopithecus*)," *Wikipedia.*

12. "*Homo habilis,*" *Wikipedia.*

13. White et al., "Pleistocene *Homo sapiens* from Middle Awash, Ethiopia."

14. "Burial," *Wikipedia.*

15. Coghlan, "Oldest Artist's Workshop in the World Discovered."

16. Hand, *Awakening the Planetary Mind.*

17. Vogt, "World's Oldest Ritual Discovered."

18. Vogt, Belardinelli, and afrol News staff, "World's Oldest Religion Discovered in Botswana."

19. "Rainbow serpent," *Wikipedia*.

20. Hand, *Awakening the Planetary Mind*.

21. "History of writing," *Wikipedia*.

22. Calleman, *The Global Mind and the Rise of Civilization*, 12.

23. Ibid., 154–58.

24. "Kali Yuga," *Wikipedia*.

25. Calleman, *The Global Mind and the Rise of Civilization*, 87–94.

26. Tedlock, *Popol Vuh*, 73.

27. Kimball, *Quetzalcoatl: The Ancient Legend*.

28. "Fuxi," *Wikipedia*.

29. Calleman, *The Global Mind and the Rise of Civilization*, 17–33.

30. "Pythia," *Wikipedia*.

31. "Ningishzida," *Wikipedia*.

32. Exodus 4:2.

CHAPTER 4.
THE HOLOGRAM OF GOOD AND EVIL

1. "Tree of Life," *Wikipedia*.

2. "Axis mundi," *Wikipedia*.

3. Longo, "Does the Universe Have a Handedness?"

4. Pantovic, "Tree of Life."

5. "Axis mundi," *Wikipedia*.

6. Alchin, "Ancient Egyptian Gods and Goddesses for Kids: The Tree of Life," Land of Pyramids, March 2015, www.landofpyramids.org/tree-of-life.htm.

7. "Yggdrasil," *Wikipedia*.

8. "*Agathis australis*," *Wikipedia*.

9. "Mesoamerican world tree," *Wikipedia*.

10. Alchin, "Ancient Egyptian Gods and Goddesses for Kids: The Tree of Life," Land of Pyramids, March 2015, www.landofpyramids.org/tree-of-life.htm.

11. Calleman, *The Global Mind and the Rise of Civilization*, 175–82.

12. Hutsemékers, Cabanac, Lamy, and Sluse, "Mapping Extreme-scale Alignments of Quasar Polarization Vectors."

13. Singal, "A Large Anisotropy in the Sky."

14. Calleman, *The Global Mind and the Rise of Civilization*, 12.

15. Codex Magliabecchiano, FAMSI, www.famsi.org/research/graz /magliabechiano/img_page012.html.

16. "Dingir," *Wikipedia*.

17. "Bagua," *Wikipedia*.

18. Sweeney, *The Egyptian Book of the Dead, Nuclear Physics and the Substratum*.

19. "Cave of Altamira," *Wikipedia*.

20. Evehema, "A Message for Mankind."

21. "Me (mythology)," *Wikipedia*.

22. Avatar (official movie site), www.avatarmovie.com.

23. "Ancient Egyptian creation myths," *Wikipedia*.

24. "Upper Paleolithic," *Wikipedia*.

25. "Slavery," *Wikipedia*.

26. "Neolithic," *Wikipedia*.

27. "Prehistoric warfare," *Wikipedia*.

28. "Cemetery 117," *Wikipedia*.

29. "Me (mythology)," *Wikipedia*.

30. Icke, *The Perception Deception*.

31. Sitchin, *The 12th Planet*.

CHAPTER 5.
ASHUR, YAHWEH, THE CHURCH
AND THE TRANSCENDENCE OF DUALITY

1. "Venus of Hohle Fels," *Wikipedia*.

2. "Lion-man," *Wikipedia*.

3. http://firstlegend.info/thetreeoflife.html.

4. "Tree of life (Kabbalah)," *Wikipedia*.

5. "Hermetic Qabalah," *Wikipedia*.

6. Daniali, "The Fascinating Balanced Sacred Assyrian Tree of Life."

7. Parpola, "The Assyrian Tree of Life: Tracing the Origins of Jewish Monotheism and Greek Philosophy."

8. Nicole Brisch, "Marduk (god)," Ancient Mesopotamian Gods and Goddesses, Oracc and the UK Higher Education Academy, 2016, http://oracc.museum.upenn.edu/amgg/listofdeities/marduk.

9. "Tiamat," *Wikipedia.*

10. Greenwood, "Consciousness Began When the Gods Stopped Speaking."

11. "Old Testament," *Wikipedia.*

12. Genesis 1:1–2:3.

13. "Tree of life (biblical)," *Wikipedia.*

14. "Fuxi," *Wikipedia.*

15. "Maya Hero Twins," *Wikipedia.*

16. "Augustine of Hippo," *Wikipedia.*

17. "Moses," *Wikipedia.*

18. "Axial Age," *Wikipedia.*

19. "613 commandments," *Wikipedia.*

20. "Aphasia," *Wikipedia.*

21. "Moses in Islam," *Wikipedia.*

22. "James (brother of Jesus)," *Wikipedia.*

23. "Gnosticism," *Wikipedia.*

24. "Paul," *Wikipedia.*

25. "Council of Jerusalem," *Wikipedia.*

26. "Crisis of the Third Century," *Wikipedia.*

27. "Treaty of Verdun," *Wikipedia.*

28. "Marcion of Sinope," *Wikipedia.*

29. The Gnostic Society Library, the Nag Hammadi Library, http://gnosis.org/naghamm/hypostas.html.

30. "Nicene Christianity," *Wikipedia.*

31. "Arianism," *Wikipedia.*

32. "Library of Alexandria," *Wikipedia.*

33. Jacobovici and Wilson, *The Lost Gospel.*

34. "Nicene Christianity," *Wikipedia.*

35. Meyer, *The Gnostic Gospels of Jesus,* 149–83.

36. Ibid., 163.

37. "Messianic age," *Wikipedia.*

CHAPTER 6.
THE SEVENTH WAVE

1. "James Cook," *Wikipedia.*
2. "Transit of Venus," *Wikipedia.*
3. Roys, *The Book of Chilam Balam at Chumayel,* figure 29.
4. "Man a Machine," *Wikipedia.*
5. Atkinson, "Who Discovered Electricity?"
6. "World Wide Web," *Wikipedia.*
7. "Elisha Gray," *Wikipedia.*
8. "Parliamentary system," *Wikipedia.*
9. Cobban, *The Eighteenth Century,* 172.
10. "Occupational burnout," *Wikipedia.*
11. "Universal natural history and theory of heaven," *Wikipedia.*

CHAPTER 7.
APPROACHING THE PRESENT TIME

1. "World Wide Web," http://info.cern.ch/hypertext/WWW/TheProject .html.
2. Internet Live Stats, www.internetlivestats.com/internet-users/#trend.
3. Ibid.
4. Saez, "Striking It Richer: The Evolution of Top Incomes in the United States."
5. "Moore's law," *Wikipedia.*
6. "Gender Equality in Sweden," https://sweden.se/society/gender-equality -in-sweden.
7. Roberts, "For Young Earners in Big City, a Gap in Women's Favor."
8. Phillips, "China on Course to Become 'World's Most Christian Nation' within 15 Years."
9. "Apocalypse Now," *Newsweek,* March 28, 2011.
10. "The Protester," person of the year, *Time,* December 26, 2011.
11. Calleman, "The Ninth Wave Continues," www.calleman.com/content /articles/The9thWaveContinues.htm; Calleman, "Some New Reflections," www.calleman.com/content/articles/SomeNewReflections.htm.
12. Van Stone, *2012: Science & Prophecy of the Ancient Maya,* 62–72.

CHAPTER 8.
THE DEACTIVATION OF THE
HOLOGRAM OF GOOD AND EVIL

1. "Pope Francis," *Wikipedia*.
2. "Cahokia," *Wikipedia;* "Tula (Mesoamerican site)," *Wikipedia;* Hardoy, *Pre-Columbian Cities;* "Chichen-Itza," *Wikipedia*, see also www .exploratorium.edu/ancientobs/chichen/HTML/chichen4.html; "Chaco Culture National Historical Park," *Wikipedia;* "Mesa Verde National Park," *Wikipedia*.
3. "Cahokia," *Wikipedia*.
4. "British empire," *Wikipedia*.
5. "Mongol Empire," *Wikipedia*.
6. "Union of the Crowns," *Wikipedia*.
7. "Scottish independence referendum, 2014," *Wikipedia*.
8. "United Kingdom European Union membership referendum, 2016," *Wikipedia*.
9. "Iraq War," *Wikipedia*.
10. "Nation state," *Wikipedia*.
11. "Peace of Westphalia," *Wikipedia*.
12. "Maastricht Treaty," *Wikipedia*.
13. "European migrant crisis," *Wikipedia*.
14. Calleman, "May 27 and 28, 2006," www.calleman.com/content/articles /midpoint_of_FourthNIGHT.htm.
15. "Göbekli Tepe," *Wikipedia*.
16. "Shia–Sunni relations," *Wikipedia*.
17. Gilson and Perot, "It's the Inequality, Stupid."

CHAPTER 9.
MANIFESTING THE DESTINY OF
HUMANITY THROUGH THE NINTH WAVE

1. "Tandava," *Wikipedia*.
2. "Chinese dragon," *Wikipedia*.
3. Van Stone, *2012: Science & Prophecy of the Ancient Maya*, 58–61.

4. "Jewish eschatology," *Wikipedia*.

5. "Great Year," *Wikipedia*.

6. "Robert Kegan," *Wikipedia*.

7. Evolutionary Collective website, http://evolutionarycollective.com.

8. Oneness University website, https://onenessuniversity.org.

9. "Mayan/Gregorian Calendar of the Continuing Ninth Wave," www.4
-ahau.com, image at http://ahau.pagesperso-orange.fr/wave20152016
.jpg.

10. "Ninth Wave Calculator," www.xzone.com.au/9thwave.html.

11. "Ninth Wave Mayan Calendar and Tzolkin Day Calendar," www.2near
.com/edge/carl.

12. Al-Islam.org, "Divine Love," www.al-islam.org/perspectives-concept
-love-islam-mahnaz-heydarpoor/divine-love.

Bibliography

Argüelles, José. *The Mayan Factor.* Rochester, Vt.: Bear and Co., 1987.

Alchin, Linda. "Ancient Egyptian Gods and Goddesses for Kids: The Tree of Life." Land of Pyramids, March 2015. www.landofpyramids.org /tree-of-life.htm.

Aron, Jacob. "Planck Shows Almost Perfect Cosmos—Plus Axis of Evil." *New Scientist,* March 21, 2013. www.newscientist.com/article/dn23301 -planck-shows-almost-perfect-cosmos-plus-axis-of-evil.

Atkinson, Nancy. "Who Discovered Electricity?" Universe Today: Space and Astronomy News, March 3, 2014. www.universetoday.com/82402 /who-discovered-electricity.

Audouze, Jean, and Guy Israel, eds. *The Cambridge Atlas of Astronomy.* Cambridge, U.K.: Cambridge University Press, 1994.

Beauregard, Mario. *Brain Wars: The Scientific Battle over the Existence of the Mind and the Proof That Will Change the Way We Live Our Lives.* New York: HarperOne, 2012.

Bennett, C. L., et al. "First Year Wilkinson Microwave Anisotropy Probe (WMAP) Observations: Preliminary Maps and Basic Results." *Astrophysical Journal Supplement Series* 148 (2003): 1–27. astro-ph /0302207.

Bianki, V. L., and E. B. Fillipova. *Sex Differences in Lateralization in the Animal Brain.* Amsterdam: Harwood Academic Publishers, 2000.

Binney, James, and Scott Tremaine. *Galactic Dynamics.* Princeton Series in Astrophysics. Princeton, N.J.: Princeton University Press, 1987.

Bohm, David. *Wholeness and the Implicate Order.* London: Routledge, 2002.

Born, Max, and Albert Einstein. *The Born-Einstein Letters: Friendship, Politics and Physics in Uncertain Times.* New York: Walker, 1971.

Calleman, Carl Johan. *The Global Mind and the Rise of Civilization: The Quantum Evolution of Consciousness.* Rochester, Vt.: Bear and Co., 2016. First published in 2014 as *The Global Mind and the Rise of Civilization: A Novel Theory of Our Origins* by Two Harbors Press, Minneapolis, Minn.

———. *The Mayan Calendar and the Transformation of Consciousness.* Rochester, Vt.: Inner Traditions, 2004.

———. *The Purposeful Universe: How Quantum Theory and Mayan Cosmology Explain the Origin and Evolution of Life.* Rochester, Vt.: Inner Traditions, 2009.

———. *Solving the Greatest Mystery of Our Time: The Mayan Calendar.* London and Coral Springs, Fla.: Garev, 2001.

Campbell, Neil A., Jane B. Reece, and Lawrence G. Mitchell. *Biology.* 5th ed. Menlo Park, Calif.: Addison-Wesley, 1999.

Carp, Gerald. *Cell and Molecular Biology.* 2nd ed. New York: John Wiley & Sons, 1999.

Cho, A. "A Singular Conundrum: How Odd Is Our Universe?" *Science* 317 (2007): 1848–50.

Cobban, Alfred, ed. *The Eighteenth Century: Europe in the Age of Enlightenment.* New York: McGraw-Hill, 1969.

Coe, Michael D. *Breaking the Maya Code.* London: Thames and Hudson, 1992.

———. *The Maya.* New York: Thames and Hudson, 1993. Originally published in 1966.

Coghlan, Andy. "Oldest Artist's Workshop in the World Discovered." *New Scientist,* October 13, 2011. www.newscientist.com/article /dn21046-oldest-artists-workshop-in-the-world-discovered.

Curtis, Helena, and Sue Barnes. *Biology.* New York: Worth, 1989.

Daniali, Benjamin. "The Fascinating Balanced Sacred Assyrian Tree of Life." *Assyria Times,* May 24, 2010. http://goo.gl/eRhnMC.

Darwin, Charles. *The Origin of Species by Means of Natural Selection or the*

Preservation of Favoured Races in the Struggle for Life. London: Collier-MacMillan, 1962. First published in 1859.

Davies, Paul. *The Mind of God: The Scientific Basis for a Rational World.* London: Orion Production, 1992.

Dawkins, Richard. *The Blind Watchmaker.* New York: W. W. Norton, 1986.

————. *The Selfish Gene.* London: Paladin Books, 1978.

Denton, Michael. *Evolution: A Theory in Crisis.* London: Burnett Books, 1985.

de Oliveira-Costa, Angelica, Max Tegmark, Matias Zaldarriaga, and Andrew Hamilton. "The Significance of the Largest Scale CMB Fluctuations in WMAP." *Physical Review D* 69, no. 6 (2003): 063516. doi/10.1103/PhysRevD.69.063516.

Diamond, Jared. *Guns, Germs, and Steel: The Fates of Human Societies.* New York: W. W. Norton, 1999.

Dossey, Larry. *One Mind: How Our Individual Mind Is Part of a Greater Consciousness and Why It Matters.* Carlsbad, Calif.: Hay House, 2013.

Evehema, Dan. "A Message for Mankind." Hopi Prophecy on the 5th World. www.5thworld.com/Paradigm/Postings/!Expectations/Hopi%20Prophecy.htm.

Ferguson, Kitty. *The Fire in the Equations: Science, Religion, and the Search for God.* London: Bantam, 1994.

Fisher, Richard, and Rachel Courtland. "Found: Hawking's Initials Written into the Universe." *New Scientist,* February 7, 2010. www.newscientist.com/article/dn18489-found-hawkings-initials-written-into-the-universe.

Ford, Martin. *Rise of the Robots: Technology and the Threat of a Jobless Future.* New York: Basic Books, 2015.

Freidel, David, Linda Schele, and Joy Parker. *Maya Cosmos: Three Thousand Years on the Shaman's Path.* New York: Morrow, 1993.

Frank, Adam, and Marcelo Gleiser. "A Crisis at the Edge of Physics." *New York Times,* June 5, 2015. www.nytimes.com/2015/06/07/opinion/a-crisis-at-the-edge-of-physics.html?_r=0.

Gardner, James N. *Biocosm: The New Scientific Theory of Evolution: Intelligent Life Is the Architect of the Universe.* Maui, Hawaii: Inner Ocean Publishing, 2003.

Ghosh, Pallab. "Universe Evolution Recreated in Lab." BBC News, May 7, 2014. www.bbc.com/news/science-environment-27299017?utm_source.

Gilson, Dave, and Carolyn Perot. "It's the Inequality, Stupid." *Mother Jones,* March 2011. www.motherjones.com/politics/2011/02/income-inequality -in-america-chart-graph.

Gonzalez, Guillermo, and Jay Richards. *The Privileged Planet: How Our Place in the Cosmos Is Designed for Discovery.* Washington, D.C.: Regnery, 2004.

Goswami, Amit. *Physics of the Soul: The Quantum Book of Living, Dying, Reincarnation, and Immortality.* London: Hampton Roads, 2001.

Greenwood, Veronique. "Consciousness Began When the Gods Stopped Speaking: How Julian Jaynes' famous 1970s theory is faring in the neuroscience age." Nautilus, May 28, 2015. http://nautil.us/issue/24/error /consciousness-began-when-the-gods-stopped-speaking.

Hameroff, Stuart. *Ultimate Computing: Biomolecular Consciousness and Nanotechnology.* Holland: Elsevier Science, 1987.

Hand Clow, Barbara. *Awakening the Planetary Mind: Beyond the Trauma of the Past to a New Era of Creativity.* Rochester, Vt.: Bear and Co., 2011.

———. *Revelations of the Ruby Crystal.* Rochester, Vt.: Bear and Co., 2015.

Hardoy, Jorge E. *Pre-Columbian Cities.* New York: Walker, 1973.

Hawking, Stephen W. *A Brief History of Time: From the Big Bang to Black Holes.* London: Bantam Press, 1988.

Hedman, Matthew. *The Age of Everything: How Science Explores the Past.* Chicago, Ill.: University of Chicago Press, 2008.

Hutsemékers, D., R. Cabanac, H. Lamy, and D. Sluse. "Mapping Extreme-Scale Alignments of Quasar Polarization Vectors." *Astronomy and Astrophysics* 441 (2005): 915–30.

Icke, David. *The Perception Deception.* Ryde, U.K: David Icke Books, 2013.

Jacobovici, Simcha, and Barrie Wilson. *The Lost Gospel: Decoding the Ancient Text that Reveals Jesus' Marriage to Mary the Magdalene.* New York: Pegasus Books, 2014.

Jaynes, Julian. *The Origin of Consciousness in the Breakdown of the Bicameral Mind.* Boston and New York: Mariner Books, 2000.

Jones, Steve, Robert Martin, and David Pilbeam, eds. *The Cambridge Encyclopedia of Human Evolution*. Cambridge, N.Y.: Cambridge University Press, 1992.

Kimball, Richard W., ed. *Quetzalcoatl: The Ancient Legend*. Albuquerque, N.M.: Tiguex Books, 1985.

Koestler, Arthur. *The Act of Creation*. London: Penguin, 1990.

———. *The Case of the Midwife Toad*. London: Hutchinson, 1971.

Kragh, Helge. *Cosmology and Controversy: The Historical Development of Two Theories of the Universe*. Princeton, N.J.: Princeton University Press, 1996.

Land, Katharine. "Exploring Anomalies in the Cosmic Microwave Background." Thesis, University of London, 2006.

Land, Katharine, and Joao Magueijo. "The Axis of Evil." http://arxiv.org/abs/astro-ph/0502237.

Longo, Michael J. "Does the Universe Have a Handedness?" University of Michigan, Ann Arbor. astro-ph/0703325, arxiv.org/pdf/astro-ph/0703325.pdf.

Lovelock, James. *The Ages of Gaia: The Biography of a Living Planet*. New York: Oxford University Press, 1990.

Magueijo, Joao, and Katharine Land. "Examination of Evidence for a Preferred Axis in the Cosmic Radiation Anisotropy." *Physical Review Letters* 95 (2005): 071301.

McFadden, Johnjoe. *Quantum Evolution: How Physics' Weirdest Theory Explains Life's Biggest Mystery*. New York: W. W. Norton, 2002.

McKee, Jeffrey K., Frank E. Poirier, and Scott W. McGraw. *Understanding Human Evolution*. Englewood Cliffs, N.J.: Prentice Hall, 2004.

McTaggart, Lynne. *The Field Updated Ed: The Quest for the Secret Force of the Universe*. New York: Harper Paperbacks, 2008.

Meyer, Marvin. *The Gnostic Gospels of Jesus: The Definite Collection of Mystical Gospels and Secret Books about Jesus of Nazareth*. New York: HarperOne, 2005.

Milton, Richard. *Shattering the Myths of Darwinism*. Rochester, Vt.: Park Street Press, 2000.

Palmer, Edwin H., ed. *The Holy Bible: New International Version*. London:

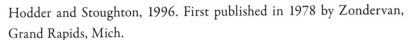

Hodder and Stoughton, 1996. First published in 1978 by Zondervan, Grand Rapids, Mich.

Pantovic, Natasa. "Tree of Life: What is the Meaning of the Tree of Life?" Art of 4 Elements. http://artof4elements.com/entry/43/tree-of-life.

O'Dubhaim, Searles. "The Elements of the Dúile from Ogham Divination: A Study in Recreating and Discovering the Ancient Ways of the Druids." Imbas, 1997. www.imbas.org/articles/elements_duile.html.

Parker, Steve. *The Dawn of Man*. Edited by Michael Day. New York: Crescent Books, 1992.

Parpola, Simo. "The Assyrian Tree of Life: Tracing the Origins of Jewish Monotheism and Greek Philosophy." *Journal of Near Eastern Studies* 52 (1993): 161–208. www.jstor.org/stable/545436.

Penrose, Roger. *Shadows of the Mind: A Search for the Missing Science of Consciousness*. New York: Oxford University Press, 1996.

Phillips, Tom. "China on Course to Become 'World's Most Christian Nation' within 15 Years." *Telegraph* (London), April 19, 2014. www.telegraph.co.uk/news/worldnews/asia/china/10776023/China-on-course-to-become-worlds-most-Christian-nation-within-15-years.html.

Poirier, Frank E. *Understanding Human Evolution*. 2nd ed. New York: Prentice-Hall, 1990.

Prothero, Donald R. *Evolution: What the Fossils Say and Why It Matters*. New York: Columbia University Press, 2007.

Quipoloa, J. "The Aztec Universe." The Aztec Gateway, 2002–2007. http://nyx.meccahosting.com/~a00001f1/cuezali/universe.html.

Radin, Dean. *Entangled Minds: Extrasensory Experiences in a Quantum Reality*. New York: Paraview Pocket Books, 2006.

Redd, Nola Taylor. "How Big Is the Universe?" Space.com, December 24, 2013. www.space.com/24073-how-big-is-the-universe.html.

Rees, Martin. *Just Six Numbers: The Deep Forces That Shape the Universe*. New York: Basic Books, 2001.

Richards, E. G. *Mapping Time: The Calendar and Its History*. Oxford, U.K.: Oxford University Press, 1998.

Roberts, Sam. "For Young Earners in Big City, a Gap in Women's Favor."

New York Times, August 3, 2007. www.nytimes.com/2007/08/03 /nyregion/03women.html?_r=0.

Rogers, Lesley J., and Andrew Richard, eds. *Comparative Vertebrate Lateralization.* Cambridge, U.K.: Cambridge University Press, 2002.

Rosenblum, Bruce, and Fred Kuttner. *Quantum Enigma: Physics Encountered Consciousness.* Oxford, U.K.: Oxford University Press, 2006.

Roys, Ralph. *The Book of Chilam Balam of Chumayel.* Oklahoma City: University of Oklahoma Press, 1967.

Ruse, Michael. *Darwinism Defended.* Upper Saddle River, N.J.: Addison-Wesley, 1982.

Saez, Emmanuel. "Striking It Richer: The Evolution of Top Incomes in the United States." University of California, Berkeley, September 3, 2013. http://eml.berkeley.edu//~saez/saez-UStopincomes-2012.pdf.

Schele, Linda, and David Freidel. *A Forest of Kings: The Untold Story of the Ancient Maya.* New York: Morrow, 1990.

Schneider, M. S. *A Beginner's Guide to Constructing the Universe: The Mathematical Archetypes of Nature, Art and Science.* New York: HarperCollins 1995.

Shlain, Leonard. *The Alphabet versus the Goddess: The Conflict between Word and Image.* New York: Viking Penguin, 1998.

Singal, Ashok K. "A Large Anisotropy in the Sky Distribution of 3CRR Quasars and Other Radio Galaxies." *Astrophysics and Space Science* 357, no. 2, article 152 (2015).

Sitchin, Zecharia. *12th Planet.* Bk. 1 of 7 bks. The Earth Chronicles. New York: Harper, 2007.

Smoot, G. F., C. L. Bennett, A. Kogut, E. L. Wright, J. Aymon, M. W. Boggess, E. S. Cheng, et al. "Structure in the COBE DMR First Year Maps." *Astrophysical Journal Letters* 396 (1992): L1–L5.

Styer, Daniel F. *The Strange World of Quantum Mechanics.* Cambridge, U.K.: Press Syndicate of the University of Cambridge, 2000. www .oberlin.edu/physics/dstyer/StrangerQM/intro.html.

Sweeney, John Frederick. *The Egyptian Book of the Dead, Nuclear Physics and the Substratum.* October 16, 2013. http://vixra.org/pdf/1310.0130v1 .pdf.

Talbot, Michael. *The Holographic Universe.* New York: Harper, 1991.

Taylor, A. R., and P. Jagannathan. "Alignments of Radio Galaxies in Deep Radio Imaging of ELAIS N1." Cornell University Library, 2016. Available at arXiv:1603.02418.

Tedlock, Dennis, trans. *Popol Vuh: The Mayan Book of the Dawn of Life.* New York: Simon and Schuster, 1985.

Tegmark, Max, Angelica de Oliveira-Costa, and Andrew Hamilton. "High Resolution Foreground Cleaned CMB Map from WMAP." *Physical Review D* 68 (2003): 123523.

Tegmark, Max, Michael A. Strauss, Michael R. Blanton, Kevork Abazajian, Scott Dodelson, Havard Sandvik, Xiaomin Wang, et al. "Cosmological Parameters from SDSS and WMAP." *Physical Review D* 69 (2004). http://arxiv.org/abs/astro-ph/0310723.

Tiwari, Prabhakar, Rahul Kothari, Abhishek Naskar, Shavari Nadkarni-Ghosh, and Pankaj Jain. "Dipole Anisotropy in Sky Brightness and Source Count Distribution in Radio NVSS Data." *Astroparticle Physics* 61 (2015): 1–11.

Van Stone, Mark. *2012: Science & Prophecy of the Ancient Maya.* San Diego, Calif.: Tlacaelel Press, 2010.

Vogelsberger, Mark, Shy Genel, Volker Springer, Paul Torrey, Debora Sijacki, Dandan Xu, Gregory F. Snyder, et al. "Properties of Galaxies Reproduced by a Hydrodynamic Simulation." *Nature* 509 (May 8, 2014): 177–82. doi:10.1038/nature13316.

Vogt, Yngve. "World's Oldest Ritual Discovered. Worshipped the Python 70,000 Years Ago." *Apollon Research Magazine,* University of Oslo, February 1, 2012. www.apollon.uio.no/english/articles/2006/python -english.html.

Vogt, Yngve, Alan Louis Belardinelli, and afrol News staff. "World's Oldest Religion Discovered in Botswana." afrol News, December 1, 2014. www .afrol.com/articles/23093.

Ward, Peter, and Donald Brownlee. *Rare Earth: Why Complex Life Is Uncommon in the Universe.* New York: Springer, 2003.

Weinberg, Steven. *The First Three Minutes.* New York: Basic Books, 1993.

White, T. D., B. Asfaw, D. DeGusta, H. Gilbert, G. D. Richards, G. Suwa, and F. C. Howell. "Pleistocene *Homo sapiens* from Middle Awash, Ethiopia." *Nature* 423 (2003): 742–47.

Whitfield, Philip. *From So Simple a Beginning: The Book of Evolution*. New York: MacMillan, 1993.

Zhao, Wen, Puxun Wu, and Zhang Yang. "Anisotropy of Cosmic Acceleration." *International Journal of Modern Physics D* 22, no. 9 (2013): 1350060.

Index

Numbers in *italics* indicate illustrations

About the Author

Carl Johan Calleman was born in Stockholm, Sweden. He received a Ph.D. in physical biology from the University of Stockholm in 1984. He has been a senior researcher at the Department of Environmental Health at the University of Washington, Seattle, and has served as an expert on cancer for the World Health Organization. He has authored or coauthored articles that have been quoted more than 1,500 times in the scientific literature. Calleman is recognized as the main proponent of the idea that the Mayan calendar reflects the evolution of consciousness. He has previously written four books on this topic: *Solving the Greatest Mystery of Our Time: The Mayan Calendar* (Garev, 2001), *The Mayan Calendar and the Transformation of Consciousness* (Inner Traditions, 2004, translated into thirteen different languages), *The Purposeful Universe* (Inner Traditions, 2009), and *The Global Mind and the Rise of Civilization* (Bear & Company, 2016). His website is
www.calleman.com.

BOOKS OF RELATED INTEREST

The Global Mind and the Rise of Civilization
The Quantum Evolution of Consciousness
by Carl Johan Calleman, Ph.D.

The Purposeful Universe
How Quantum Theory and Mayan Cosmology
Explain the Origin and Evolution of Life
by Carl Johan Calleman, Ph.D.

The Mayan Calendar and the Transformation of Consciousness
by Carl Johan Calleman, Ph.D.

The Mayan Code
Time Acceleration and Awakening the World Mind
by Barbara Hand Clow
Foreword by Carl Johan Calleman, Ph.D.

The 8 Calendars of the Maya
The Pleiadian Cycle and the Key to Destiny
by Hunbatz Men

The Mayan Factor
Path Beyond Technology
by José Argüelles

Awakening the Planetary Mind
Beyond the Trauma of the Past to a New Era of Creativity
by Barbara Hand Clow

Time of the Quickening
Prophecies for the Coming Utopian Age
by Susan B. Martinez, Ph.D.

INNER TRADITIONS • BEAR & COMPANY
P.O. Box 388
Rochester, VT 05767
1-800-246-8648
www.InnerTraditions.com

Or contact your local bookseller